365 Easy Meals

Quick, Simple, Delicious Meals For Every Day of the Year

365 Easy Meals
Quick, Simple, Delicious Meals For Every Day of the Year

1st Printing - September 2006
2nd Printing - May 2007
3rd Printing - November 2007

International Standard Book No. 978-1-59769-015-7

Library of Congress No. 2006905416

Library of Congress Catalog Data
Main Title: 365 Easy Meals : Quick, Simple, Delicious Meals for Every Day of the
Year / [illustrations by Nancy Bohanan].
Variant Title: Three Hundred Sixty-five Easy Meals
Description: 397 p. : ill. ; 24 cm.
Notes: Includes index.
Subjects: 1. Cookery, American. 2. Quick and easy cookery.
TX715 .A1133 2006

Cover and Illustrations by Nancy Bohanan

Edited, Designed and Published in the United States of America
and Manufactured in China by
Cookbook Resources, LLC
541 Doubletree Drive
Highland Village, Texas 75077
Toll free 866-229-2665

www.cookbookresources.com

cookbook
resources LLC
Bringing Family and Friends to the Table

What's For Dinner?

An eternal question…yesterday, today and tomorrow!

365 Easy Meals not only answers the question, but gives you the recipes for easy meals for family and friends every day of the year.

All the ingredients for these easy meals are probably in your pantry already. If not, they are easy to find at your favorite grocery store. Planning your week is easy when you have something to go by… something that helps you think and gives you ideas.

365 Easy Meals is designed to make life a little easier by helping you plan and prepare meals for family and friends. Here are some examples of the menus and recipes inside these pages.

Chicken-Country Casserole
Nutty Green Salad
•
Fried Chicken Breasts
Mashed Potatoes and Gravy
Divine Strawberries
•
Chiffon-Cheese Breakfast Soufflé
Bacon Nibblers
•
Grilled Swordfish Steaks with
Mango Salsa
Creamy Baked Potatoes
•
Speedy Gonzales Special
Sunshine Salad
•
Bless My Sole
Herbed New Potatoes
•
Broccoli-Noodle Soup
Cornbread Muffins
Blueberry Tarts

Skillet Nachos
Guacamole Salad
Haystacks
•
Steakhouse Stew
Cream-Style Corn Sticks
Stuffed Celery
•
Zesty Orange Chicken
Hawaiian Coleslaw
Hawaiian Bread
•
Pasta Salad Bowl
Party Sandwiches
•
Yummy Barbecued Grilled Chicken
Twice-Baked Potatoes
•
Easy Enchiladas
Baked Refried Beans
•
Slow Cooker Steak Deluxe
Party Potatoes
Buffet-Asparagus Casserole

CONTENTS

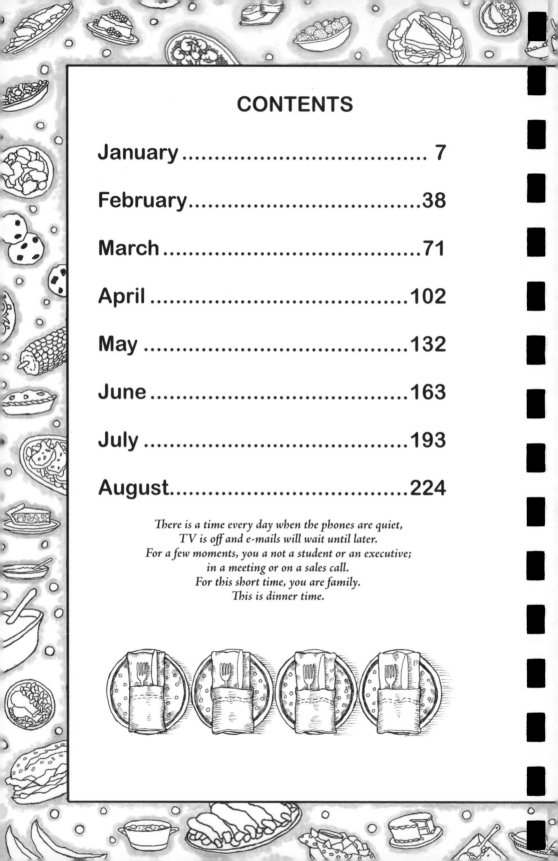

There is a time every day when the phones are quiet,
TV is off and e-mails will wait until later.
For a few moments, you a not a student or an executive;
in a meeting or on a sales call.
For this short time, you are family.
This is dinner time.

CONTENTS

When we recognize the importance of sharing meals together, our families are stronger, our nation is stronger and our own little part of the world feels safer and a little more loving.

Potato Soup

1 large baking potato, cubed	
1 (14 ounce) can chicken broth	396 g
1 cup shredded Velveeta® cheese	240 ml
1 (8 ounce) carton whipping cream	227 g

- Boil potato, drain and mash with fork. Add broth, cheese and cream. Heat and serve. Serves 4.

Lucky Black-Eyed Pea Salad

1 (15 ounce) can black-eyed peas, drained	425 g
3 green onions with tops, chopped	
¼ cup chopped fresh parsley	60 ml
½ cup chopped green bell peppers	120 ml
⅓ cup chopped celery	80 ml
⅓ cup Italian dressing	80 ml

- Stir all ingredients and a little pepper together and chill. Serves 3 to 4.

❄ *January* ❄

1- New Year's Day
15 - Martin Luther King's Birthday
20 - Inauguration Day

1
2
3
4
5
6
7
8
9
10
11
12
13
14
15
16
17
18
19
20
21
22
23
24
25
26
27
28
29
30
31

1
2
3
4
5
6
7
8
9
10
11
12
13
14
15
16
17
18
19
20
21
22
23
24
25
26
27
28
29
30
31

Chili

1 pound lean ground beef	.5 kg
2 teaspoons garlic powder	10 ml
2 tablespoons chili powder	30 ml
1 tablespoon flour	15 ml
1 (8 ounce) can tomato sauce	227 g

- Brown hamburger meat with garlic powder. Drain excess fat. Add chili powder, flour and 1 teaspoon (5 ml) salt. Stir and mix well.
- Add tomato sauce and 1 cup (240 ml) water. Heat to boiling, reduce heat and simmer 20 minutes. Stir often. Serves 3 to 4.

Cheddar Biscuits

2 cups biscuit mix	480 ml
⅔ cup milk	160 ml
½ cup shredded cheddar cheese	120 ml
2 tablespoons butter, melted	30 ml
½ teaspoon garlic powder	2 ml

- Preheat oven to 450° (230° C). Mix biscuit mix, milk and cheese to form soft dough.
- Drop by tablespoonfuls onto unsprayed cookie sheet. Bake 8 to 10 minutes. Mix butter and garlic powder. Brush over warm biscuits. Makes 9 biscuits.

One Big German Pancake

½ cup flour	120 ml
3 eggs, slightly beaten	
½ cup milk	120 ml
2 tablespoons butter, melted	30 ml

- Preheat oven to 425° (220° C). Beat flour and eggs together. Stir in remaining ingredients and ¼ teaspoon (1 ml) salt.
- Pour into sprayed 9-inch (23 cm) pie pan. Bake for 20 minutes. Pancake will puff into big bubbles while baking. Cut into wedges and dust with powdered sugar. Serve with melted butter and maple syrup. Serves 3 to 4.

Maple-Bacon Bake

1 pound hickory-smoked bacon	.5 kg
Maple syrup	
Cracked black pepper	

- Preheat oven to 325° (162° C). Separate bacon, lay slices across broiler pan and sprinkle each slice with pepper. Brush with maple syrup. Bake for 45 minutes.

Fruit Cup

1 mango, peeled, chopped	
2 kiwifruit, chopped, peeled	
1 (15 ounce) can pineapple tidbits, drained	425 g
1 tablespoon lime juice	15 ml
Granola cereal	

- Mix ingredients and serve sprinkled with granola cereal. Serves 3 to 4.

Breakfast or Brunch

1
2
3
4
5
6
7
8
9
10
11
12
13
14
15
16
17
18
19
20
21
22
23
24
25
26
27
28
29
30
31

Broccoli-Noodle Soup

1 (12 ounce) package egg noodles	340 g
1 (16 ounce) package, frozen, chopped broccoli	.5 kg
1 (1 pint) carton half-and-half cream	.5 kg
1 (14 ounce) can chicken broth	396 g
1 (16 ounce) box Velveeta® cheese, cubed	.5 kg

• Cook noodles and broccoli according to package directions. Set aside. Combine half-and-half, chicken broth and cheese. Heat on low and stir until cheese melts. Add noodles and broccoli and simmer until mixture heats thoroughly.

• Serves 4 to 6.

Cornbread Muffins

1 (8 ounce) box cornbread muffin mix	227 g
1 egg	
⅓ cup milk	80 ml

• Prepare according to package directions.

• Serves 4 to 6.

Blueberry Tarts

8 mini graham cracker piecrusts	
1 (20 ounce) can blueberry pie filling	567 g
1 (8 ounce) carton whipped topping	227 g

• Fill piecrusts with pie filling. Top each blueberry tart with dollop of whipped topping. Serves 6 to 8.

Chicken Spaghetti

3 boneless, skinless chicken breast halves, cooked
1 (10 ounce) can tomatoes and green chilies   280 g
1 (10 ounce) can cream of mushroom soup   280 g
1 (8 ounce) package shredded cheddar cheese   227 g
1 (8 ounce) package shredded Velveeta® cheese   227 g
1 (12 ounce) package spaghetti   340 g

- Preheat oven to 350° (176° C). Shred cooked chicken into large bowl. Add tomatoes, soup and both cheeses.
- Boil spaghetti according to package directions. Drain. Add to chicken mixture. Mix.
- Pour into 3-quart (3 L) baking dish, cover and bake for 35 minutes. Serves 4 to 5.

Cucumber Salad

4 cucumbers, peeled, sliced
1 medium onion, sliced into rings

Dressing:
1½ cups mayonnaise   360 ml
½ cup sugar   120 ml
½ cup vinegar   120 ml

- Cover cucumbers and onions with dressing and let stand overnight in refrigerator in covered plastic bowl. Sprinkle a little salt over salad. Serves 4 to 6.

New Orleans Franks

3 tablespoons butter, melted	45 ml
1 medium onion, chopped	
1 clove garlic, minced	
2 (15 ounce) cans diced tomatoes	2 (425 g)
6 - 10 frankfurters, divided	
5 cups cooked rice	1.3 L

- Saute onion and garlic in butter in saucepan until tender. Add ½ teaspoon (2 ml) salt, dash of pepper and tomatoes. Mix well.
- Dice 2 frankfurters and add to tomato mixture. Cook over low heat for 15 to 20 minutes. Add remaining whole frankfurters. Cook until frankfurters are plump and sauce is thick.
- Arrange frankfurters on rice and pour sauce over all. Serves 4 to 6.

Baked Bean Creole

3 slices bacon, diced	
½ cup minced onion	120 ml
½ cup finely minced green pepper	120 ml
1 (15 ounce) can baked beans	425 g
1 (15 ounce) can stewed tomatoes	425 g
1 teaspoon sugar	5 ml

- Preheat oven to 425° (220° C). Fry bacon until crisp. Remove from pan. Brown onions and green pepper in bacon grease and combine with bacon.
- Arrange beans and bacon-vegetable mixture in alternate layers in 3-quart (3 L) baking dish. Mix tomatoes and sugar and pour over all. Bake for about 30 minutes. Serves 4 to 6.

The calendar days listed in the left margin: 1, 2, 3, 4, 5, 6, 7, 8, 9, 10, 11, 12, 13, 14, 15, 16, 17, 18, 19, 20, 21, 22, 23, 24, 25, 26, 27, 28, 29, 30, 31

Fruited Pork Tenderloin

3 - 5 pound boneless pork loin	1.3 kg
Vegetable oil	
Garlic salt	
1 (18 ounce) jar strawberry preserves	510 g

- Preheat oven to 350° (176° C). Rub pork loin with oil. Season all sides with garlic salt and pepper. Wrap loin in foil with no holes to vent. Bake for 20 to 25 minutes per pound.

- During last 30 minutes of baking time, remove from oven and open top of foil. Spoon preserves over entire top of loin and return to oven. Let pork loin rest 10 to 15 minutes before serving. Serves 6 to 8.

Romaine-Strawberry Salad

1 (10 ounce) package chopped romaine lettuce	280 g
2 cups broccoli slaw	480 ml
1½ cups quartered fresh strawberries	360 ml
4 fresh green onions, sliced diagonally	

- In salad bowl, toss ingredients. When ready to serve, use about ½ cup (120 ml) raspberry vinaigrette salad dressing and toss. Serves 6 to 8.

Simple Side Dish: Herbed Rice

- Cook 1 (7 ounce/198 g) box herb-butter rice and pasta according to package directions.

1
2
3
4
5
6
7
8
9
10
11
12
13
14
15
16
17
18
19
20
21
22
23
24
25
26
27
28
29
30
31

Barbecups

1 pound lean ground beef	**.5 kg**
½ cup barbecue sauce	**120 ml**
1 (10 count) can biscuits	
½ cup shredded cheddar cheese	**120 ml**

- Preheat oven to 400° (204° C). Brown ground beef. Drain. Stir in barbecue sauce. Separate dough into 10 biscuits.

- Place biscuits into 10 sprayed cups. Firmly press in bottom and on sides. Spoon ¼ cup (60 ml) meat into each biscuit. Sprinkle with cheese. Bake for 10 to 12 minutes. Cool 1 minute and remove from pan. Serves 4 to 6.

Frito Salad

1 head iceberg lettuce	
1 onion, chopped	
1 (16 ounce) package shredded cheddar cheese	**.5 kg**
3 tomatoes, chopped	
1 (15 ounce) can ranch-style beans, rinsed, drained	**425 g**
1 (8 ounce) bottle Catalina dressing	**227 g**
1 (13 ounce) package Fritos corn chips, crushed	**370 g**

- Tear lettuce into bite-size pieces. Add onion, cheese, tomatoes, beans and dressing. Just before serving, toss with corn chips. Serves 4 to 6.

Simple Side Dish: **Baked Beans**

- Heat 2 (15 ounce/425g) cans baked beans in saucepan. Stir several times.

Sausage Casserole

2 (8 ounce) cans refrigerated crescent rolls	**2 (227 g)**
1 pound sausage	**.5 kg**
1 (8 ounce) package shredded cheddar cheese	**227 g**
6 eggs	
2 cups milk	**480 ml**

- Preheat oven to 350° (176° C). Spread dough in bottom of 9 x 13-inch (23 x 33 cm) pan. Brown and drain sausage. Sprinkle sausage over rolls.
- Sprinkle with cheese. Beat eggs with milk. Pour mixture over sausage and add a little salt and pepper. Bake for 35 to 40 minutes. Serves 4 to 6.

Baked Grapefruit

Ruby red grapefruit	
2 teaspoons sugar and ½ teaspoon cinnamon	
** per grapefruit half**	**10 ml/2 ml**
Fresh fruit or mint leaf	

- Preheat oven to 200° (93° C). Slice grapefruit in half. Cut between and loosen grapefruit sections. Sprinkle with cinnamon-sugar mixture. Bake until grapefruit is warm. Remove and garnish each slice with fresh fruit or mint leaf.

Simple Bread Idea: **Hot Buttered Biscuits**

- Bake 1 (22 ounce/ 624 g) package frozen flaky layer biscuits according to package directions.

Breakfast or Brunch

Ham Slices With Cranberry Relish

1 (3 pound) boneless, cooked ham	1.3 kg
1 (16 ounce) can whole cranberry sauce	.5 kg
1 cup orange marmalade	240 ml
1 (8 ounce) can crushed pineapple, drained	227 g
¾ cup coarsely chopped pecans	180 ml

- Preheat oven to 250° (121° C). Slice enough ham for each person. Serve room temperature or warmed. To warm ham, place slices in foil and heat for 15 minutes. In small bowl, combine relish ingredients and place in freezer to chill just until ready to serve. This relish can be served cold or warm over ham. Serves 6 to 8.

Sour Cream Potato Salad

6 medium potatoes	
¼ cup oil	60 ml
¾ cup sour cream	180 ml
½ cup mayonnaise	120 ml
2 eggs, hard-boiled, chopped	

- Peel potatoes and cut into uniform cubes. Cook in boiling, salted water until done. Drain. Chill potatoes in refrigerator. Stir oil into chilled potatoes. Add sour cream, mayonnaise, eggs and a little salt and pepper and mix well. Serves 6.

1
2
3
4
5
6
7
8
9
10
11
12
13
14
15
16
17
18
19
20
21
22
23
24
25
26
27
28
29
30
31

Shrimp Etouffee

½ cup (1 stick) butter	120 ml
1 bunch green onions, chopped	
1 pound shrimp, peeled, veined	.5 kg
Fluffy cooked rice	

• In skillet, saute onions in butter. Pour in shrimp and simmer until shrimp turns pink. Serve over rice. Serves 4 to 6.

English Pea Casserole

1 (15 ounce) can green peas, drained	425 g
1 (10 ounce) can cream of mushroom soup	280 g
2 strips bacon, diced	
1 small onion, chopped	

• Preheat oven to 350° (176° C). Place peas in sprayed 9-inch (23 cm) square baking pan and add soup. Cook bacon and onion in skillet. Pour over peas and soup. Bake for 25 minutes. Serves 4 to 6.

Spring Salad

1(10 ounce) package spring-mix salad greens	280 g
2 cups fresh broccoli florets	480 ml
1 seedless cucumber, peeled, sliced	
1 (8 ounce) bottle ranch salad dressing	227 g

• Combine greens, broccoli and cucumber and toss with as much dressing as needed. Serves 4 to 6.

1
2
3
4
5
6
7
8
9
10
11
12
13
14
15
16
17
18
19
20
21
22
23
24
25
26
27
28
29
30
31

One-Pot Dinner

1 pound lean ground beef	.5 kg
1 small onion, chopped	
¼ cup ketchup	60 ml
1 (10 ounce) can tomatoes and green chilies	280 g
1 (8 ounce) can green peas, drained	227 g
1 beaten egg	
2 cups instant mashed potatoes, prepared	480 ml
½ cup shredded cheddar cheese	120 ml

• Preheat oven to 350° (176° C). Brown meat and onions. Place in sprayed 3-quart (3 L) baking dish and stir in ketchup. Sprinkle with a little salt and pepper. Sprinkle tomatoes and peas on top of meat.

• Mix egg into mashed potatoes, spread over top of vegetables. Cover and bake for 30 minutes. Uncover. Sprinkle top with cheese and bake for 5 minutes longer. Place under broiler if you wish top to be browner. Serves 4 to 6.

Quick Deviled Eggs

12 eggs, hard-boiled	
½ cup mayonnaise	120 ml
2 tablespoons mustard	30 ml
½ cup pickle relish	120 ml

• Cut eggs in half. Remove yolks. Mash yolks with fork and add remaining ingredients. Blend well and refill whites with mixture. Serves 6 to 8.

Ranch Sausage and Grits

1 cup instant grits	240 ml
1 pound hot sausage	.5 kg
½ teaspoon minced garlic	2 ml
1 (8 ounce) package shredded sharp cheddar	
cheese, divided	227 g
½ cup hot salsa	120 ml
¼ cup (½ stick) butter, melted	60 ml
2 eggs, beaten	

- Preheat oven to 350° (176° C). Cook instant grits according to package directions. In skillet, brown and cook sausage and garlic and drain. Combine cooked grits, sausage, half cheese, salsa, melted butter and eggs and mix well.
- Pour into sprayed 9 x 13-inch (23 x 33 cm) baking dish. Bake uncovered for 50 minutes. Remove from oven and sprinkle remaining cheese over casserole. Return to oven for 10 minutes. Serve with hot biscuits. Serves 4 to 6.

Wake-Up Fruit

1 small honeydew melon or cantaloupe	
½ cup soft-style cream cheese	120 ml
½ cup vanilla yogurt	120 ml
1 tablespoon honey	15 ml
1½ cups fresh raspberries	360 ml

- Slice and peel melon. Arrange on plate. Whip cream cheese, yogurt and honey until smooth. Drizzle mixture across fruit wedges. Top with raspberries. Serves 4 to 6.

Breakfast or Brunch

1
2
3
4
5
6
7
8
9
10
11
12
13
14
15
16
17
18
19
20
21
22
23
24
25
26
27
28
29
30
31

Easy Enchiladas

1 dozen corn tortillas	
1 pound lean ground beef	.5 kg
1 clove garlic, minced	
1 large onion, chopped	
1 (12 ounce) package shredded longhorn cheese, divided	340 g
1 (10 ounce) can cream of chicken soup	280 g
1 cup milk	240 ml

- Preheat oven to 300° (148° C). Wrap tortillas in paper towels and heat in microwave. Brown beef with garlic and onion. Season with 1 teaspoon (5 ml) pepper.
- Sprinkle each tortilla with 2 tablespoons (30 ml) cheese and top with 1½ tablespoons (22 ml) meat mixture. Roll tightly and place in sprayed 9 x 13-inch (23 x 33 cm) baking dish. Heat soup with milk. Pour over enchiladas. Sprinkle with remaining cheese. Bake for 20 to 30 minutes or until hot and bubbly. Serves 4 to 6.

Baked Refried Beans

1 (15 ounce) can refried beans	425 g
⅓ cup chunky salsa, drained	80 ml
½ teaspoon cayenne pepper	2 ml
1 (8 ounce) package shredded cheddar cheese	227 g

- Preheat oven to 350° (176° C). Place refried beans in sprayed 9-inch (23 cm) baking dish and stir in salsa and cayenne pepper. Heat uncovered for 10 minutes. Sprinkle cheese over top of beans and return to oven for 4 to 5 minutes. Serves 4 to 6.

Lemon-Pepper Fish Fillets

1½ pounds cod fillets	.7 kg
1 tablespoon plus 1 teaspoon olive oil	15 ml/5 ml
¼ teaspoon lemon pepper	1 ml

• Preheat oven to 375° (190° C). Arrange fillets in baking dish. Drizzle with oil and season with salt and lemon pepper. Bake 10 to 12 minutes or until fish is opaque. Serves 4.

Broccoli Cornbread

1 (8 ounce) box cornbread mix	227 g
2 eggs, beaten	
1 (10 ounce) package frozen chopped broccoli	280 g
½ cup chopped onion	120 ml
½ cup cottage cheese	120 ml
¾ cup (1½ sticks) butter, melted	180 ml

• Preheat oven to 350° (176° C). Combine cornbread mix with eggs. Add thawed broccoli, onion, cottage cheese and melted butter. Stir to blend. Bake in sprayed 8 x 8-inch (20 x 20 cm) pan for 35 minutes. Serves 4 to 6.

Simple Side Dish: **Easy Fruit**

• Chill 2 (24 ounce/680 g) jars refrigerated tropical fruit and serve.

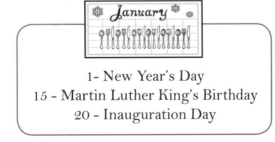

* January *

1- New Year's Day
15 - Martin Luther King's Birthday
20 - Inauguration Day

1
2
3
4
5
6
7
8
9
10
11
12
13
14
15
16
17
18
19
20
21
22
23
24
25
26
27
28
29
30
31

Cranberried Pork Chops

6 lean center-cut pork chops
1 (16 ounce) can whole cranberry sauce   **.5 kg**

- In large skillet, brown pork chops on both sides. Drain. Pour cranberry sauce over chops. Cover and simmer over low heat until tender, about 30 to 35 minutes. Serves 4 to 6.

Corn With Brussels Sprouts

1 (1 pint) carton brussels sprouts   **.5 kg**
1 (15 ounce) can whole kernel corn, drained   **425 g**
3 tablespoons butter   **45 ml**

- Wash and prepare brussels sprouts for cooking. Cook brussels sprouts in ½ cup (120 ml) water for about 10 minutes or until tender. Add corn, butter and ¼ teaspoon (1 ml) salt and dash of pepper and heat. Serves 4 to 6.

Crunchy Salad

¼ cup sesame seeds   **60 ml**
½ cup sunflower seeds   **120 ml**
½ cup sliced almonds   **120 ml**
1 head red leaf lettuce
Creamy Italian salad dressing

- Toast sesame seeds, sunflower seeds and almonds at 300° (148° C) for 10 minutes. Tear lettuce into bite-size pieces and add seed mixture. Toss with dressing. Serves 4 to 6.

Lentil And Bean Curry Soup

1 (14 ounce) can chicken broth	396 g
1 (7 ounce) package lentil pilaf mix	198 g
1 tablespoon curry powder	15 ml
1 (8 ounce) can green peas	227 g
1 (15 ounce) can diced tomatoes	425 g
1 (15 ounce) can great northern beans, drained	425 g

• Combine 3 cups (710 ml) water, broth, lentil mix, seasonings from packet and curry powder. Bring to boil. Reduce heat and simmer, covered, for 30 minutes. Add peas. Cook, uncovered for 5 minutes. Stir in tomatoes and beans. Heat. Serves 4 to 6.

Tuna Melt

6 eggs, hard-boiled	
2 (6 ounce) cans tuna	2 (168 g)
1 (8 ounce) package shredded Velveeta® cheese	227 g
4 tablespoons sweet pickle relish	60 ml
4 tablespoons chopped onions	60 ml
1 cup mayonnaise	240 ml
2 dozen small hamburger buns	

• Preheat oven to 350° (176° C). Chop eggs, flake and drain tuna. Combine all ingredients. Spoon into buns and bake for 15 minutes. Serves 4 to 6.

1
2
3
4
5
6
7
8
9
10
11
12
13
14
15
16
17
18
19
20
21
22
23
24
25
26
27
28
29
30
31

Slow Cooker Steak Delight

1½ pounds tenderized round steak, trimmed	.7 kg
1 (16 ounce) package brown gravy mix	.5 kg
1 (10 ounce) can tomatoes and green chilies	280 g
1 (1 ounce) packet onion soup mix	28 g
1½ tablespoons Cajun seasoning	22 ml

• Cut steak into serving pieces. Cook gravy mix according to package directions. Combine tomatoes and green chilies, soup mix and Cajun seasoning in blender. Put all ingredients into slow cooker and cook on HIGH for 4 hours. Serves 4 to 6.

Party Potatoes

1 (8 ounce) package cream cheese and chives	227 g
1 (22 ounce) carton refrigerated mashed potatoes	624 g

• Preheat oven to 350° (176° C). Add cream cheese to whipped potatoes. Pour into sprayed 7 x 11-inch (18 x 28 cm) baking dish. Cover and bake for 30 minutes. Serves 4 to 6.

Buffet-Asparagus Casserole

1 (15 ounce) can asparagus, drained	425 g
1 (15 ounce) can green peas, drained	425 g
½ cup shredded cheddar cheese	120 ml
1 (10 ounce) can cream of mushroom soup	280 g
1 cup seasoned breadcrumbs	240 ml

• Preheat oven to 350° (176° C). Layer vegetables and cheese in sprayed 7 x 11-inch (18 x 28 cm) baking dish. Spoon soup and breadcrumbs over vegetables. Bake for 30 minutes or until bubbly. Serves 4 to 6.

Berry Delicious Salad

1 (10 ounce) package mixed salad greens	280 g
2 cups fresh blueberries	480 ml
⅔ cup crumbled gorgonzola cheese	160 ml
⅓ cup chopped pecans, toasted	80 ml
Raspberry-vinaigrette dressing	

- In salad bowl combine salad greens, blueberries, cheese and pecans. Toss salad with dressing and chill. Serves 4.

Quick Skillet Supper

1½ pounds lean ground beef	.7 kg
⅔ cup stir-fry sauce	160 ml
1 (16 ounce) package frozen stir-fry vegetables	.5 kg
2 (3 ounce) packages Oriental-flavor ramen noodles	2 (84 g)

- Brown and crumble ground beef in large skillet. Add 2⅓ cups (560 ml) water, stir-fry sauce, vegetables and seasoning packet in noodle package.
- Cook and stir on medium heat about 5 minutes.
- Break noodles, add to beef-vegetable mixture and cook about 6 minutes. Stir to separate noodles as they soften and serve hot. Serves 4 to 6.

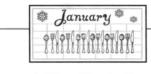

❄ January ❄

1- New Year's Day
15 - Martin Luther King's Birthday
20 - Inauguration Day

1
2
3
4
5
6
7
8
9
10
11
12
13
14
15
16
17
18
19
20
21
22
23
24
25
26
27
28
29
30
31

Italian Green Salad

1 (10 ounce) package Italian-blend salad greens	280 g
1 seedless cucumber, peeled, sliced	
1 small zucchini with peel, sliced	
1 (8 ounce) bottle creamy Italian salad dressing	227 g
⅓ cup sunflower seeds	80 ml

- In salad bowl, combine salad greens, cucumber and zucchini. When ready to serve, toss with creamy Italian dressing and sprinkle sunflower seeds on top. Add croutons, if desired. Serves 4.

Super Simple Main Dish: **Sam's Lasagna**

- Heat 1 (57 ounce/2 kg) carton frozen lasagna, thawed according to package directions.

Deluxe Coconut Cake

1 (18 ounce) package yellow cake mix	510 g
3 eggs	
⅓ cup oil	80 ml
1 (14 ounce) can sweetened condensed milk	396 g
1 (10 ounce) can cream of coconut	280 g
1 (4 ounce) can flaked coconut	114 g
1 (8 ounce) carton whipped topping	227 g

- Preheat oven to 350° (176° C). Prepare yellow cake mix according to package directions using eggs, oil and 1 cup (240 ml) water. Pour into sprayed, floured 9 x 13-inch (23 x 33 cm) baking pan. Bake for 30 to 35 minutes or until toothpick inserted in center comes out clean.

- While cake is warm, punch holes in top about 2 inches (5 cm) apart. Pour sweetened condensed milk over cake and spread around until all milk soaks into cake. Pour coconut cream over cake and sprinkle coconut over top. When cake is cool, frost with whipped topping. Chill before serving. Serves 8.

Vanilla French Toast

5 eggs, beaten	
1 (12 ounce) can evaporated milk	340 g
1 cup sugar	240 ml
1 teaspoon cinnamon	5 ml
1½ tablespoons vanilla	22 ml
¼ cup (½ stick) butter, melted	60 ml
1 large loaf French bread	

- Mix eggs with milk. Add sugar, cinnamon, vanilla and butter. Cut bread into ¾-inch (1.8 cm) slices. Dip bread in egg mixture and place on 350° (176° C) griddle or in skillet on medium-high heat. Grill until brown on both sides. To serve, dust with powdered sugar. Serves 6 to 8.

Tropical Fruit Soup

1 (15 ounce) can crushed pineapple with juice	425 g
1 (15 ounce) can cream of coconut	425 g
1½ cups sour cream	360 ml
1 (15 ounce) can fruit cocktail with juice	425 g
Almond slivers, toasted	

- Combine all ingredients except almonds with 1 cup (240 ml) water in blender for 15 to 20 seconds. Chill overnight. To serve, add sliced bananas and/or strawberries. Top with toasted almonds. Serves 6.

Simple Side Dish: **Fast Bacon**

- Heat 1 (8 ounce/227 g) package pre-cooked bacon according to package directions.

Breakfast or Brunch

Chicken Breast Eden Isle

1 (8 ounce) carton sour cream	227 g
1 (3 ounce) cream cheese, softened	84 g
1 (10 ounce) can cream of chicken soup	280 g
1 (2.5 ounce) jar dried beef	70 g
6 boneless, skinless chicken breast halves	
6 bacon strips	
Fluffy rice	

- Preheat oven to 350° (176° C). With mixer beat sour cream, cream cheese and soup. Line bottom of sprayed 7 x 11-inch (23 x 33 cm) baking dish with dried beef.
- Place chicken breasts, wrapped with bacon strips, onto dried beef. Spoon sour cream mixture over chicken. Cover and bake for 1 hour. Uncover last few minutes to brown. Serve over rice. Serves 4 to 6.

Elegant Green Beans

2 pounds whole fresh green beans	1 kg
1 onion, thinly sliced	
6 tablespoons olive oil	90 ml
2 teaspoons sugar	10 ml
1 tablespoon white wine vinegar	15 ml
1 tablespoon fresh lemon juice	15 ml

- Steam beans with onion 10 minutes or until crisp and tender. Drain and place in medium bowl.
- Mix all other ingredients with 1 teaspoon (5 ml) salt and ½ teaspoon (2 ml) pepper and pour over beans. Cover and chill several hours. Serves 4 to 6.

Sausage-Potato Casserole

2 (10 ounce) cans cream of mushroom soup	2 (280 g)
1 cup milk	240 ml
1 pound ground sausage, divided	.5 kg
2 (15 ounce) cans sliced potatoes, drained, divided	2 (425 g)
1 (8 ounce) package shredded cheddar cheese, divided	227 g

- Preheat oven to 375° (190° C). Combine soup and milk. Brown sausage until thoroughly cooked.
- Line potatoes in sprayed 9 x 13-inch (23 x 33 cm) baking dish. Pour half soup mixture over potatoes and half sausage. Spread with half cheese. Repeat layers. Bake for 25 minutes. Serves 6 to 8.

Red-Neck Salad

2 (15 ounce) cans shoe-peg corn, drained	2 (425 g)
2 (15 ounce) cans black-eyed peas, drained	2 (425 g)
1 tomato, diced	
1 red onion, sliced	
1 (16 ounce) bottle zesty Italian dressing	.5 kg

- Combine corn and peas in bowl. Add tomato and onion. Pour about half dressing over mixture, add more as needed and refrigerate 4 to 5 hours. Serves 6.

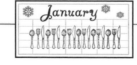

January

1- New Year's Day
15 - Martin Luther King's Birthday
20 - Inauguration Day

1
2
3
4
5
6
7
8
9
10
11
12
13
14
15
16
17
18
19
20
21
22
23
24
25
26
27
28
29
30
31

Five-Can Soup

1 (14 ounce) can chicken broth	396 g
1 (10 ounce) can cream of chicken soup	280 g
1 (12 ounce) can chicken breast	340 g
1 (15 ounce) can ranch-style beans	425 g
1 (10 ounce) can tomatoes and green chilies	280 g
Tortilla chips	
Shredded cheese	
Sour cream	

• In saucepan combine broth, soup, chicken, beans and tomatoes and green chilies and simmer 30 minutes. Serve over a few crushed tortilla chips and top with cheese and sour cream. Serves 5 to 6.

Jalapeno Fudge

1 (16 ounce) package shredded cheddar cheese	.5 kg
3 - 4 jalapeno peppers, chopped	
4 eggs, lightly beaten	

• Preheat oven to 350° (176° C). Mix all ingredients. Pour into sprayed 9-inch (23 cm) baking dish and bake until golden brown, about 25 minutes. Cut into squares. Serves 4 to 5.

Simple Bread Idea: **Toasted French Bread**

• Butter each bread slice in 1 loaf French bread and broil until light brown.

Cheese Omelet

12 eggs
1 cup milk   **240 ml**
2 drops hot sauce
1 (8 ounce) package shredded sharp cheddar cheese 227 g
1 (8 ounce) package shredded Monterrey Jack cheese 227 g

- Preheat oven to 325° (162° C). Beat all ingredients and ⅛ teaspoon (.5 ml) salt. Pour into unsprayed 9-inch (23 cm) baking dish. Bake for one hour or until puffy. Serves 4 to 6.

Quick, Creamy Biscuits

2½ cups biscuit mix   **600 ml**
1 (8 ounce) carton whipping cream   **227 g**

- Preheat oven to 375° (190° C). Mix biscuit mix and cream. Place on floured board. Knead several times. Pat out to ½-inch (1.2 cm) thick. Cut with biscuit cutter or 2-inch (5 cm) glass and place biscuits on sprayed baking sheet. Bake for 12 to 15 minutes. Serves 4 to 6.

Simple Side Dish: Crispy Bacon

- Fry 1 pound (.5 kg) bacon and drain. As long as you are frying bacon, fry another pound, drain and crumble. Freeze to use in another dish later.

Breakfast or Brunch

1
2
3
4
5
6
7
8
9
10
11
12
13
14
15
16
17
18
19
20
21
22
23
24
25
26
27
28
29
30
31

Grilled Catfish

4 catfish fillets
Olive oil
½ teaspoon garlic powder   **2 ml**
½ teaspoon lemon pepper   **2 ml**

- Sprinkle catfish fillets with olive oil and rub in. Sprinkle fillets with seasonings plus ½ teaspoon (2 ml) salt. Place fish on grill rack directly over medium hot coals and grill about 3 to 5 minutes per side or until fish flakes easily. Serves 4.

Italian Pasta Salad

1 (6.4 ounce) box Italian pasta salad mix   **180 g**
½ cup zesty Italian salad dressing   **120 ml**
Parmesan cheese

- Prepare pasta according to package directions and toss with salad dressing. Sprinkle parmesan on top. Serves 4.

Simple Bread Idea: **Buttered French Bread**

- Butter and heat 1 loaf sliced French bread according to package directions.

Hot Tamale Pie

1 (24 ounce) package corn chips	680 g
2 (16 ounce) cans chili without beans	2 (.5 kg)
1 (16 ounce) can tamales	.5 kg
12 - 15 slices Velveeta® cheese	.5 kg

- Preheat oven to 350° (176° C). Arrange corn chips in lightly sprayed 9 x 13-inch (23 x 33 cm) baking dish. Spread chili over chips. Slice tamales and arrange over chili. Top with cheese slices. Bake for 20 to 30 minutes. Serves 4 to 6.

Mexican-Fiesta Rice

1 (6 ounce) package Mexican fiesta rice	168 g
1 cup chopped celery	240 ml
1 (8 ounce) package cubed Mexican Velveeta® cheese	227 g

- In saucepan, heat 2 cups (480 ml) water to boil and add rice and celery. Return to boiling, reduce heat and simmer 5 minutes. Stir occasionally. Place in serving bowl and sprinkle with cheese. Serves 4 to 6.

Simple Side Dish: **Guacamole Salad**

Shredded lettuce
1 (16 ounce) carton refrigerated guacamole   .5 kg
1 bunch fresh green onions, chopped

- For each serving, place shredded lettuce on salad plate with about ⅓ cup (80 ml) guacamole on top. Place green onions on each serving. Serves 4 to 6.

January
1
2
3
4
5
6
7
8
9
10
11
12
13
14
15
16
17
18
19
20
21
22
23
24
25
26
27
28
29
30
31

1
2
3
4
5
6
7
8
9
10
11
12
13
14
15
16
17
18
19
20
21
22
23
24
25
26
27
28
29
30
31

Planet Pizza

1 (8 ounce) can crescent dinner rolls	227 g
1 (8 ounce) can tomato sauce	227 g
½ pound sliced bacon, fried	227 g
½ cup sliced fresh mushrooms	120 ml
1 teaspoon ground oregano	5 ml
1 cup shredded Mozzarella cheese	240 ml

• Preheat oven to 375° (190° C). Place dough on cookie sheet. Flatten to form rectangle. Spread tomato sauce over dough evenly and crumble bacon over tomato sauce. Sprinkle with mushrooms, oregano and cheese. Bake for 15 minutes or until cheese bubbles. Serves 4.

Green Salad

1 (10 ounce) package spring-mix salad greens	280 g
1 bunch red radishes, sliced	
1 small zucchini with peel, sliced	
1 cup fresh broccoli florets	240 ml
1 (8 ounce) bottle honey-mustard vinaigrette dressing	227 g

• In salad bowl, combine salad greens, radishes, zucchini and broccoli florets. Toss with salad dressing. Serves 4.

January

1- New Year's Day
15 - Martin Luther King's Birthday
20 - Inauguration Day

French Toast On The Town

½ cup (1 stick) butter	120 ml
1 cup firmly packed light brown sugar	240 ml
3 tablespoons corn syrup	45 ml
7 slices white bread, crust removed	
6 eggs, beaten	
1½ cups half-and-half cream	360 ml
½ teaspoon vanilla	2 ml
1 teaspoon almond extract	5 ml
¼ teaspoon ground cinnamon	1 ml

- In saucepan melt butter, add brown sugar and corn syrup and stir until they blend well. Pour mixture into 9 x 13-inch (23 x 33 cm) baking dish. Place bread slices over butter-sugar mixture in single layer. (Six slices will fit in baking dish. Cut 1 remaining bread slice to fit around edges of dish.)
- Combine eggs, cream, vanilla, almond extract, cinnamon and ½ teaspoon (2 ml) salt and mix until they blend well. Slowly pour over bread slices.
- Cover and refrigerate overnight.
- Uncover and bake at 350º (176º C) for about 35 minutes or until golden brown. When serving, cut into squares and lift up with square spatula so brown sugar mixture comes with each serving. Serves 4 to 6.

Super Simple Side Dish: **Fast Bacon**

- Heat 1 package pre-cooked bacon slices or sausage links in microwave-safe dish according to package directions.

Breakfast or Brunch

1
2
3
4
5
6
7
8
9
10
11
12
13
14
15
16
17
18
19
20
21
22
23
24
25
26
27
28
29
30
31

Pepper Steak

1½ pounds round steak	.7 kg
1 (14 ounce) can beef broth	396 g
¼ cup soy sauce	60 ml
½ cup chopped bell pepper	120 ml
1 (15 ounce) can bean sprouts	425 g
2 (8 ounce) cans sliced water chestnuts, drained	2 (227 g)
1 (4 ounce) can sliced mushrooms	114 g
Cornstarch	
Fluffy rice	

• Cut steak into bite-size pieces. Season with black pepper and brown in small amount of oil. Add broth, soy sauce, and vegetables. Cook over medium heat. Make paste with 2 tablespoons (30 ml) cornstarch and 1 tablespoon (15 ml) water. Add to mixture. Cook on low heat 30 to 45 minutes. Serve over rice. Serves 4.

Ramen Noodle Coleslaw

1 (16 ounce) package coleslaw mix	.5 kg
1 cup sunflower seeds	240 ml
1 green bell pepper, seeded, chopped	
1 bunch green onions, chopped	
2 (3 ounce) packages chicken-flavored ramen	2 (84 g)
1 (16 ounce) bottle Italian salad dressing	.5 kg

• Combine coleslaw, sunflower seeds, bell pepper, onions, ramen noodles and seasoning packets. Break ramen noodles into smaller pieces and add to coleslaw mixture. Toss with dressing and refrigerate. Serves 4.

No-Panic Crab Casserole

2 (6 ounce) cans crabmeat, drained, flaked	2 (168 g)
1 cup half-and-half cream	240 ml
1½ cups mayonnaise	360 ml
6 eggs, hard-boiled, finely chopped	
1 cup seasoned breadcrumbs, divided	240 ml
1 tablespoon dried parsley flakes	15 ml
1 (8 ounce) can sliced water chestnuts, drained	227 g
2 tablespoons butter, melted	30 ml

- Preheat oven to 350° (176° C). Combine crabmeat, cream, mayonnaise, hard-boiled eggs, ½ cup (120 ml) breadcrumbs, parsley, water chestnuts and a little salt and mix well. Pour into sprayed 2-quart (2 L) baking dish. Combine remaining breadcrumbs and butter and sprinkle over top of casserole. Bake uncovered for 40 minutes. Serves 4.

Italian-Broiled Tomatoes

Roma tomatoes
Olive Oil
Lemon pepper
Garlic powder
Parmesan cheese

- Cut roma tomatoes in half. Drizzle with olive oil.
- Sprinkle with lemon pepper, garlic powder and parmesan cheese. Broil in oven or toaster oven. Serves 4.

1
2
3
4
5
6
7
8
9
10
11
12
13
14
15
16
17
18
19
20
21
22
23
24
25
26
27
28

Favorite Onion Soup

½ pound white onions, sliced	227 g
¼ cup (½ stick) butter	60 ml
2 tablespoons oil	30 ml
3 tablespoons flour	45 ml
1 quart chicken broth	1 L
1 quart beef broth	1 L
½ cup shredded Swiss cheese	120 ml
½ cup shredded parmesan cheese	120 ml
8 slices French bread	

• In large saucepan, saute onions in butter and oil until onions are transparent, but not brown. When tender, turn heat to simmer, sprinkle with flour and stir vigorously. Stir in broths. Heat thoroughly and divide among 8 ovenproof bowls.

• Mix both cheeses with 1 tablespoon (15 ml) water to form a smooth paste and spread over bread. Float slice of bread on top each serving. Place all bowls on oven rack 4 inches (10 cm) from broiler. Heat and broil until cheese melts. Serves 4 to 6.

Russian Salad

1 (10 ounce) package fresh spinach	280 g
3 eggs, hard-boiled, sliced	
1 bunch green onions, chopped	
1 (8 ounce) fresh mushrooms, sliced	227 g
½ pound bacon, fried, crumbled	227 g
1 (8 ounce) can sliced water chestnuts, drained	227 g
1½ cups fresh beans sprouts, drained	360 ml
Catalina dressing	

• Combine all salad ingredients and toss with desired amount of dressing. Serves 4 to 6.

1
2
3
4
5
6
7
8
9
10
11
12
13
14
15
16
17
18
19
20
21
22
23
24
25
26
27
28

Grilled Chicken

Boneless, skinless chicken breast halves
Oil
Thyme
Garlic powder
Pinch brown sugar

- In large mixing bowl, combine chicken breasts and 1 tablespoon (15 ml) oil per breast to coat. Sprinkle with seasonings and a little salt. Refrigerate for 15 to 20 minutes. Grill for 8 to 10 minutes on each side.

Macaroni And Cheese

2 (10 ounces) packages Stouffer's frozen welsh rarebit, thawed	**2 (280 g)**
1 cup elbow macaroni	**240 ml**
1 cup sour cream	**240 ml**
¼ cup grated cheddar cheese	**60 ml**

- Preheat oven to 400° (204° C). Heat welsh rarebit in top of double boiler for 15 to 20 minutes.

- Cook macaroni according to package directions. Drain. Pour welsh rarebit into 2-quart (2 L) baking dish. Add cooked macaroni, 1 teaspoon (5 ml) salt and sour cream. Stir to combine. Sprinkle with grated cheese. Bake for 20 minutes. Serves 4 to 6.

Simple Bread Idea: **French Bread**

- Butter each slice 1 loaf sliced French bread and toast.

1
2
3
4
5
6
7
8
9
10
11
12
13
14
15
16
17
18
19
20
21
22
23
24
25
26
27
28

Chicken Pockets

1 (3 ounce) package cream cheese, softened	84 g
1 (12 ounce) can chicken	340 g
3 tablespoons butter, softened	45 ml
2 tablespoons milk	30 ml
1 tablespoon chopped chives	15 ml
1 (8 ounce) can crescent rolls	227 g
Parmesan cheese	
Breadcrumbs	

- Preheat oven to 350° (176° C). With mixer, blend cream cheese, chicken and butter. Add, milk and chives plus ⅛ teaspoon (.5 ml) salt.
- Separate dough into 4 rectangles and press seams together. Spoon mixture into center of dough. Pull 4 corners up and twist together.
- Seal sides by pinching together. Sprinkle top with parmesan cheese and breadcrumbs.
- Bake on unsprayed baking sheet for 20 to 25 minutes. Serves 4.

Broccoli Salad

1 cup mayonnaise	240 ml
⅓ cup sugar	80 ml
2 teaspoons vinegar	10 ml
1½ bunches broccoli, chopped	
1 pound bacon, fried, crumbled	.5 kg
1 cup raisins	240 ml
1 cup cashew nuts	240 ml
1 medium onion, chopped	

- Combine mayonnaise, sugar and vinegar. Set aside. Mix remaining ingredients and toss with dressing. Serves 4 to 6.

Swiss Tuna Grill

1 (6 ounce) can white tuna, drained, flaked	168 g
½ cup shredded Swiss cheese	120 ml
1 rib celery, finely chopped	
¼ onion, finely chopped	
¼ cup mayonnaise	60 ml
¼ cup sour cream	60 ml
Rye bread	
Butter, softened	

• Combine tuna, cheese, celery, onion, mayonnaise, sour cream, ½ teaspoon (2 ml) salt and ¼ teaspoon (1 ml) pepper and mix well. Spread on rye bread and top with another slice rye bread. Spread top of sandwiches with butter and place on hot griddle. Over medium heat, brown sandwich tops and bottoms and serve hot. Serves 4.

Spicy Turkey Soup

3 - 4 cups cooked, chopped turkey	710 ml
2 (14 ounce) cans chicken broth	2 (396 g)
2 (10 ounce) cans diced tomatoes and green chilies	2 (280 g)
1 (15 ounce) can whole kernel corn	425 g
1 large onion, chopped	
1 (10 ounce) can tomato soup	280 g
1 teaspoon garlic powder	5 ml
1 teaspoon dried oregano	5 ml
3 tablespoons cornstarch	45 ml

• In large roasting pan, combine turkey, broth, tomatoes and green chilies, corn, onion, tomato soup, garlic powder and oregano. Mix cornstarch with 3 tablespoons (45 ml) water and add to soup mixture. Bring mixture to a boil, reduce heat and simmer for 2 hours. Stir occasionally. Serves 4 to 6.

1
2
3
4
5
6
7
8
9
10
11
12
13
14
15
16
17
18
19
20
21
22
23
24
25
26
27
28

Smothered Steak

1½ pounds (¾ inch/1.8 cm) thick beef round steak	.7 kg
⅓ cup flour	80 ml
3 tablespoons oil	45 ml
3 medium onions, sliced	
1 (10 ounce) can beef broth	280 g
1 tablespoon lemon juice	15 ml
1 teaspoon garlic powder	5 ml

• Cut meat into serving-size pieces. Pound flour into steak with meat tenderizer. In large skillet, brown steak in oil and top with onion slices. In medium bowl, combine remaining ingredients. Pour over steak, bring to boil and reduce heat to simmer. Cover and cook slowly for 1 hour. Check steak while cooking and add a little water if needed. Serves 4.

Spinach Salad

1 (10 ounce) package baby spinach	280 g
1 bunch fresh parsley, chopped	
1 cup grated Romano cheese	240 ml
1 (4 ounce) package blue cheese, crumbled	114 g
Vinaigrette dressing	

• Combine spinach and parsley in large bowl. Just before serving, pour enough dressing to moisten greens. Toss well. Sprinkle with cheeses. Toss again. Season with pepper. Serves 4.

One-Pan Banana Bread

⅓ cup oil	80 ml
1½ cups mashed ripe bananas	360 ml
½ teaspoon vanilla	2 ml
3 eggs	
2⅔ cups biscuit mix	640 ml
1 cup sugar	240 ml
½ cup chopped nuts	120 ml

• Preheat oven to 350° (176° C). Mix all ingredients and pour into sprayed, floured 9 x 5-inch (23 x 13 cm) loaf pan. Bake for 55 to 65 minutes. Cool 5 minutes and remove from pan. Cool on wire rack. Serves 4 to 6.

Baked Eggs

1 pound pork breakfast sausage	.5 kg
10 eggs, beaten	
⅓ cup flour	80 ml
¾ teaspoon baking powder	4 ml
1 (16 ounce) package shredded Monterey Jack cheese	5 kg
1½ cups cottage cheese	360 ml
¾ cup fresh mushrooms, sliced	180 ml

• Preheat oven to 375° (190° C). Cook sausage in skillet. Drain and crumble. Beat eggs, flour and baking powder. Add sausage, cheeses and mushrooms. Mix well.

• Pour into sprayed 9 x 13-inch (23 x 33 cm) baking dish. Bake for 35 to 40 minutes. Serves 4 to 6.

Breakfast or Brunch

1
2
3
4
5
6
7
8
9
10
11
12
13
14
15
16
17
18
19
20
21
22
23
24
25
26
27
28

Santa Fe Stew

1½ pounds ground round beef	.7 kg
1 (1 ounce) packet taco seasoning	28 g
1 (1 ounce) packet ranch-style dressing mix	28 g
1 (15 ounce) can whole kernel corn with liquid	425 g
1 (15 ounce) can kidney beans with liquid	425 g
2 (15 ounce) cans stewed tomatoes with liquid	425 g
2 (15 ounce) cans pinto beans with liquid	2 (425 g)
1 (10 ounce) can tomatoes and green chilies	280 g

• Cook beef until brown. Drain well if necessary. Add both packages of seasonings and mix well. Add corn, kidney beans, stewed tomatoes, pinto beans, tomatoes and green chilies and mix well. Simmer for 25 minutes. If you want it really hot, use 2 cans tomatoes and green chilies. Serves 4 to 6.

Jalapeno Bites

1 (8 ounce) package cream cheese, softened	227 g
1 (5 ounce) grated parmesan cheese	143 g
3 tablespoons chopped fresh jalapeno peppers	45 ml
2 egg yolks	
2 cups dry breadcrumbs	480 ml

• Preheat oven to 350° (176° C). Beat cream cheese, parmesan cheese, jalapeno peppers and egg yolks in bowl. Mix to form paste. Shape ½ tablespoon (7 ml) at a time into ¼-inch (.6 cm) rounds. Roll in breadcrumbs. Place on unsprayed baking sheet. Bake for 10 to 15 minutes. Serves 4 to 6.

Teriyaki Chicken

1½ - 2 pounds chicken pieces, skinned	.7 kg
½ cup soy sauce	120 ml
¼ cup dry sherry	60 ml
2 tablespoons sugar	30 ml
2 tablespoons grated fresh ginger root	30 ml
4 cloves garlic, crushed	
2 tablespoons oil	30 ml

- Rinse chicken, pat dry and arrange in baking dish. Combine soy sauce, sherry, sugar, ginger root, garlic and oil. Pour over chicken and toss to coat.

- Cover and marinate in refrigerator 6 hours and turn occasionally. Drain. Pat chicken dry and place on hot grill. Cook and turn occasionally for 30 minutes or until chicken is tender. Serves 4 to 6.

Grilled Mixed Vegetables

1 yellow squash, washed, cubed	
1 zucchini, (1 inch) sliced	2.5 cm
1 green bell pepper, seeded, quartered	
1 small onion, quartered	
6 large mushrooms, halved	
1 (8 ounce) bottle Italian dressing	227 g

- Mix vegetables and spread on aluminum foil. Sprinkle dressing over all. Close foil tightly to make flat package and place on grill rack. Grill for about 15 minutes or until vegetables are tender. Serves 4.

1
2
3
4
5
6
7
8
9
10
11
12
13
14
15
16
17
18
19
20
21
22
23
24
25
26
27
28

Cherry Brisket

1 (5 pound) brisket	2.2 kg
Soy sauce	
Worcestershire sauce	
1 (1 ounce) packet dry onion soup mix	28 g
Caraway seeds	
1 (20 ounce) can cherry pie filling	567 g

- Season brisket with soy and Worcestershire sauce. Sprinkle soup mix and caraway seeds over brisket. Cover tightly with plastic wrap and marinate in refrigerator for 2 days.

- Wrap brisket in 2 layers of aluminum foil. Place on baking sheet and bake at 325° (162° C) for 4 hours. Let cool before unwrapping. Pour juices into container. Refrigerate juices and brisket. Scrape seasonings off meat and slice.

- Place juices in bottom of baking pan and top with brisket slices. Pour pie filling over top. Bake at 350° (176° C) for 30 to 45 minutes. Serves 4 to 6.

Strawberry-Spinach Salad

1 pound fresh spinach, cut up	.5 kg
1 pint strawberries, sliced	.5 kg
French dressing	

- Prepare spinach and strawberries and return to refrigerator to chill. Just prior to serving, toss spinach and strawberries with enough dressing just to coat spinach leaves. Serves 4 to 6.

Sweet-And-Sour Chicken

1 cup apricot preserves	240 ml
1 (1 ounce) packet onion soup mix	28 g
1 (8 ounce) small bottle Russian dressing	227 g
1 (2 pound) package frozen chicken tenders, thawed	1 kg
Fluffy rice	

• Preheat oven to 400° (204° C). Mix preserves, soup mix and dressing. In sprayed 9 x 13-inch (23 x 33 cm) baking pan, pour mixture over chicken and bake for 40 minutes to 1 hour or until chicken cooks fully. Serve over rice. Serves 4 to 6.

Angel Whip Salad

1 (16 ounce) carton whipped topping	.5 kg
1 (20 ounce) can cherry pie filling	567 g
1 (14 ounce) can sweetened condensed milk	396 g
1 (8 ounce) can crushed pineapple, drained	227 g
1 (3 ounce) can flaked coconut	84 g
1 cup miniature marshmallows	240 ml

• Combine all ingredients and chill. Serves 4 to 6.

Simple Side Dish: **Chicken-Broccoli Linguine**

• Cook 2 (4.7 ounce/143 g) boxes chicken and broccoli linguine according to package directions.

1
2
3
4
5
6
7
8
9
10
11
12
13
14
15
16
17
18
19
20
21
22
23
24
25
26
27
28

Gold Rush Casserole

1 (5 ounce) box dry hash brown potato mix	143 g
4 tablespoons butter	60 ml
¼ cup flour	60 ml
2 cups milk	480 ml
1 cup sour cream	240 ml
2 tablespoons dried minced parsley	30 ml
8 slices Canadian bacon	
8 eggs	

• Preheat oven to 300° (148° C). Prepare potatoes according to package directions. In skillet, melt butter and blend in flour and ½ teaspoon (2 ml) salt. Gradually stir in milk. Cook, stir until thick and remove from heat. Add sour cream, parsley and hash browns and mix well. Spoon into sprayed 9 x 13-inch (23 x 33 cm) baking dish. Arrange bacon on top. Bake for 20 minutes. Break eggs in depressed areas made with spoon. Bake 15 minutes or until eggs set. Serves 4 to 6.

Fresh Green Salad

1 (16 ounce) package field greens	.5 kg
Tomato wedges or red onion rings	
4 slices bacon	

• Combine greens and tomato wedges or red onion rings in bowl. Place bacon on paper towels and cook in microwave until crisp. Break bacon into pieces and drain. Toss with greens and serve with ranch-style dressing. Serves 4.

(Continued on page 49.)

365

(Continued from page 48.)

Yogurt-Granola-Fruit Medley

2 bananas, sliced	
1 (8 ounce) carton vanilla yogurt	227 g
1 cup granola	240 ml
1¼ cups seedless grapes, halved	300 ml

- Layer half banana slices in serving bowl. Spread with one-fourth yogurt, sprinkle with one-fourth granola and half the grapes.
- Sprinkle with one-fourth more granola. Repeat these layers. Cover and chill up to 3 hours before serving. Serves 4.

Simple Bread Idea: **Hot Biscuits**

- Bake 1 (22 ounce/624 g) package frozen flaked biscuits according to package directions and serve hot.

1- National Freedom Day
2- Groundhog Day
12 - Lincoln's Birthday
14 - Valentine's Day
22 - Washington's Birthday

1
2
3
4
5
6
7
8
9
10
11
12
13
14
15
16
17
18
19
20
21
22
23
24
25
26
27
28

Italian Toast

2 large firm, ripe tomatoes, chopped, drained	
1 cup loosely packed, chopped fresh basil	240 ml
¼ cup chopped Belgian endive	60 ml
¼ cup olive oil	60 ml
1 loaf Italian bread	

- Mix tomatoes, basil, endive and olive oil in medium bowl. Let stand at room temperature. Add a little salt and pepper. Slice bread, arrange on baking sheet and toast under broiler until golden brown on both sides. Top hot toasts with tomato mixture. Serves 4 to 6.

Incredible Broccoli-Cheese Soup

1 (10 ounce) package frozen chopped broccoli	280 g
3 tablespoons butter	45 ml
¼ onion, finely chopped	
¼ cup flour	60 ml
1 (16 ounce) carton half-and-half cream	.5 kg
1 (14 ounce) can chicken broth	396 g
⅛ teaspoon cayenne pepper	.5 ml
1 (8 ounce) package cubed mild Mexican Velveeta® cheese	227 g

- Punch several holes in broccoli package and microwave for 5 minutes. Turn package and cook additional 4 minutes. Leave in microwave for 3 minutes.
- In large saucepan, melt butter and saute onion, but do not brown. Add flour, stir and gradually add cream, chicken broth, cayenne pepper, ½ teaspoon (2 ml) salt and ¼ teaspoon (1 ml) pepper.
- Stir constantly and heat until mixture is slightly thick. Do NOT let mixture come to boil. Add cheese, stir and heat until cheese melts. Add cooked broccoli. Serve piping hot. Serves 4 to 6.

Bacon And Onion Quiche

4 tablespoons butter, divided	60 ml
2 onions, chopped	
4 eggs	
1½ cups milk	360 ml
¾ pound bacon, fried crisp	340 g
1 (8 ounce) package shredded Swiss cheese	227 g

- Preheat oven to 325° (162° C). Spread 1 tablespoon (15 ml) butter evenly into 9-inch (23 cm) pie pan. Melt remaining butter in skillet. Add onions and saute until soft but not brown. Beat eggs, milk and a little salt and pepper until they blend.

- Line bottom of pie pan with bacon strips and scatter cheese on top. Pour in egg mixture. Bake for 25 to 30 minutes or until custard is brown and set. No crust. Serves 4 to 6.

Endive-Orange Salad

2 bunches curly endive	
2 bunches watercress	
1 (11 ounce) can mandarin oranges, drained	312 g
4 shallots, finely chopped	
½ cup olive oil	120 ml
4 tablespoons lemon juice	60 ml
1 teaspoon sugar	5 ml

- Wash endive and break in small pieces. Wash watercress and rip off stems. Combine in large bowl. Top with orange sections before serving. Combine shallots, oil, lemon juice, sugar and a little salt and pepper. Blend with fork. Pour over greens and toss well. Serves 4 to 6.

1
2
3
4
5
6
7
8
9
10
11
12
13
14
15
16
17
18
19
20
21
22
23
24
25
26
27
28

Grilled and Dilled Salmon

1 pint plain yogurt	.5 kg
1 tablespoon lemon juice	30 ml
2 cloves garlic, minced	
1 tablespoon chopped fresh dill	15 ml
Dash hot sauce	
½ cucumber, peeled, thinly sliced	
6 (8 ounce) salmon steaks or fillets	6 (227 g)

- Combine yogurt with lemon juice, garlic, dill, ⅛ teaspoon (.5 ml) each of salt and pepper and hot sauce in medium bowl. Gently stir in cucumber. Place oven rack about 3 inches (8 cm) from heat. Broil or grill salmon for 10 to 20 minutes or until fish flakes easily. Turn once. Spread yogurt dill sauce over salmon before serving. Serves 6.

Carrots And Mashed Potatoes

4 potatoes, peeled, cubed	
1 large carrot, peeled, cubed	
⅓ cup milk	80 ml
1 teaspoon dried dill	5 ml
¼ cup (½ stick) butter	60 ml

- Place potatoes and carrots in water. Boil for 25 minutes. Drain. Return to pot and mash. Stir in milk, dill and butter. Season with a little salt and pepper.   Serves 4 to 6.

(Continued on page 53.)

(Continued from page 52.)

Italian Green Salad

1 (10 ounce) package Italian-blend salad greens   **280 g**
⅓ cup sunflower seeds   **80 ml**
Creamy Italian dressing

• Combine salad greens and sunflower seeds. Toss with
  desired amount of salad dressing.   Serves 4 to 6.

Chocolate Chip Valentine Cookie

1 package refrigerator chocolate chip cookie dough

• Press entire package of dough into sprayed heart-
  shaped baking pan. Bake according to package
  directions. Add extra time necessary for size of
  cookie. Cool. Remove carefully and place on serving
  platter. Decorate if you have time.

❤ *February* ☃

1- National Freedom Day
2- Groundhog Day
12 - Lincoln's Birthday
14 - Valentine's Day
22 - Washington's Birthday

1
2
3
4
5
6
7
8
9
10
11
12
13
14
15
16
17
18
19
20
21
22
23
24
25
26
27
28

White Wine Chicken Livers

6 strips bacon	
6 green onions, chopped	
1 (2.5 ounce) can mushroom pieces, drained	70 g
6 - 8 chicken livers	
1 (14 ounce) can beef broth	396 g
½ cup white wine	120 ml
Fluffy rice	

- Cook bacon in skillet until crisp. Remove from pan and crumble. Saute onions and mushrooms in bacon drippings for 1 minute. Add livers, broth and wine and cook 10 more minutes. Stir in bacon and serve over cooked rice. Serves 6 to 8.

Green Bean Casserole

1 (10 ounce) can cream of mushroom soup	280 g
½ cup milk	120 ml
1 teaspoon soy sauce	5 ml
2 (15 ounce) cans cut green beans, drained	2 (425 g)
1 (3 ounce) can french-fried onions	84 g

- Preheat oven to 350° (176° C). Combine soup, milk, soy sauce and dash of pepper. Stir in beans and ½ can of onions. Bake for 25 minutes. Top with remaining onions. Bake 5 minutes or until onions are golden brown. Serves 6 to 8.

(Continued on page 55.)

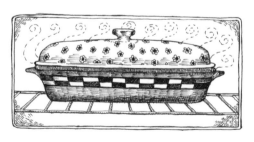

(Continued from page 54.)

"No Need to Knead" Rolls

2 cups lukewarm water	240 ml
2 (¼ ounce) packages dry yeast	2 (10 g)
1 egg	
¼ cup shortening	60 ml
6½ cups flour	1.5 L

- Preheat oven to 400° (204° C). In bowl, combine all ingredients and 1½ teaspoons (7 ml) salt; mix well and shape into rolls. Place rolls in sprayed round cake pans.
- Cover and let rise for 1 hour 30 minutes to 2 hours or until double in size. Bake rolls for 15 to 20 minutes. Serves 6 to 8.

Mom's Banana Pudding

1 (5 ounce) package banana pudding mix	143 g
3 cups milk	710 ml
1 (12 ounce) box vanilla wafer cookies	340 g
4 - 6 bananas, sliced	

- Prepare banana pudding according to package directions with milk. Make cookie crust by placing whole vanilla wafers in bottom and along sides of glass dish. Layer pudding, sliced bananas and cookies. Repeat until all ingredients are used. Refrigerate for 2 to 4 hours to blend flavors. Serves 6 to 8.

1
2
3
4
5
6
7
8
9
10
11
12
13
14
15
16
17
18
19
20
21
22
23
24
25
26
27
28

Ham Sandwiches

½ cup (1 stick) butter, softened	120 ml
8 onion rolls, split	
1 small onion, chopped	
2 tablespoons poppy seeds	30 ml
1 teaspoon dry mustard	5 ml
1 pound shaved ham	.5 kg
8 ounces sliced Swiss cheese	227 g

- Preheat oven to 350° (176° C). Spread butter on cut sides of rolls and reserve 1 tablespoon (15 ml) butter. Saute onion in remaining butter in skillet until soft, about 5 minutes. Add poppy seeds and dry mustard. Mix well.
- Layer ham, cheese slice and some of onion mixture on bottom half of each roll. Replace roll tops and wrap in foil. Place on baking sheet and bake for 20 minutes. Serves 8.

Blue Cheese-Bacon Potatoes

20 small red new potatoes with peel	
½ pound bacon, fried, crumbled	227 g
1 cup mayonnaise	240 ml
¼ cup whipping cream, slightly whipped	60 ml
¼ cup Roquefort cheese	60 ml
Parsley, finely chopped	

- Boil potatoes until tender. Combine mayonnaise, cream and cheese. Fold dressing into potatoes.
- Garnish with crumbled bacon and parsley. Serves 6 to 8.

Scalloped Oysters

1 cup dry breadcrumbs	240 ml
2 cups cracker crumbs	480 ml
1 cup (2 sticks) butter, melted	240 ml
1 (1 quart) carton oysters with liquor	1 L
4 tablespoons oyster liquor	60 ml
4 tablespoons cream	60 ml

- Preheat oven to 425° (220° C). Mix bread and cracker crumbs. Stir crumbs into butter. Put one-third crumb mixture sprayed 7 x 11-inch (18 x 28 cm) baking dish.
- Drain liquor from oysters. Cover with half oysters. Sprinkle with a little salt and pepper. Add half oyster liquor and cream. Repeat. Cover top with remaining crumbs. Bake for 30 minutes. Serves 4 to 6.

Strawberry-Slaw Salad

1 (10 ounce) package romaine lettuce, torn	280 g
1 cup broccoli slaw	240 ml
1 pint large fresh strawberries, quartered	.5 kg
½ red onion, coarsely chopped	

- In salad bowl, toss all ingredients. When ready to serve, use raspberry vinaigrette salad dressing. Serves 4 to 6.

Simple Side Dish: Broccoli-Rice Au Gratin

- Cook 1 (16 ounce/.5 kg) box broccoli au gratin rice and pasta according to package directions.

1
2
3
4
5
6
7
8
9
10
11
12
13
14
15
16
17
18
19
20
21
22
23
24
25
26
27
28

Chicken and Broccoli Casserole

1 (10 ounce) can cream of chicken soup	280 g
½ cup mayonnaise	120 ml
2 tablespoons lemon juice	30 ml
¼ teaspoon curry powder	1 ml
1 (16 ounce) package frozen broccoli florets	.5 kg
6 chicken breast halves, cooked, cubed	
1 cup crushed cornbread dressing	240 ml

- Preheat oven to 350° (176° C). Combine soup, mayonnaise, lemon juice and curry powder. Season with a little salt and pepper. Layer broccoli, chicken and soup mixture in 1-quart (1 L) baking dish. Top with layer of dressing crumbs. Heat for 30 to 40 minutes. Serves 4 to 6.

Cashew-Pea Salad

1 (16 ounce) package baby peas, thawed, drained	.5 kg
¾ cup chopped celery	180 ml
¼ cup chopped red bell pepper, chilled	60 ml
1 cup cashew pieces, chilled	240 ml
½ cup mayonnaise	120 ml

- Combine peas, celery, bell pepper and cashews. Toss. Add ½ cup (120 ml) mayonnaise and mix well. Refrigerate. Serves 4 to 6.

365

Sauerkraut and Ribs

1 (32 ounce) can sauerkraut	1 kg
½ cup packed brown sugar	120 ml
6 - 7 country-style pork ribs	
½ red apple with peel, finely diced	

- Preheat oven to 325° (162° C). Spread kraut in sprayed 9 x 13-inch (23 x 33 cm) baking dish. Mix in 1 cup (240 ml) water and brown sugar.
- Lay ribs on top. Cover snugly with foil wrap. Bake for about 4 hours. Drain off some fatty liquid. Stir red apple into kraut for some color. Bake uncovered for another 30 minutes. Serves 6 to 7.

Corn and Green Bean Casserole

1 (15 ounce) can French green beans with liquid	425 g
1 (8 ounce) can frozen whole kernel corn, drained	227 g
¾ cup broken pecans	180 ml
⅔ cup shredded cheddar cheese	160 ml
1½ cups cracker crumbs	360 ml
½ cup (1 stick) butter, melted	120 ml

- Preheat oven to 350° (176° C). In large baking dish, place in layers half beans, half corn and half pecans. Pour ½ cup (120 ml) bean juice over top.
- Repeat layers of beans, corn and pecans. Sprinkle with cheese and crumbs. Pour butter over all. Bake for 30 minutes. Serves 4 to 6.

Sausage-Apple Quiche

½ pound pork sausage	227 g
1½ cups chopped apple	360 ml
½ teaspoon ground cinnamon	2 ml
½ teaspoon ground nutmeg	2 ml
1 cup shredded cheddar cheese	240 ml
4 eggs, beaten	
1 cup half-and-half cream	240 ml
½ cup biscuit mix	120 ml

- Preheat oven to 375° (190° C). Cook sausage until brown, stir to crumble and drain. Combine apple, spices, cheese and sausage. Place in sprayed 9-inch (23 cm) quiche dish or pie pan. Combine eggs, cream and biscuit mix in large bowl. Mix well. Pour over apple mixture. Bake for 40 minutes or until set. Serves 4 to 6.

Stuffed Lettuce

1 head iceberg lettuce	
1 (8 ounce) package cream cheese, softened	227 g
2 tablespoons Roquefort® cheese	30 ml
2 tablespoons grated carrot	30 ml
2 tablespoons diced fresh tomato	30 ml
1 teaspoon minced onion	5 ml

- Wash lettuce and remove core; make hole large enough for 1 cup (240 ml) filling. Drain well. Beat together remaining ingredients and ¾ teaspoon (4 ml) salt and ⅛ teaspoon (.5 ml) pepper.
- Pack firmly into cavity of lettuce head. Wrap in clean, damp cloth. Chill several hours. Slice crosswise or in wedges so each portion has cheese center. Serves 4 to 6.

1 2 3 4 5 6 7 8 9 10 11 12 13 14 15 16 17 18 19 20 21 22 23 24 25 26 27 28

Rump Roast

4 - 5 pound beef rump roast	**1.8 kg**
Lemon pepper	
2 (10 ounce) cans cream of mushroom soup	**2 (280 g)**
2 (10 ounce) cans French onion soup	**2 (280 g)**

- Preheat oven to 325° (162° C). Sprinkle roast with lemon pepper. Place roast in roasting pan. Pour soups over roast. Cover and bake for 4 to 5 hours. Serves 4 to 6.

Cheesy Potatoes

4 - 5 cups instant mashed potatoes, prepared	**1 L**
1 (10 ounce) can cream of chicken soup	**280 g**
2 green onions, chopped	
1 cup shredded cheddar cheese	**240 ml**

- Preheat oven to 350° (176° C). Mix ingredients and a dash of salt. Spoon into sprayed 2-quart (2 L) baking dish. Cover and bake for 25 minutes. Serves 4 to 6.

Honey-Fruit Salad

1 (15 ounce) can pineapple chunks with juice	**425 g**
2 oranges, peeled, sectioned	
1 apple, cored, diced	
1 banana, sliced	
½ cup chopped pecans	**120 ml**
¼ cup honey	**60 ml**
1 tablespoon lemon juice	**15 ml**

- Combine all ingredients in salad bowl and refrigerate. Serves 4 to 6.

Cheesy Vegetable Soup

1 (16 ounce) bag frozen mixed vegetables	.5 kg
3 (14 ounce) cans chicken broth	3 (396 g)
1 (8 ounce) package shredded Velveeta® cheese	227 g
1 (10 ounce) can tomatoes and green chilies	280 g

- Cook vegetables in broth. Add cheese and melt. Add tomatoes and green chilies. Heat thoroughly and mash vegetables slightly. Serves 4 to 6.

Stuffed Mushrooms

1 (16 ounce) package pork sausage	.5 kg
½ onion, chopped	
½ green pepper, seeded, chopped	
20 - 30 whole mushrooms	
1 (8 ounce) package cream cheese	227 g

- Preheat oven to 300° (148° C). Brown sausage. Add onion and pepper. Cook over medium heat and drain. While mixture cooks, clean mushrooms and remove stems.
- Heat cream cheese in microwave about 1 minute or until soft. Mix with sausage. Stuff mushrooms and place on baking sheet. Bake for 20 to 25 minutes or until mushrooms are tender. Serves 4 to 6.

February

1- National Freedom Day
2- Groundhog Day
12 - Lincoln's Birthday
14 - Valentine's Day
22 - Washington's Birthday

1
2
3
4
5
6
7
8
9
10
11
12
13
14
15
16
17
18
19
20
21
22
23
24
25
26
27
28

Cranberries And Chicken

1 (16 ounce) can whole cranberry sauce	.5 kg
1 (8 ounce) bottle Catalina salad dressing	227 g
1 (1 ounce) packet dry onion soup mix	28 g
6 boneless, skinless chicken breast halves	

• Mix cranberry sauce, dressing and onion soup. Pour over chicken breasts in sprayed 9 x 13-inch (23 x 33 cm) glass baking dish. Marinate overnight. Bake at 350° (176° C) for 1 hour. Serves 6.

Spring Greens

1 (10 ounce) package spring-mix salad greens	280 g
1 seedless cucumber, sliced	
1 bunch red radishes, sliced	
1 (16 ounce) jar refrigerated honey-mustard dressing	.5 kg

• In salad bowl, toss greens, cucumber and radishes. Toss with one-half salad dressing. Add more if needed. Serves 4 to 6.

Onion Biscuits

2 cups biscuit mix	480 ml
¼ cup milk	60 ml
1 (8 ounce) carton French onion dip	227 g

• Preheat oven to 375° (190° C). Combine all ingredients and mix well. Drop dough by tablespoons in mounds onto sprayed baking sheet. Bake for 12 minutes. Serves 4 to 6.

1
2
3
4
5
6
7
8
9
10
11
12
13
14
15
16
17
18
19
20
21
22
23
24
25
26
27
28

Onion-Smothered Pork Chops

6 (½ inch) thick pork chops	**6 (1.2 cm)**
1 tablespoon oil	**15 ml**
½ cup (1 stick) butter, divided	**120 ml**
1 onion, chopped	
1 (10 ounce) can cream of onion soup	**280 g**
3 cups instant brown rice	**710 ml**

- Preheat oven to 325° (162° C). In skillet, brown pork chops in oil and simmer about 10 minutes. Place pork chops in sprayed shallow baking pan.

- In same skillet, add half butter and saute chopped onion. (Pan juices are brown from pork chops so onions will be brown from juices already in skillet.)

- Add onion soup and ½ cup (120 ml) water and stir well. Sauce will have a pretty, light brown color. Cook rice according to package directions and add remaining butter to rice.

- Place pork chops over rice in sprayed 9 x 13-inch (23 x 33 cm) baking pan. Pour onion-soup mixture over pork chops. Cover and bake for 40 minutes. Serves 6.

(Continued on page 65.)

❤ *February* ☃

1- National Freedom Day
2- Groundhog Day
12 - Lincoln's Birthday
14 - Valentine's Day
22 - Washington's Birthday

(Continued from page 64.)

Sweet Potato Delight

3 cups mashed sweet potatoes	710 ml
6 tablespoons (¾ stick) butter	90 ml
2 eggs	
¼ cup sugar	60 ml
1 teaspoon vanilla	5 ml

Topping:

⅓ cup flour	80 ml
1 cup packed brown sugar	240 ml
1 cup chopped nuts	240 ml
6 tablespoons (¾ stick) butter	90 ml

- Preheat oven to 350° (176° C). Combine sweet potatoes, 6 tablespoons (90 ml) butter, eggs, ¼ cup (60 ml) sugar and vanilla. Pour into sprayed 9-inch (23 cm) square baking pan. Combine topping ingredients and spread over sweet potato mixture. Bake for 30 minutes. Serves 4 to 6.

Beer Muffins

2 cups biscuit mix	480 ml
2 teaspoons sugar	10 ml
⅔ cup beer	160 ml
1 egg, slightly beaten	

- Preheat oven to 400° (204° C). Spray 12 muffin cups. Mix biscuit mix and sugar. Add beer and egg. Fill muffin cups two-thirds full. Bake for 15 minutes or until golden brown. Serves 4 to 6.

1
2
3
4
5
6
7
8
9
10
11
12
13
14
15
16
17
18
19
20
21
22
23
24
25
26
27
28

Three-Cheese Chicken Casserole

1 (10 ounce) package small egg noodles	280 g
3 tablespoons butter	45 ml
1 green and 1 red bell pepper, chopped	
½ cup chopped celery	120 ml
½ cup chopped onion	120 ml
1 (10 ounce) can cream of chicken soup	280 g
½ cup milk	120 ml
1 (6 ounce) jar sliced mushrooms, drained	168 g
1 (16 ounce) carton small curd cottage cheese, drained	.5 kg
4 cups, cooked, diced chicken or turkey breasts	1 L
1 (12 ounce) package shredded cheddar cheese	340 g
¾ cup freshly grated parmesan	180 ml

- Preheat oven to 325° (162° C). Cook noodles according to package directions and drain. Melt butter in skillet and saute peppers, celery and onion.

- In large bowl, combine noodles, sauteed mixture, chicken soup, milk, mushrooms, ½ teaspoon (2 ml) pepper, cottage cheese, chicken and cheddar cheese. Pour into sprayed 9 x 13-inch (23 x 33 cm) baking dish.

- Cover and bake for 35 to 40 minutes or until it bubbles around edges of casserole. Remove from oven, sprinkle parmesan cheese over casserole and return to oven for 5 minutes. Serves 4 to 6.

(Continued on page 67.)

(Continued from page 66.)

Bell Pepper Salad

1 medium red bell pepper, sliced
1 medium green bell pepper, sliced
1 medium yellow bell pepper, sliced
¼ cup vinaigrette dressing   60 ml

- Mix peppers in large bowl and toss with dressing. Refrigerate until ready to serve. Serves 4.

Granola Sundae

1 cup vanilla yogurt   240 ml
1 cup granola mix   240 ml
2 cups sliced bananas   480 ml
1 pint strawberries, sliced   .5 kg

- Layer yogurt, granola and fruit in 4 (8 ounce/227 g) stemmed glasses or bowls. Refrigerate until ready to serve. Serves 4.

1- National Freedom Day
2- Groundhog Day
12 - Lincoln's Birthday
14 - Valentine's Day
22 - Washington's Birthday

Pork Chop Cheddar Bake

8 boneless pork chops	
1 (10 ounce) can cream of mushroom soup	280 g
1 cup rice	240 ml
1½ cups shredded cheddar cheese, divided	360 ml
½ cup minced onion	120 ml
⅓ cup chopped bell pepper	80 ml
1 (4 ounce) can sliced mushrooms, drained	114 g
1 (3 ounce) can french-fried onions	84 g

- Preheat oven to 325° (162° C). Brown pork chops lightly. Drain and place in sprayed 9 x 13-inch (23 x 33 cm) baking dish. In same skillet, combine soup, 1¼ cups (300 ml) water, rice, ½ cup (120 ml) cheese, onion, bell pepper and mushrooms and mix well. Pour over pork chops. Cover with foil and bake for 1 hour 10 minutes. Uncover and top with remaining cheese and french-fried onions. Return to oven just until cheese melts. Serves 8.

Tangy Spinach Salad

1 (10 ounce) package baby spinach	280 g
1 cup cottage cheese	240 ml
1 red bell pepper, thinly sliced	
½ cup honey-mustard salad dressing	120 ml

- Combine above ingredients and toss with dressing. Serves 4 to 6.

Simple Bread Idea: **Texas Toast**

- Heat 1 package frozen garlic Texas Toast according to package directions and serve hot.

Fiesta Eggs

1 pound sausage	.5 kg
½ green bell pepper, seeded, chopped	
3 green onions, chopped	
1 (10 ounce) can tomatoes and green chilies	280 g
½ cup hot, chunky salsa	120 ml
4 ounces cubed Velveeta® cheese	114 g
10 eggs, slightly beaten	
½ cup sour cream	120 ml
⅔ cup milk	160 ml

- Preheat oven to 325° (162° C). Brown sausage, pepper and onions. Spoon mixture onto paper towels to drain. Dry skillet with more paper towels. Pour tomatoes and green chilies, salsa and cheese in skillet and cook, stir constantly, until cheese melts. Remove from heat.

- Beat eggs in bowl with 1½ teaspoons (7 ml) salt, sour cream and milk. Fold in sausage mixture and tomato-cheese mixture. Transfer to sprayed 7 x 11-inch (18 x 28 cm) baking dish. Bake uncovered for about 25 minutes or until center sets. Serves 4 to 6.

Simple Bread Idea: **Honey-Bran Muffins**

- Prepare 2 (7.4 ounce/210 g) package honey-bran muffin mix with 1⅓ cups (320 ml) milk according to package directions.

Breakfast or Brunch

Golden Catfish Fillets

2 eggs	
¾ cup flour	**180 ml**
¾ cup cornmeal	**180 ml**
1 teaspoon garlic powder	**5 ml**
6 - 8 (4 - 8 ounce) catfish fillets	**6 - 8 (114 g)**

- In shallow bowl, beat eggs and 2 tablespoons (30 ml) water until foamy. In another shallow bowl, combine flour, cornmeal, garlic powder and little salt. Dip fillets in eggs then coat with cornmeal mixture.

- Heat ¼-inch (.6 cm) oil in large skillet. Fry fish over medium-high heat for about 4 minutes on each side or until fish flakes easily with fork. Serves 6 to 8.

Sour Cream Cornbread

1 cup self-rising cornmeal	**240 ml**
1 (8 ounce) can cream-style corn	**227 g**
1 (8 ounce) carton sour cream	**227 g**
3 large eggs, lightly beaten	
¼ cup oil	**60 ml**

- Preheat oven to 400° (204° C). Heat lightly sprayed 8-inch (20 cm) cast-iron skillet at 400° (204° C). Combine all ingredients and stir just until moist. Remove prepared skillet from oven and spoon batter into hot skillet. Bake for 20 minutes or until golden. Serves 4 to 6.

Simple Side Dish: **Baked Beans**

- You can't beat baked beans with catfish! Open your favorite flavor canned beans or prepare the easy recipe on page 84.

Spinach-Chicken Salad

2 (10 ounce) packages fresh baby spinach	2 (280 g)
1 pound boneless, skinless chicken breasts, cooked	.5 kg
2 tablespoons lemon pepper	30 ml
1 cup mayonnaise	240 ml

- Place spinach in large bowl. Shred chicken breasts and add to spinach. Toss spinach and chicken with lemon pepper and mayonnaise. Serves 4 to 6.

Crispy Herb Bread

1½ teaspoons basil	7 ml
1 teaspoon rosemary	5 ml
½ teaspoon thyme	2 ml
1 cup (2 sticks) butter, melted	240 ml
1 package hot dog buns	

- Preheat oven to 300° (148° C). Combine all ingredients except buns and let stand several hours at room temperature. Spread on buns and cut into strips. Bake for 15 to 20 minutes or until crisp. Serves 4 to 6.

Deluxe Stuffed Eggs

12 large eggs, hard-boiled	
1 (4 ounce) package crumbled blue cheese	114 g
¼ cup half-and-half cream	60 ml
2 tablespoons lime juice	30 ml
2 tablespoons black caviar	30 ml

- Cut eggs in half lengthwise and carefully remove yolks. Mash yolks with fork. Add cheese, cream and lime juice and stir until smooth. Spoon mixture back into egg whites. Top with caviar. Refrigerate. Serves 4 to 6.

1
2
3
4
5
6
7
8
9
10
11
12
13
14
15
16
17
18
19
20
21
22
23
24
25
26
27
28
29
30
31

Tuna Souffle

6 slices white bread, torn
1 (12 ounce) can evaporated milk   **340 g**
2 eggs, beaten
2 (6 ounce) cans tuna, drained   **2 (168 g)**
2 (10 ounce) cans chicken noodle soup   **2 (280 g)**
1 (10 ounce) can cream of mushroom soup   **280 g**

- Preheat oven to 350° (176° C). Soak torn bread in evaporated milk. Stir in eggs. Add tuna and chicken noodle soup and blend. Pour into 9 x 13-inch (23 x 33 cm) baking pan. Bake for 30 minutes. Heat cream of mushroom soup and spoon over top of souffle. Serves 6.

Hearts Of Palm Salad

2 heads Boston lettuce, torn
6 green onions, sliced
1 (14 ounce) can hearts of palm, drained, sliced   **396 g**
½ cup vinaigrette dressing   **120 ml**

- Toss lettuce, onions and hearts of palm. Pour dressing over salad and serve. Serves 4 to 6.

No-Rise Rolls

1 (¼ ounce) package dry yeast   **10 g**
4 cups self-rising flour   **1 L**
½ cup sugar   **120 ml**
1 egg, beaten
1 cup (2 sticks) butter, melted   **240 ml**

- Preheat oven to 400° (204° C). Mix yeast with 2 cups (480 ml) warm water. Add flour, sugar, egg and butter and mix well.
- Fill sprayed muffin cups three-fourths full. Bake until brown, about 20 minutes. Unused dough can be kept in refrigerator. Serves 4 to 6.

Turkey Steaks With Mushrooms

1 (16 ounce) package frozen turkey tenderloin	.5 kg
¼ cup (½ stick) butter	60 ml
½ cup fresh, sliced mushrooms	120 ml
2 small onions, quartered	
½ teaspoon instant beef bouillon	2 ml

- Melt butter in skillet on medium high heat. When butter begins to brown, cook turkey 3 minutes and turn. Reduce heat and add mushrooms and onions.

- Cover and cook 5 minutes. Remove turkey to platter. Combine bouillon and ¼ cup (60 ml) water. Add to skillet. Stir and heat 1 minute. Pour over turkey. Serves 4 to 6.

Show-Stopper Vegetables

2 (10 ounce) packages frozen peas	2 (280 g)
2 (10 ounce) packages frozen French-style green beans	2 (280 g)
1 (10 ounce) package frozen lima beans	280 g
1 (8 ounce) carton whipping cream	227 g
1½ cups mayonnaise	360 ml
½ cup grated parmesan cheese	120 ml

- Preheat oven to 350° (176° C).
- Cook vegetables separately according to package directions. Drain and mix vegetables.
- Combine whipping cream and mayonnaise. Fold mixture into vegetables and spoon into sprayed 3-quart (3 L) baking dish. Sprinkle with parmesan cheese. Bake for 15 to 20 minutes or until thoroughly hot. Serves 4 to 6.

1
2
3
4
5
6
7
8
9
10
11
12
13
14
15
16
17
18
19
20
21
22
23
24
25
26
27
28
29
30
31

Hawaiian Spareribs

3 pounds pork spareribs	**1.3 kg**
⅓ cup soy sauce	**80 ml**
½ cup firmly packed brown sugar	**120 ml**
Fluffy rice	

- Preheat oven to 350° (176° C). Cut ribs into serving-size pieces (3 to 4 ribs per person). Place in single layer in 9 x 13-inch (23 x 33 cm) baking dish.
- Combine soy sauce with 1 cup (240 ml) water and pour over ribs. Sprinkle with ½ teaspoon (2 ml) salt and brown sugar. Bake for 2 hours and turn occasionally for even browning. Serve pan liquid over rice.

Asparagus Casserole

2 (15 ounce) cans asparagus spears	**2 (425 g)**
2 (15 ounce) cans petite peas	**2 (425 g)**
1 (10 ounce) can cream of mushroom soup	**280 g**
¾ cup shredded sharp cheddar cheese	**180 ml**
1 cup soft breadcrumbs	**240 ml**
2 tablespoons butter, melted	**30 ml**

- Chill cans of asparagus for 2 to 3 hours. About 40 minutes before serving, open cans and drain. Arrange half of asparagus in sprayed 6-cup (1.5 L) baking dish.
- Gently mix peas, soup and cheese. Spoon half mixture into baking dish. Add remaining asparagus and top with remaining pea mixture. Toss crumbs with butter. Sprinkle on top of vegetables. Bake at 350° (176° C) for 30 minutes. Serves 4 to 6.

Peach Melba Breakfast Shortcake

1 (10 count) box frozen waffles, thawed, lightly toasted	
½ cup cottage cheese	120 ml
½ cup bran cereal with peaches, raisins, almonds	120 ml
1 (15 ounce) can peach slices, drained	425 g

- Top each waffle with cottage cheese, cereal and fruit. If desired, substitute peaches for favorite fruit.

Quesadilla Pie

1 (4 ounce) can chopped green chilies, drained	114 g
½ pound sausage, cooked, drained	227 g
1 (16 ounce) package grated cheddar cheese	.5 kg
3 eggs, well beaten	
1½ cups milk	360 ml
¾ cup biscuit mix	180 ml
Hot salsa	

- Preheat oven to 350° (176° C). Sprinkle green chilies, cooked sausage and cheddar cheese in sprayed 9-inch (23 cm) pie pan. In separate bowl, combine eggs, milk and biscuit mix. Pour mixture over chilies, sausage and cheese and bake for 30 to 40 minutes. Serve with salsa on top of each slice. Serves 4 to 6.

Breakfast or Brunch

1
2
3
4
5
6
7
8
9
10
11
12
13
14
15
16
17
18
19
20
21
22
23
24
25
26
27
28
29
30
31

Meatball Hoagies

1 small onion, diced	
1 small green bell pepper, diced	
1 (15 ounce) can sloppy Joe sauce	425 g
1 (18 ounce) package frozen, cooked meatballs, thawed	510 g
4 hoagie buns	

- Saute onion and pepper in a little oil. Add sauce and meatballs, cook 10 minutes or until thoroughly hot and stir often. Spoon evenly onto hoagie buns. Serves 4.

Sassy Potato Salad

12 medium red potatoes with peels	
1 cup sour cream	240 ml
1 cup mayonnaise	240 ml
½ teaspoon prepared horseradish	2 ml
1 teaspoon celery seed	5 ml
1 cup chives or chopped green onions	240 ml

- Boil potatoes and cool. Mix sour cream, mayonnaise, horseradish, celery seed and dash of salt in mixing bowl.
- Slice potatoes and place half in 9 x 13-inch (23 x 33 cm) baking pan. Pour half of mayonnaise mixture over potatoes. Sprinkle with half chives (green onions). Repeat with second half.
- Serves 4 to 6.

Marinated Cucumbers

⅓ cup vinegar	80 ml
2 tablespoons sugar	30 ml
1 teaspoon dried dill weed	5 ml
3 cucumbers, peeled, sliced	

- Combine vinegar, sugar, 1 teaspoon (5 ml) salt, dill weed and ¼ teaspoon (1 ml) pepper. Pour over cucumbers. Refrigerate 1 hour before serving. Serves 4.

Grilled Ham And Apples

½ cup orange marmalade	120 ml
1 tablespoon butter	15 ml
¼ teaspoon ground ginger	1 ml
1 (1 pound/½ inch) thick ham slices	.5 kg (1.2 cm)
2 apples, cut into ½-inch thick slices	1.2 cm

- Combine marmalade, butter and ginger in a glass measuring cup. Microwave 1 minute, stirring once. Place ham slices on grill and cover grill lid.

- Grill about 5 to 10 minutes, turn occasionally and baste with marmalade mixture. Place apple slices on ham and grill additional 5 to 10 minutes. Serves 4 to 6.

Corn And Green Chilies Casserole

2 (10 ounce) packages frozen corn	2 (280 g)
2 tablespoons butter	30 ml
1 (8 ounce) package cream cheese	227 g
1 tablespoon sugar	15 ml
1 (4 ounce) can chopped green chilies	114 g

- Preheat oven to 350° (176° C). Cook corn according to package directions, drain and set aside. Melt butter in saucepan over low heat and add cream cheese. Stir until they melt. Stir in corn, sugar and green chilies. Spoon into sprayed 2-quart (2 L) baking dish. Cover and bake for 25 minutes. Serves 4 to 6.

1
2
3
4
5
6
7
8
9
10
11
12
13
14
15
16
17
18
19
20
21
22
23
24
25
26
27
28
29
30
31

Southwest Spaghetti

1½ pounds lean ground beef	.7 kg
1 tablespoon chili powder	15 ml
1 (15 ounce) can tomato sauce	425 g
1 (10 ounce) package spaghetti, broken up, cooked	280 g
1 tablespoon beef bouillon granules	15 ml
Shredded cheddar-Jack cheese	

- Brown beef until no longer pink. Drain and place in slow cooker. Add chili powder, tomato sauce, spaghetti, 2⅓ cups (560 ml) water and beef bouillon. Mix well. Cover and cook on LOW for 6 to 7 hours. When ready to serve, cover generously with cheese. Serves 4 to 6.

Hot, Parmesan Bread

1 (16 ounce) unsliced loaf Italian bread	.5 kg
½ cup Caesar dressing	120 ml
⅓ cup grated parmesan cheese	80 ml

- Cut 24 (½ inch/1.2 cm) thick slices from loaf. In small bowl, combine dressing and cheese. Spread 1 teaspoon (5 ml) dressing mixture onto each bread slice. Place bread on baking sheet and broil until golden brown. Serves 4 to 6.

Green And Red Salad

4 cups torn mixed salad greens	1 L
3 fresh green onions with tops, chopped	
2 medium red apples with peel, cored, diced	
1 cup fresh raspberries	240 ml
½ cup poppy seed dressing	120 ml

- Toss salad greens, onions and fruit. Drizzle with dressing and toss. Serves 4 to 6.

Broiler Sandwiches

5 slices bacon, cooked, crumbled
2 eggs, hard-boiled, chopped
1 (8 ounce) package shredded Velveeta® cheese   227 g
1 small onion, chopped
1 cup chili sauce   240 ml
8 sandwich buns, split

- Combine bacon, eggs, cheese, onion and chili sauce. Spread mixture on bun halves. Toast under broiler until brown. Serves 8.

Deviled Eggs

6 eggs, hard-boiled
2 tablespoons sweet pickle relish   30 ml
3 tablespoons mayonnaise   45 ml
Paprika

- Peel eggs and cut in half lengthwise. Take yolks out and mash with fork. Add relish and mayonnaise to yolks. Place yolk mixture back into egg white halves. Sprinkle with paprika. Serves 4 to 6.

Simple Side Dish: **Chilled Apricots**

- Serve 2 (24 ounce/680 g) jars refrigerated apricot halves. These jars of fruit are great time-savers.

March

2nd Sunday - Daylight Savings Begins
17 - Saint Patrick's Day

1
2
3
4
5
6
7
8
9
10
11
12
13
14
15
16
17
18
19
20
21
22
23
24
25
26
27
28
29
30
31

Mexican Meatloaf

1½ pounds lean ground beef	.7 kg
1 (10 ounce) can tomatoes and green chilies	280 g
1½ cups soft breadcrumbs	360 ml
1 egg	
3 tablespoons onion flakes	45 ml
¾ cup shredded cheddar cheese	180 ml

- Preheat oven to 375° (190° C). Mix together ground beef, tomatoes and green chilies, breadcrumbs, egg, onion flakes and 1¼ teaspoons (6 ml) salt. Shape into loaf and place in sprayed shallow pan. Bake for 1 hour. Sprinkle cheese on top. Return to oven until cheese melts. Serves 4 to 6.

Mexican Spoon Bread

1 cup yellow cornmeal	240 ml
1 tablespoon sugar	15 ml
½ teaspoon baking soda	2 ml
¾ cup milk	180 ml
⅓ cup oil	80 ml
2 eggs, beaten	
1 (15 ounce) can cream-style corn	425 g
1 (4 ounce) can chopped green chilies	114 g
2 cups shredded cheddar cheese, divided	480 ml

- Preheat oven to 350° (176° C). In mixing bowl, combine and mix cornmeal, sugar, 1 teaspoon (5 ml) salt and baking soda. Stir in milk and oil and mix well. Add eggs and corn.
- Spoon half batter into sprayed 9 x 13-inch (23 x 33 cm) baking pan. Sprinkle half green chilies and half cheese over batter. Repeat layers, ending with cheese. Bake uncovered for 45 minutes or until light brown. Serve from pan. Serves 4 to 6.

Speedy Pea Soup

1 (15 ounce) can green peas with juice	425 g
1 cup half-and-half cream	240 ml
¼ medium onion, chopped	
3 tablespoons butter	45 ml
Croutons	

- Heat green peas and cream. Pour into blender. Add onion, butter, ¼ teaspoon (1 ml) salt and dash of pepper. Blend until smooth, about 1 minute. Pour from container into saucepan and heat thoroughly. Pour into soup bowls and garnish with croutons. Serves 4 to 6.

Bitsy Quiches

1 (16 ounce) container cottage cheese	.5 kg
½ cup ricotta cheese	120 ml
3 tablespoons sour cream	45 ml
½ cup biscuit mix	120 ml
3 eggs, beaten	
½ cup (1 stick) butter, melted	120 ml
1 (8 ounce) package shredded Swiss cheese	227 g

- Preheat oven to 350° (176° C). Mix all ingredients. Spray muffin cups and fill almost full. Bake for 30 minutes. Serves 4 to 6.

1
2
3
4
5
6
7
8
9
10
11
12
13
14
15
16
17
18
19
20
21
22
23
24
25
26
27
28
29
30
31

Chili Soup

3 (15 ounce) cans chili with beans	3 (425 g)
1 (15 ounce) can whole kernel corn	425 g
1 (14 ounce) can beef broth	396 g
2 (15 ounce) cans Mexican stewed tomatoes	2 (425 g)
2 teaspoons ground cumin	10 ml
2 teaspoons chili powder	10 ml

- Combine all ingredients in saucepan. Bring to a boil, reduce heat and simmer 15 minutes. Serves 4 to 6.

Butterfingers

2 cups buttermilk baking mix	480 ml
1 tablespoon dried onion flakes	15 ml
1 egg	
⅓ cup milk	80 ml
½ cup (1 stick) butter	120 ml
2 tablespoons dried parsley flakes	30 ml
1½ teaspoons Italian herb seasoning	7 ml
½ teaspoon paprika	2 ml
⅓ cup grated parmesan cheese	80 ml

- Preheat oven to 375° (190° C). Combine mix, onion flakes, egg and just enough milk to make thick dough. Turn dough out on lightly floured surface and knead lightly. Pat into rectangle shape about 9 x 13-inch (23 x 33 cm). Add butter to 10 x 15-inch (25 x 38 cm) pan and melt in hot oven.

- Cut dough into 12 or 14 strips with sharp knife or pizza cutter. Cut each strip in half and place evenly on top of melted butter in pan. Combine parsley flakes, Italian seasoning, paprika and parmesan and sprinkle mixture over strips. Bake for 10 to 12 minutes or until golden brown. Serve hot. Serves 4 to 6.

Provolone-Pepper Burgers

⅓ cup grated provolone cheese	80 ml
¼ cup diced roasted red peppers	60 ml
¼ cup finely chopped onion	60 ml
1 pound lean ground beef	.5 kg
4 hamburger buns, split	

- In bowl, combine cheese, red peppers, onion and a little salt and pepper. Add beef and mix well. Shape into 4 patties. Grill, covered, over medium-hot heat for 5 minutes on each side or until meat is no longer pink. Serves 4.

Pineapple-Cheese Casserole

2 (20 ounce) cans unsweetened pineapple chunks, drained	2 (567 g)
1 cup sugar	240 ml
5 tablespoons flour	75 ml
1½ cups shredded cheddar cheese	360 ml
1 stack round, buttery crackers, crushed	
½ cup (1 stick butter), melted	120 ml

- Preheat oven to 350° (176° C). Spray 9 x 13-inch (23 x 33 cm) baking dish. Layer ingredients in following order: pineapple, sugar-flour combination, cheese and cracker crumbs. Drizzle butter over casserole. Bake for 25 minutes or until bubbly. Serves 4 to 6.

1
2
3
4
5
6
7
8
9
10
11
12
13
14
15
16
17
18
19
20
21
22
23
24
25
26
27
28
29
30
31

Chicken-Cornbread Casserole

4 cups cornbread, crumbled	1 L
¼ cup chopped green bell pepper	60 ml
⅓ cup chopped onion	80 ml
⅓ cup chopped celery	80 ml
2 cups cooked, chopped chicken	480 ml
1 (10 ounce) can cream of chicken soup	280 g
1 (14 ounce) can chicken broth	396 g

- Preheat oven to 350° (176° C). Combine cornbread, green pepper, onion and celery. Mix well. Place half mixture in 2-quart (2 L) baking dish. Spread chicken over cornbread. Combine soup and chicken broth and pour over chicken. Place other half of cornbread over chicken and press down. Bake for 45 minutes. Serves 4 to 6.

Nutty Green Salad

6 cups torn, mixed salad greens	1.5 L
1 medium zucchini, sliced	
1 (8 ounce) can sliced water chestnuts, drained	227 g
½ cup peanuts	120 ml
⅓ cup Italian salad dressing	80 ml

- Toss greens, zucchini, water chestnuts and peanuts. When ready to serve, add salad dressing and toss. Serves 4 to 6.

Simple Side Dish: **Easy Baked Beans**

- Heat 2 (15 ounce/425 g) cans baked beans and serve.

Crab-Stuffed Baked Potatoes

4 large baking potatoes	
½ cup (1 stick) butter	120 ml
½ cup whipping cream	120 ml
1 bunch fresh green onions, chopped	
2 (6 ounce) cans crabmeat, drained, flaked	2 (168 g)
¾ cup shredded cheddar cheese	180 ml
2 tablespoons minced fresh parsley	30 ml

• Bake potatoes at 375° (190° C) for 1 hour or until well done. Halve each potato lengthwise, scoop out flesh and leave skins intact. In large bowl, mash potatoes with butter.

• Add whipping cream, ¾ teaspoon (4 ml) salt, ½ teaspoon (2 ml) pepper and green onions. Stir in crabmeat. Fill reserved potato skins with potato mixture. Sprinkle with cheese. Bake at 350° (176° C) for 15 minutes. Sprinkle with parsley. Serves 4.

Spinach Salad

½ cup sliced almonds	120 ml
1 (8 ounce) package fresh baby spinach	227 g
2 eggs, hard-boiled, sliced	
1 sweet red bell pepper, seeded, julienne strips	
1 (8 ounce) bottle raspberry-vinaigrette salad dressing	227 g

• Toast almonds on baking sheet at 275° (135° C) for 10 minutes. Combine all ingredients. Just before serving, pour about one-third bottle of dressing over salad and toss. Serves 4.

1
2
3
4
5
6
7
8
9
10
11
12
13
14
15
16
17
18
19
20
21
22
23
24
25
26
27
28
29
30
31

Shepherd's Pie

1 pound lean ground beef	.5 kg
1 (1 ounce) packet taco seasoning mix	28 g
1 cup shredded cheddar cheese	240 ml
1 (11 ounce) can Mexicorn®, drained	312 g
2 cups instant mashed potatoes, prepared	480 ml

- Preheat oven to 350° (176° C). In skillet, brown beef and cook 10 minutes. Drain. Add taco seasoning and ¾ cup (180 ml) water and cook 5 more minutes.

- Spoon beef mixture into sprayed 8-inch (20 cm) baking pan. Sprinkle cheese on top. Spread corn over beef and cheese. Spread mashed potatoes over top. Bake for 25 minutes or until top is golden brown. Serves 4 to 6.

Broccoli-Cauliflower Salad

1 small head cauliflower	
3 bunches broccoli	
1 cup mayonnaise	240 ml
1 tablespoon vinegar	15 ml
1 tablespoon sugar	15 ml
1 bunch green onions, chopped	
1 (8 ounce) shredded mozzarella cheese	227 g

- Cut up cauliflower and broccoli into florets. Combine mayonnaise, vinegar and sugar. Combine cauliflower, broccoli, mayonnaise mixture, onions and cheese. Add a little salt, toss and chill. Serves 4 to 6.

Easy Oven Soup

1 (1 ounce) packet dry onion soup mix	28 g
1 (10 ounce) can cream of mushroom soup	280 g
1 cup red wine	240 ml
1 (16 ounce) package frozen stew meat	.5 kg

- In large, heavy pan, mix soups, wine, ½ cup (120 ml) water and a little pepper. Stir in meat. Cover and bake at 300° (148° C) for 3 to 4 hours. Serves 4.

Green Spring Salad Mix

2 (10 ounce) bags spring-mix salad greens	2 (280 g)
Fresh green onions, sliced	
1 (8 ounce) bottle creamy Italian salad dressing	227 g
1 (16 ounce) box seasoned croutons	.5 kg

- In salad bowl, toss salad, onion and half dressing. Use more dressing if needed. Top with croutons. Serves 4 to 6.

Cornbread Muffins

2 (8 ounce) packages corn muffin mix	2 (227 g)
⅔ cup milk	160 ml
2 eggs	

- Preheat oven to 400° (204° C). In mixing bowl, combine all ingredients and pour into 12 sprayed muffin cups. Serves 6 to 8.

Tip: For a special St. Patrick's Day touch, add 3 to 4 drops green food coloring . The leprechauns will like it.

1
2
3
4
5
6
7
8
9
10
11
12
13
14
15
16
17
18
19
20
21
22
23
24
25
26
27
28
29
30
31

Bacon and Banana Sandwiches

Peanut butter
8 slices English muffins
2 bananas
8 slices bacon, cooked, crispy
Butter, softened

- Spread layer of peanut butter over 8 slices of muffins. Slice bananas and arrange on top of 4 slices. Place 2 strips of bacon on each of the 4 slices. Top with remaining muffin slices. Spread top slice with butter. Brown sandwiches, buttered side down. Turn, spread butter and cook other side until golden brown. Serve hot. Serves 4 to 6.

Happy Orange Slush

1 (6 ounce) can frozen orange juice concentrate	168 g
1 teaspoon vanilla	5 ml
12 ice cubes	
¼ cup sugar	60 ml
½ cup dry milk	120 ml

- Combine all ingredients in blender with 1¾ cups (420 ml) water and process. Serves 4.

Sunny Day Salad

1 (6 ounce) carton plain yogurt	168 g
1 tablespoon honey	15 ml
1 (8 ounce) can sliced pineapple	227 g

- Mix yogurt with honey. Place 1 slice pineapple onto each salad plate. Spoon 1 tablespoon (15 ml) yogurt in middle. Serves 4 to 6.

Dressed-Up Spaghetti

½ pound lean bacon, diced	227 g
1 pound spaghetti, cooked, drained	.5 kg
⅔ cup romano cheese	160 ml

• Cook bacon until crisp. Retain bacon drippings. Place spaghetti in serving bowl. Toss bacon drippings with spaghetti. Sprinkle with bacon and cheese. Serves 4.

Spinach Salad With Sprouts

1 (10 ounce) package baby spinach	280 g
2 cups fresh bean sprouts	480 ml
1 (8 ounce) can water chestnuts, sliced, drained	227 g
½ cup mayonnaise	120 ml

• Mix above ingredients and serve. Serves 4.

Mozzarella Loaf

1 (16 ounce) loaf French bread	15 kg
12 slices mozzarella cheese	
¼ cup grated parmesan cheese	60 ml
6 tablespoons (¾ stick) butter, softened	90 ml
½ teaspoon garlic salt	2 ml

• Preheat oven to 375° (190° C). Cut loaf into 12 slices. Place slices of mozzarella cheese between bread slices. Combine parmesan cheese, butter and garlic salt. Spread on each side of bread. Reshape loaf, pressing firmly together. Brush remaining butter mixture on outside of loaf. Bake for 8 to 10 minutes. Serves 4 to 6.

1
2
3
4
5
6
7
8
9
10
11
12
13
14
15
16
17
18
19
20
21
22
23
24
25
26
27
28
29
30
31

Ham With Red-Eye Gravy

6 (¼ inch) thick slices country ham	6 (.6 cm)
¼ cup butter	60 ml
¼ cup firmly packed brown sugar	60 ml
½ cup strong black coffee	120 ml

- Saute ham in butter over low heat until light brown and turn several times. Remove ham from skillet and cover with foil to keep warm. Stir brown sugar into pan drippings, heat until sugar dissolves and stir constantly. Add coffee and simmer 5 minutes. Season with a little salt and pepper. Serve over ham. Serves 4 to 6.

Frontier Potatoes

6 - 8 red potatoes with peel	
3 strips bacon	
½ red or orange bell pepper	
2 tablespoons butter	30 ml
1 teaspoon cumin seeds	5 ml

- Boil potatoes in saucepan with water until tender. Chop up bacon and slice pepper into julienne strips. Drain potatoes when done and cut into chunky slices. Melt butter in large skillet. Add bacon and bell pepper and fry until pepper just starts to become tender. Add potatoes and cumin seeds. Cook until brown. Serves 4 to 6.

Quick, Creamy Biscuits

2½ cups biscuit mix	600 ml
½ pint whipping cream	227 g

- Preheat oven to 375° (190° C). Mix biscuit mix and cream. Place on floured board. Knead several times. Pat out to ½-inch (1.2 cm) thickness. Cut with biscuit cutter.
- Bake for 12 to 15 minutes or until light brown.

Hot Cornbread Sandwich

2 (8 ounce) packages corn muffin mix	**2 (227 g)**
2 eggs, beaten	
⅔ cup milk	**160 ml**
12 slices American cheese	
6 slices deli ham	

- Preheat oven to 400° (204° C). In bowl, combine muffin mix, eggs and milk and mix well. Pour half of mixture into sprayed 7 x 11-inch (18 x 28 cm) baking dish. Carefully place 6 slices cheese, then ham slices and remaining cheese slices on top of ham. Spoon remaining cornbread batter over top of cheese. Bake for 25 minutes or until cornbread is golden brown. Cut into squares and serve hot. Serves 4 to 6.

Crunchy Salad

¼ cup sesame seeds	**60 ml**
½ cup sunflower seeds	**120 ml**
½ cup slivered almonds	**120 ml**
1 head red leaf lettuce	
Creamy Italian dressing	

- Toast sesame seeds, sunflower seeds and almonds at 300° (148° C) for about 10 minutes or until light brown. Tear lettuce into bite-size pieces and add seed mixture. Toss with creamy Italian dressing. Serves 4 to 6.

March

2nd Sunday - Daylight Savings Begins
17 - Saint Patrick's Day

1
2
3
4
5
6
7
8
9
10
11
12
13
14
15
16
17
18
19
20
21
22
23
24
25
26
27
28
29
30
31

Sirloin In Rich Mushroom Sauce

1 pound boneless beef sirloin, cut into strips	.5 kg
1 (14 ounce) can beef broth	396 g
2 teaspoons minced garlic	10 ml
1 (10 ounce) can cream of mushroom soup	280 g
1 (4 ounce) can sliced mushrooms	114 g
Angel hair pasta	

- Heat 2 tablespoons (30 ml) oil in heavy skillet over medium-high heat. Brown steak strips. Add broth, garlic, a little black pepper and ½ can water. Heat to boiling. Reduce heat and simmer 15 minutes.
- Spoon mushroom soup, mushrooms and 1 cup (240 ml) water in saucepan and heat just enough to mix well. Pour over steak and simmer 5 minutes. Serve over angel hair pasta. Serves 4 to 6.

Tossed Zucchini Salad

½ cup oil	120 ml
3 tablespoons vinegar	45 ml
1½ teaspoons sugar	7 ml
1 teaspoon minced garlic	5 ml
2 tomatoes, cut in wedges	
2 cups thinly sliced zucchini	480 ml
2 cups torn iceberg lettuce	480 ml
2 cups torn romaine lettuce	480 ml

- Combine oil, vinegar, sugar, garlic, ¼ teaspoon (1 ml) salt and dash of pepper in jar with lid. Shake to mix. Chill 1 to 2 hours. In large bowl, toss tomatoes, zucchini, lettuce and romaine. Toss salad with desired amount of dressing. Serves 4 to 6.

Seafood Myriad

2 (6 ounce) cans small, veined shrimp, drained	2 (168 g)
1 (6 ounce) can crabmeat, drained, flaked	168 g
2 (10 ounce) cans corn chowder	2 (280 g)
2 cups seasoned breadcrumbs, divided	480 ml

- Preheat oven to 375° (190° C). Combine shrimp, crabmeat, chowder and ¾ cup (180 ml) breadcrumbs. Spoon into sprayed, glass pie pan. Sprinkle remaining breadcrumbs over top of casserole and bake for 25 minutes. Serves 4 to 6.

Three-Bean Salad

1 (15 ounce) can cut green beans, drained	425 g
1 (15 ounce) can cut wax beans, drained	425 g
1 (15 ounce) can kidney beans, drained	425 g
1 (8 ounce) bottle Italian salad dressing	227 g
1 (4 ounce) jar pimentos, drained	114 g

- Combine ingredients and chill. Season to taste. Add chopped onions and cherry tomato halves, if desired. Serves 6 to 8.

Hush Puppies

1½ cups cornmeal	360 ml
¼ cup flour	60 ml
2 teaspoons baking powder	10 ml
1 cup milk	240 ml
1 egg	
½ cup chopped onion	120 ml
Oil	

- Stir cornmeal, flour, baking powder and 1¼ teaspoons (6 ml) salt together. Beat milk and egg. Add it and onion to cornmeal mixture. Drop by heaping teaspoons into hot oil. Serves 4 to 6.

1
2
3
4
5
6
7
8
9
10
11
12
13
14
15
16
17
18
19
20
21
22
23
24
25
26
27
28
29
30
31

Vegetarian Chili

2 (15 ounce) cans stewed tomatoes	2 (425 g)
1 (15 ounce) can kidney beans, rinsed, drained	425 g
1 (15 ounce) can pinto beans with liquid	425 g
1 onion, chopped	
1 green bell pepper, seeded, chopped	
1 tablespoon chili powder	15 ml
1 (7 ounce) package elbow macaroni	198 g
¼ cup (½ stick) butter, sliced	60 ml
Cheddar cheese	

• Combine tomatoes, both cans of beans, onion, bell
  pepper, chili powder and 1 cup (240 ml) water in slow
  cooker. Cover and cook on LOW for 4 to 5 hours
  or HIGH for 2 hours. Cook macaroni according to
  package directions, drain and stir butter into hot
  noodles. Fold into chili. Sprinkle with cheese.
  Serves 4 to 6.

Mexican Cornbread

1 cup cornmeal	240 ml
½ teaspoon baking soda	2 ml
¼ cup milk	60 ml
2 eggs, slightly beaten	
⅓ cup butter, melted	80 ml
1 (15 ounce) can cream-style corn	425 g
1 (4 ounce) can green chilies	114 g
1 (8 ounce) package shredded cheddar cheese	227 g

• Preheat oven to 350° (176° C). Mix dry ingredients
  with 1 teaspoon (5 ml) salt. Add milk, eggs and butter
  and mix well. Fold in corn, chilies and cheese. Pour
  into sprayed 9 x 13-inch (23 x 33 cm) pan. Bake for
  45 minutes. Let stand 10 minutes before cutting into
  squares. Serves 4 to 6.

Bacon And Sour Cream Omelet

2 eggs
2 strips bacon
⅓ cup sour cream   **80 ml**
3 green onions, chopped
1 tablespoon butter   **15 ml**

- Beat eggs with 1 tablespoon (15 ml) water. Fry bacon, crumble when cool and save pan drippings. Combine crumbled bacon and sour cream. Saute onions in bacon drippings. Mix with bacon-sour cream. Melt butter in omelet pan. Pour in egg mixture and cook. When omelet sets, spoon sour cream mixture along center and fold omelet onto warm plate.

Monkey Bread

½ cup sugar   **120 ml**
¼ cup (½ stick) butter   **60 ml**

- Bring sugar and butter to boil for 1 minute. Set aside.

4 tablespoons plus extra sugar   **60 ml**
2 teaspoons plus extra cinnamon   **10 ml**
1 (12 ounce) can biscuits, quartered   **340 g**

- Preheat oven to 350° (176° C). Combine sugar and cinnamon in plastic bag. Add biscuits and shake to coat. Arrange biscuits in sprayed, floured 8-inch (20 cm) cake pan. Pour liquid mixture over biscuits and sprinkle additional sugar and cinnamon on top. Bake for 35 minutes.   Serves 4 to 6.

1
2
3
4
5
6
7
8
9
10
11
12
13
14
15
16
17
18
19
20
21
22
23
24
25
26
27
28
29
30
31

Tuna Potatoes

4 medium potatoes, baked
1 (6 ounce) can tuna, drained   168 g
1 (8 ounce) package shredded cheddar cheese,
    divided   227 g
½ cup mayonnaise   120 ml
½ cup chopped onion   120 ml

- Halve baked potatoes, scoop flesh out of skin
  carefully and save shell. Mix potato with tuna, half
  cheese, mayonnaise and onion. Spoon into potato
  shell. Put remaining cheese on top of potatoes and
  bake at 400° (204° C) to melt. Serves 4.

Snappy Salad

Several lettuce leaves
1 (15 ounce) can peach halves, drained   425 g
1 (16 ounce) carton small curd cottage cheese,
    drained   .5 kg

- Place lettuce leaf on individual plates with 1 or 2 peach
  halves. Spoon heaping tablespoon (15 ml) cottage
  cheese in center of each peach half. Serves 4.

Cherry-Vanilla Trifle

2 (8 ounce) containers cherry-vanilla yogurt   2 (227 g)
4 (3.6 ounce) containers vanilla pudding snacks   4 (100 g)
1 prepared angel food cake, torn into bite-size pieces
1 (20 ounce) can cherry pie filling   567 g

- Combine yogurt and pudding. Place layer of cake
  pieces with layer of yogurt-pudding mix. Sprinkle
  with cherries. Repeat layers. Cover and refrigerate.
  Serves 4.

365

Broiled Salmon Steaks

2 (8 ounce) salmon steaks, halved	**2 (227 g)**
1 teaspoon dried marjoram	**5 ml**

- Spray salmon with butter spray. Sprinkle with half of marjoram and a little pepper. Spray broiler rack and broil steaks 4 inches (10 cm) from heat source until first side is light brown (about 5 to 8 minutes). Turn, spray and sprinkle with remaining marjoram and a little black pepper. Broil 5 to 8 minutes longer or until fish flakes easily with fork. Serves 2.

Veggie Rice

3 cups cooked brown rice	**710 ml**
1 (15 ounce) can peas, drained	**425 g**
2 tablespoons dried parsley	**30 ml**
¼ cup (½ stick) butter, melted	**60 ml**

- In medium saucepan, combine ingredients. Stir until mixture heats thoroughly. Serves 2.

Tarragon Asparagus

1 pound fresh asparagus spears	**.5 kg**
1 tablespoon tarragon	**15 ml**

- Wash asparagus and break off at tender point. Steam over boiling water for 6 minutes or until barely tender. Remove from heat and drain. Spray with butter spray and sprinkle with tarragon and ¼ teaspoon (1 ml) pepper. Serves 2 to 4.

1
2
3
4
5
6
7
8
9
10
11
12
13
14
15
16
17
18
19
20
21
22
23
24
25
26
27
28
29
30
31

Ham and Cheese Bars

2 cups biscuit mix	480 ml
1 cup cooked, finely chopped ham	240 ml
1 cup shredded cheddar cheese	240 ml
½ onion, finely chopped	
½ cup grated parmesan cheese	120 ml
¼ cup sour cream	60 ml
1 teaspoon garlic powder	5 ml
1 cup whole milk	240 ml
1 egg	

• Preheat oven to 350° (176° C). Combine all
  ingredients with ½ teaspoon (2 ml) salt. Mix by
  hand. Spread in sprayed 9 x 13-inch (23 x 33 cm)
  pan. Bake for 30 minutes or until light brown. Cut in
  rectangles, about 2 x 1-inch (5 x 2.5 cm). Serve hot
  or at room temperature. Serves 4 to 6.

Broccoli Soup

1 (12 ounce) package egg noodles	340 g
1 (16 ounce) package frozen chopped broccoli	.5 kg
1 pint half-and-half cream	.5 kg
1 (14 ounce) can chicken broth	396 g
1 (16 ounce) box Velveeta® cheese, cubed	.5 kg

• Cook noodles and broccoli according to package
  directions. Set aside and combine cream, broth and
  cheese. Heat on low and stir until cheese melts.
  Add noodles and broccoli and simmer until mixture is
  thoroughly hot. Serves 4 to 6.

Creamy Mushroom Pork Chops

5 - 6 pork chops
1 (10 ounce) can cream of mushroom soup   280 g
1 soup can of milk

- Fry pork chops in large skillet until almost done. Drain. Put back into pan and add soup and milk. Cover and simmer about 30 minutes or until done. Serves 4 to 6.

Chive-Potato Souffle

3 eggs, separated
2 cups hot prepared instant mashed potatoes   480 ml
½ cup sour cream   120 ml
2 tablespoons chopped chives   30 ml

- Preheat oven to 350° (176° C). Beat egg whites until stiff. Set aside. Beat yolks until smooth and add to potatoes. Fold in beaten egg whites, sour cream, chives and 1 teaspoon (5 ml) salt. Pour into sprayed 2-quart (2 L) baking dish. Bake for 45 minutes. Serves 4 to 6.

Spinach and Apple Salad

1 (10 ounce) package fresh spinach   280 g
⅓ cup frozen orange juice concentrate, thawed   80 ml
¼ cup mayonnaise   60 ml
1 red apple with peel, diced
5 slices bacon, fried, crumbled

- Place spinach in salad bowl. Mix orange juice concentrate and mayonnaise. When ready to serve, mix spinach and apple. (Cut apple at the last minute.) Pour dressing over salad and top with bacon. Serves 4 to 6.

1
2
3
4
5
6
7
8
9
10
11
12
13
14
15
16
17
18
19
20
21
22
23
24
25
26
27
28
29
30
31

Elegant Chicken

3 cups cooked, shredded chicken	710 ml
1 (6 ounce) package long grain-wild rice, cooked	168 g
1 (10 ounce) can cream of celery soup	280 g
1 (4 ounce) jar pimentos	114 g
1 cup mayonnaise	240 ml
1 (15 ounce) can French-style green beans, drained	425 g
1 (2.8 ounce) can fried onion rings	84 g

- Preheat oven to 350° (176° C). Combine all ingredients except onion rings. Pour into sprayed 3-quart (3 L) baking dish. Bake for 25 to 30 minutes. Top with onion rings last 10 minutes of cooking time. Serves 4 to 6.

Broccoli Salad

1 bunch fresh broccoli, cut into florets	
10 slices bacon, fried, crumbled	
3 - 4 green onions, chopped	
½ cup sunflower kernels	120 ml
½ cup mayonnaise	120 ml
½ cup sugar	120 ml
2 tablespoons red wine vinegar	30 ml

- Mix all ingredients. Chill for 2 hours. Serves 4.

Cheese Muffins

3¾ cups buttermilk-biscuit mix	890 ml
1¼ cups shredded cheddar cheese	300 ml
1 egg, beaten	
1¼ cups milk	300 ml

- Preheat oven to 325° (162° C). In large bowl, combine all ingredients and beat vigorously by hand. Pour into sprayed muffin cups. Bake for 35 minutes. Serves 4 to 6.

Bless My Sole

1½ pounds fresh or frozen sole or cod	.7 kg
1 egg, beaten	
2 tablespoons milk	30 ml
2 cups crushed corn flakes	480 ml
Oil	

- Cut fish into serving-size pieces and sprinkle with a little salt and pepper. In shallow bowl, combine egg and milk or water and place corn flake crumbs in second bowl. Dip fish in egg mixture and coat well on both sides with crushed flakes. Fry in thin layer of oil in skillet until brown on both sides, about 5 to 8 minutes on each side. Serves 4.

Herbed New Potatoes

1½ pounds new potatoes	.7 kg
½ cup (1 stick) butter, sliced	120 ml
½ cup chopped fresh parsley	120 ml
½ teaspoon dried rosemary	2 ml

- Scrub potatoes and cut in half, but do not peel. In medium saucepan, boil in lightly salted water. Cook until potatoes are tender, about 20 minutes and drain. Add butter, parsley and rosemary and toss gently until butter melts. Serve hot. Serves 4 to 6.

Savory Rib Roast

1 tablespoon dried thyme	15 ml
1 teaspoon crushed, dried rosemary	5 ml
1 teaspoon dried sage	5 ml
1 (4 pound) beef rib roast	1.8 kg

• Preheat oven to 350° (176° C). In small bowl, combine seasonings with 1 teaspoon (5 ml) pepper. Rub over roast. Place roast, fat side up, on rack in large roasting pan. Bake uncovered for 2 to 2½ hours or until meat reaches desired doneness. Let stand 10 minutes before slicing. Serves 6 to 8.

Scalloped Potatoes

6 medium potatoes	
½ cup (1 stick) butter	120 ml
1 tablespoon flour	15 ml
1 (8 ounce) package shredded cheddar cheese	227 g
¾ cup milk	180 ml

• Preheat oven to 350° (176° C). Peel and slice half of potatoes. Place in 3-quart (3 L) sprayed baking dish. Slice half of butter over potatoes and sprinkle with flour. Cover with half cheese and repeat layers. Pour milk over layers. Cover and bake at for 1 hour. Serves 6 to 8.

Zucchini Patties

1½ cups grated zucchini	360 ml
1 egg, beaten	
2 tablespoons flour	30 ml
⅓ cup finely minced onion	80 ml

• Combine all ingredients plus ½ teaspoon (2 ml) salt. Heat skillet with about 3 tablespoons (45 ml) oil. Drop zucchini mixture by tablespoonfuls onto skillet at medium-high heat. Turn and brown on both sides. Remove and drain on paper towels. Serves 6 to 8.

Chicken-Artichoke Salad

4 cups cooked, chopped chicken breasts	1 L
1 (14 ounce) can artichoke hearts, drained, chopped	396 g
½ cup chopped walnuts	120 ml
1 cup chopped red bell pepper	240 ml
⅔ cup mayonnaise	160 ml

- In bowl, combine all ingredients and add a little salt and pepper. Cover and refrigerate until ready to serve. Serves 4 to 6.

Avocado-Cream Soup

4 ripe avocados, peeled, diced	
1½ cups whipping cream	360 ml
2 (14 ounce) cans chicken broth	2 (396 g)
¼ cup dry sherry	60 ml
Paprika	

- In blender, process half avocados and half cream. Repeat with remaining avocados and cream. Bring chicken broth to a boil in saucepan, reduce heat and stir in avocado puree. Add 1 teaspoon (5 ml) salt and sherry and chill thoroughly. To serve, place in individual bowls and sprinkle a little paprika on top. Serves 4 to 6.

Pineapple Cake

1 (20 ounce) can crushed pineapple with juice	567 g
1 (18 ounce) box white or yellow cake mix	510 g
1 cup (2 sticks) butter, sliced	240 ml

- Preheat oven to 350° (176° C). Spread pineapple in well sprayed 9 x 13-inch (23 x 33 cm) dish.
- Sprinkle dry cake mix over fruit and dot with butter slices. Bake for about 35 minutes or until brown. Serves 8.

1
2
3
4
5
6
7
8
9
10
11
12
13
14
15
16
17
18
19
20
21
22
23
24
25
26
27
28
29
30

Spinach-Stuffed Shells

1 (12 ounce) package jumbo macaroni shells	340 g
2 (9 ounce) pouches frozen creamed spinach	2 (255 g)
1 (15 ounce) carton ricotta cheese	425 g
1 (8 ounce) package shredded mozzarella cheese	227 g
½ pound ground beef	227 g
1 (26 ounce) jar spaghetti sauce	737 g

- Preheat oven to 350° (176° C). Prepare pasta according to package directions and drain. Prepare spinach and slightly cool. Add ricotta, mozzarella and 1 teaspoon (5 ml) salt to spinach. Stuff shells with 1 tablespoon (15 ml) mixture. In skillet, cook meat and add spaghetti sauce. Place shells in sprayed 9 x13-inch (23 x 33 cm) baking dish and pour sauce over all. Bake for 30 minutes. Serves 6 to 8.

Romaine Salad

1 head romaine lettuce, torn	
½ cup dried sweetened cranberries	120 ml
2 small zucchini, sliced	
1 seedless cucumber, peeled, sliced	
¼ cup raspberry-vinaigrette dressing	60 ml

- Combine first 4 ingredients, add dressing and toss. Serves 4.

Chile Bread

1 loaf unsliced Italian bread	
½ cup (1 stick butter), melted	120 ml
1 (4 ounce) can diced green chilies, drained	114 g
¾ cup shredded Monterey Jack cheese	180 ml

- Preheat oven to 350° (176° C). Slice bread almost all the way through. Combine melted butter, chilies and cheese. Spread between bread slices. Cover loaf with foil. Bake for 25 minutes. Serves 4 to 6.

Alfredo Chicken

5 - 6 boneless, skinless chicken breast halves
1 (16 ounce) package frozen broccoli florets, thawed   .5 kg
1 sweet red bell pepper, seeded, chopped
1 (16 ounce) jar alfredo sauce   .5 kg

- Preheat oven to 375° (190° C). In large skillet with a little oil, brown and cook chicken breasts until juices run clear. Transfer to sprayed 9 x 13-inch (23 x 33 cm) baking dish.
- Microwave broccoli according to package directions and drain. Spoon broccoli and bell pepper over chicken. In small saucepan, heat alfredo sauce with ¼ cup (60 ml) water. Pour over chicken and vegetables. Cover and bake 15 to 20 minutes. Serves 6 to 8.

Fruit Salad

1 (14 ounce) can sweetened condensed milk   396 g
2 tablespoons lemon juice   30 ml
2 (15 ounce) cans fruit cocktail, chilled,
**   well drained   2 (425 g)**
1 (20 ounce) can pineapple tidbits, chilled,
**   drained   567 g**
1 (8 ounce) carton whipped topping   227 g

- In large bowl, combine condensed milk and lemon juice. Mix well, add fruit cocktail and pineapple and mix gently. Fold in whipped topping and spoon into crystal bowl. Serves 6 to 8.

1
2
3
4
5
6
7
8
9
10
11
12
13
14
15
16
17
18
19
20
21
22
23
24
25
26
27
28
29
30

Hot Bunwiches

8 hamburger buns
8 slices Swiss cheese
8 slices ham
8 slices turkey
8 slices American cheese

- Lay out all 8 buns. On bottom bun, place slices of Swiss cheese, ham, turkey and American cheese. Place top bun over American cheese. Wrap each bunwich individually in foil and place in freezer. When ready to serve, take out of freezer 2 to 3 hours before serving. Leave bunwiches in foil, heat at 325° (162 ° C) for 30 minutes and serve hot. Serves 6 to 8.

Frozen Pistachio Salad

1 (4 ounce) package instant pistachio pudding	**114 g**
1 (15 ounce) can crushed pineapple with juice	**425 g**
1 (8 ounce) carton whipped topping	**227 g**
⅔ cup chopped pecans	**160 ml**

- Stir instant pudding and pineapple together and fold in whipped topping. Pour into shallow pan and freeze. To serve, cut into squares. Serves 4 to 6.

Simple Side Dish: **Pasta With White Cheddar**

- Prepare 1 (6 ounce) box shells and white cheddar pasta according to package directions.

Sausage Souffle

8 slices white bread, cubed	
1 (8 ounce) package shredded sharp cheddar cheese	227 g
1½ pounds link sausage, cut in thirds	680 g
5 eggs	
2¼ cups milk	540 ml
¾ teaspoon dry mustard	4 ml
1 (10 ounce) can cream of mushroom soup	280 g
½ cup milk	120 ml

- Spray 9 x 13-inch (23 x 33 cm) pan. Place bread cubes in dish and top with cheese. Brown and drain sausage and place on top of cheese. Beat eggs with 2¼ cups (540 ml) milk and mustard and pour over sausage. Cover and refrigerate overnight.
- Heat soup and milk in saucepan just enough to mix well and pour over bread and sausage. Bake at 300° (148° C) for 1 hour 30 minutes until set. Serves 6 to 8.

Vanilla Muffins

2 cups biscuit mix	480 ml
2 tablespoons sugar	30 ml
1 egg	
⅔ cup milk	160 ml
1 teaspoon vanilla	5 ml

- Preheat oven to 400° (204° C). Spray 12 muffin cups. Combine all ingredients and beat 30 seconds. Fill muffin cups two-thirds full. Bake for about 15 minutes or until golden brown. Serves 6 to 8.

April 1 2 3 4 5 6 7 8 9 10 11 12 13 14 15 16 17 18 19 20 21 22 23 24 25 26 27 28 29 30

1
2
3
4
5
6
7
8
9
10
11
12
13
14
15
16
17
18
19
20
21
22
23
24
25
26
27
28
29
30

Sausage And Wild Rice

2 tablespoons butter	30 ml
1 medium onion, chopped	
1 (4 ounce) can mushroom pieces, drained	114 g
1 pound smoked sausage, thinly sliced	.5 kg
Dash poultry seasoning	
1 (6 ounce) box long grain-wild rice	168 g

• Melt butter in large skillet. Add onions and mushrooms and saute until translucent and tender. Add sausage and cook 10 to 15 minutes. Add a little poultry seasoning. Cook rice according to package directions. When done, stir in sausage mixture and toss. Serves 2 to 4.

Asparagus Amandine

¼ cup milk	60 ml
1 (10 ounce) can cream of chicken soup	280 g
3 eggs, hard-boiled, sliced	
1 cup cubed American cheese	240 ml
1 (10 ounce) package frozen cut asparagus, cooked	280 g
1 cup sliced almonds	240 ml
½ cup breadcrumbs	120 ml
2 tablespoons butter, melted	30 ml

• Preheat oven to 350° (176° C). Combine milk and soup. Stir in eggs, cheese and asparagus. Pour mixture into sprayed baking dish. Cover with almonds and crumbs. Drizzle with butter. Bake for 30 to 40 minutes or until bubbly and slightly brown on top. Serves 4 to 6.

Red Beans And Rice

1 pound dry red beans	.5 kg
1 meaty ham bone or ham hocks	
2 onions, chopped	
¼ teaspoon garlic powder	1 ml
2 bay leaves	
Hot sauce	
Fluffy white rice	

- Combine all ingredients, except rice, with 8 cups (2 L) water and a little salt and pepper. Place in large, heavy pan. Bring to a boil. Lower heat, simmer and stir occasionally for 4 hours. When soft enough, mash some beans against side of pot to thicken sauce. Serve over hot, cooked rice. Serves 4 to 6.

Cowboy Corn Cakes

2 cups yellow cornmeal	480 ml
½ cup flour	120 ml
2 tablespoons oil	30 ml

- Combine cornmeal and flour with 2 teaspoons (10 ml) salt. Stir in 2 cups (480 ml) boiling water and form mixture into 10 to 12 patties. Heat oil in large skillet over medium-high heat. Fry patties 3 to 5 minutes on each side or until brown. Serves 4 to 6.

Chilled Cucumbers

2 seedless cucumbers, peeled, sliced	
1 (8 ounce) carton sour cream	227 g

- Place sliced cucumbers in bowl, stir in sour cream and a little salt. Refrigerate. Serves 4 to 6.

Chili-Cheese Dogs

1 (8 ounce) package shredded cheddar cheese	227 g
¼ cup chili sauce	60 ml
¼ cup pickle relish	60 ml
8 franks	
8 hot dog buns	

- Preheat oven to 400° (204°C). Combine cheese, chili sauce and relish and mix well. Split franks lengthwise and fill with mixture. Place franks into buns. Place on individual foil rectangles and seal. Heat for 15 minutes. Serves 6 to 8.

Pumpkin Seeds

2 cups pumpkin seeds	480 ml
2 tablespoons butter	30 ml

- Preheat oven to 275° (135° C). Wash seeds. Drain and pat dry. In large skillet, saute seeds with 1 teaspoon (5 ml) salt in butter. Stir 3 minutes until all seeds coat with butter. Bake for 30 minutes. If not roasted enough, bake additional 15 minutes or until brown. Drain on paper towels. Eat them, shell and all. Serves 4 to 6.

Stuffed Apples

4 - 6 apples, washed
Peanut butter
Raisins

- Core apple. Mix peanut butter with raisins and stuff apple with peanut butter mixture. Slice or serve whole. Serves 6 to 8.

Liver And Onions

Bacon drippings or vegetable oil	
1 pound calves liver	.5 kg
Flour	
1 (10 ounce) can French onion soup	280 g
½ soup can water	

• Heat bacon drippings or oil in large skillet over medium-high heat. Season liver with a little salt and pepper and dredge in flour. Brown both sides in skillet. Pour soup and water over liver and stir to loosen crumbs. Cover and reduce heat. Cook about 15 to 20 minutes more or until gravy thickens. Serves 4.

English Pea Salad

1 (16 ounce) bag frozen green peas, thawed	.5 kg
1 bunch fresh green onions, chopped	
½ cup chopped celery	120 ml
½ cup sweet pickle relish	120 ml
Mayonnaise	

• Mix peas, onions, celery and relish. Add enough mayonnaise to hold salad together. Refrigerate. Serves 4.

Simple Side Dish: **Hash Brown Potatoes**

• Prepare 1 (5 ounce/143 g) box hash brown potatoes with 3 tablespoons butter and serve hot.

1
2
3
4
5
6
7
8
9
10
11
12
13
14
15
16
17
18
19
20
21
22
23
24
25
26
27
28
29
30

Mexicali Pork Chops

1 (1 ounce) packet taco seasoning	28 g
4 (½ inch) thick boneless pork loin chops	4 (1.2 cm)
1 tablespoon oil	15 ml
Salsa	

• Rub taco seasoning over pork chops. In skillet, brown pork chops in oil over medium heat. Add 2 tablespoons (30 ml) water, turn heat to low, cover and simmer pork chops about 40 minutes. Spoon desired amount of salsa over pork chops. Serves 4.

Red Rice

1 ham hock (very meaty)	
2 cups instant rice	480 ml
1 (15 ounce) can diced tomatoes with juice	425 g
1 (10 ounce) can tomato soup	280 g

• Cover ham hock with 3 cups (710 ml) water and simmer for 40 minutes or until meat is easy to remove from bone. Drain in colander and save broth. Combine broth and rice. Cook until water absorbs and rice is tender. Add ham bits, tomatoes and soup and cook until excess moisture is gone. Serves 4.

April

1 - April Fool's Day
15 - Federal Tax Day
22 - Earth Day
Last Friday - Arbor Day

Ham Quiche Biscuit Cups

1 (8 ounce) package cream cheese, softened	227 g
2 tablespoons milk	30 ml
2 eggs	
½ cup shredded Swiss cheese	120 ml
2 tablespoons chopped green onions	30 ml
1 (10 count) can flaky biscuits	
½ cup finely chopped ham	120 ml

- Preheat oven to 350° (176° C). Beat cream cheese, milk and eggs until smooth. Stir in Swiss cheese and green onions. Separate dough into 10 biscuits. Place one biscuit in each of 10 sprayed cups. Firmly press bottom and sides, forming ¼-inch (.6 cm) rim.
- Place half of ham in dough cups. Spoon about 2 tablespoons (30 ml) egg mixture over ham. Top with remaining ham and bake for about 25 minutes or until filling sets and edges of biscuits are golden brown. Remove from pan. Serves 4.

Breakfast Shake

1 cup milk	240 ml
½ cup banana or strawberry yogurt	120 ml
1 tablespoon honey	15 ml
1 banana, cubed	

- Blend all ingredients in blender until smooth. Makes 1 large shake.

Breakfast or Brunch

Baked-Crab Sandwiches

12 slices thin bread, trimmed, buttered	
2 (7 ounce) cans crabmeat, flaked	198 g
1 (8 ounce) package shredded cheddar cheese	227 g
4 eggs, beaten	
3 cups milk	710 ml
½ teaspoon curry	2 ml

- Preheat oven to 325° (162° C). Place 6 slices bread, butter side up in sprayed 9 x 13-inch (23 x 33 cm) baking dish. Spread crabmeat over bread and top with remaining 6 slices, butter-side up. Sprinkle with cheese. Mix eggs, milk and curry and pour carefully over bread. Cover and chill 4 hours. Bake for 45 minutes. Serves 6.

Creamy Cranberry Salad

1 (6 ounce) package cherry gelatin	168 g
1 (8 ounce) carton sour cream	227 g
1 (16 ounce) can whole cranberry sauce	.5 kg
1 (15 ounce) can crushed pineapple	425 g

- Dissolve gelatin in 1¼ cups (300 ml) boiling water and mix well. Stir in remaining ingredients and pour into 7 x 11-inch (18 x 28 cm) glass baking dish. Refrigerate until firm. Serves 6.

Chocolate-Orange Cake

1 (16 ounce) loaf frozen pound cake, thawed	.5 kg
1 (12 ounce) jar orange marmalade	340 g
1 (16 ounce) can ready-to-spread chocolate-fudge frosting	.5 kg

- Cut cake horizontally in 3 layers. Place 1 layer on cake platter. Spread with half of marmalade. Place second layer over first and spread remaining marmalade. Top with third cake layer and spread frosting on top and sides of cake. Refrigerate. Serves 8.

Grilled Cheeseburgers On Rye

1 pound lean ground beef	.5 kg
4 slices cheddar cheese	
1 (4 ounce) can chopped green chilies	114 g
8 slices rye bread	
¼ cup butter	60 ml

• Make 4 beef patties and cook as desired. Place slice of cheese on each and top with spoonful of green chilies. Place each patty between two slices of bread. Spread both sides of sandwich with butter and grill butter-side down in hot iron skillet. Serves 4.

Jigger Beans

2 (15 ounce) cans pork and beans	2 (425 g)
3 slices bacon, cut in (2 inch) pieces	5 cm
1 large onion, thinly sliced	
½ cup orange-drink mix	120 ml
2 tablespoons cider vinegar	30 ml
1 jigger brandy	

• Preheat oven to 300° (148° C). Mix all ingredients except bacon slices and brandy. Put in 2-quart (2 L) baking dish and top with bacon slices. Bake for 1 hour 30 minutes. Just before serving add brandy and stir casserole from bottom to mix. Serves 4 to 6.

1
2
3
4
5
6
7
8
9
10
11
12
13
14
15
16
17
18
19
20
21
22
23
24
25
26
27
28
29
30

1
2
3
4
5
6
7
8
9
10
11
12
13
14
15
16
17
18
19
20
21
22
23
24
25
26
27
28
29
30

Cornish Game Hens

2 cornish game hens	
Garlic powder	
1 - 2 apples, cored, diced	
½ cup (1 stick) butter	**120 ml**
1 medium onion, diced	
¼ cup cream sherry	**60 ml**

- Preheat oven to 350° (176° C). Rub inside hens with a little salt, pepper and garlic powder. Stuff apples inside hens. (If hens are small, only 1 apple is needed.) Place hens breast side up on rack in roasting pan. Melt butter in skillet and saute onions with sherry until onions are clear. Cover hens with mixture. Cover with foil. Bake for 30 to 40 minutes, remove cover and bake for 30 minutes more or until golden brown. Serves 2.

Festive Salad

1 (10 ounce) package mixed salad greens	**280 g**
1 red and 1 green apple, cored, diced	
1 cup shredded parmesan cheese	**240 ml**
½ cup Craisins®	**120 ml**
½ cup slivered almonds, toasted	**120 ml**
Poppy seed dressing	

- In large salad bowl, toss greens, apples, cheese, Craisins® and almonds. Drizzle dressing over salad and toss. Serves 4.

Simple Side Dish: **Easy Rice Pilaf**

- Prepare 1 (7 ounce/ 198 g) box rice pilaf according to package directions.

Ham-Broccoli Stromboli

1 (10 ounce) package refrigerated pizza dough	280 g
1 (10 ounce) package chopped broccoli	280 g
1 (10 ounce) can cream of celery soup	280 g
3 cups cooked, diced ham	710 ml
1 cup shredded cheddar cheese	240 ml

• Preheat oven to 400° (204° C). Unroll dough onto sprayed baking sheet. Set aside. Cook broccoli according to package directions. Mix broccoli, soup and ham. Spread ham mixture down center of dough. Top with cheese.

• Fold long sides of dough over filling. Pinch short side to seal. Bake uncovered for 20 minutes or until golden brown. Slice and serve. Serves 4.

Marinated Salad

1 (15 ounce) can asparagus, drained	425 g
1 (15 ounce) can English peas, drained	425 g
1 (2 ounce) can sliced mushrooms, drained	57 g
1 (8 ounce) can sliced water chestnuts, drained	227 g
Italian salad dressing	
Lettuce	

• Combine asparagus, peas, mushrooms and water chestnuts, cover and marinate in Italian dressing overnight in refrigerator. Serve on bed of lettuce. Serves 6 to 8.

Crisp Oven-Fried Fish

¼ cup milk	60 ml
1 egg, beaten	
1 cup crushed corn flake crumbs	240 ml
¼ teaspoon thyme	1 ml
¼ cup parmesan cheese	60 ml
2 pounds fish fillets	1 kg
⅓ cup butter, melted	80 ml
Lemon slices	

• Preheat oven to 500° (260° C). Mix egg and milk in shallow pan. Mix crumbs, thyme and cheese in separate pan. Dip fillet in egg-milk mixture. Roll in crumb mixture. Lay fillets side-by-side in sprayed baking dish. Drizzle with melted butter and remaining crumbs on top. Bake for 14 minutes. Serve with lemon slices. Serves 6 to 8.

Colorful Coleslaw

1 (16 ounce) package shredded cabbage	.5 kg
1 bunch green onions, sliced	
2 cups cubed cheddar cheese	480 ml
¼ cup sliced ripe olives	60 ml
1 (12 ounce) can Mexicorn®, drained	340 g
1 cup mayonnaise	240 ml
2 tablespoons sugar	30 ml
2 tablespoons vinegar	30 ml

• Combine cabbage, onions, cheese, olives and corn and mix. Add remaining ingredients and toss with slaw. Cover and refrigerate. Serves 6 to 8.

Smoked Pork Chops

1 (4 - 6 count) package thick-sliced, smoked pork chops
1 (8 ounce) jar sweet-and-sour sauce   **227 g**
¼ cup chipotle salsa   **60 ml**

- Place pork chops in skillet with just a little oil. Cook over medium heat and cook about 7 minutes on each side. (Chops do not need to brown. They will dry out if cooked too long.) While pork chops cook, combine sweet-and-sour sauce and salsa. Pour over pork chops in skillet. Heat to boiling, reduce heat, cover and simmer about 10 minutes. Serve over rice. Serves 4 to 6.

Spinach-Sprout Salad

1 (10 ounce) package baby spinach, chilled   **280 g**
1 cup fresh bean sprouts, chilled   **240 ml**
8 slices pre-cooked bacon, crumbled, chilled
Lime-basil vinaigrette salad dressing
3 eggs, hard-boiled, sliced, chilled

- In salad bowl, combine spinach, bean sprouts and crumbled bacon and toss with lime-basil vinaigrette salad dressing. Place egg slices on top and refrigerate. Serves 4 to 6.

Simple Side Dish: **Easy Cheesy Rice**

- Prepare 2 (4 ounce/114 g) packages 4-cheese rice and pasta according to package directions.

April 1 2 3 4 5 6 7 8 9 10 11 12 13 14 15 16 17 18 19 20 21 22 23 24 25 26 27 28 29 30

1
2
3
4
5
6
7
8
9
10
11
12
13
14
15
16
17
18
19
20
21
22
23
24
25
26
27
28
29
30

Porcupine Meatballs

1 cup instant rice	**240 ml**
1 egg, beaten	
1 pound lean ground beef	**.5 kg**
2 teaspoons grated onion	**10 ml**
2½ cups tomato juice	**600 ml**
½ teaspoon sugar	**2 ml**

• Mix rice, egg, beef and onion with a little salt and pepper. Shape into meatballs and brown in skillet. Add tomato juice and sugar and bring to a boil. Cover and simmer 15 to 20 minutes. Serves 4 to 6.

Cheesy Spinach

1 (16 ounce) package frozen chopped spinach	**.5 kg**
3 eggs, beaten	
½ cup flour	**120 ml**
1 (16 ounce) carton small curd cottage cheese	**.5 kg**
1 (8 ounce) package shredded cheddar cheese	**227 g**

• Preheat oven to 350° (176° C). Cook spinach and drain well. Stir in eggs, flour and cottage cheese. Fold in cheddar cheese. Pour into sprayed 1½-quart (1.5 L) baking dish. Bake uncovered for 35 minutes. Serves 4 to 6.

1 - April Fool's Day
15 - Federal Tax Day
22 - Earth Day
Last Friday - Arbor Day

Lemon-Herb Pot Roast

1 (3 - 3½ pound) boneless beef chuck roast	1.3 kg
1 teaspoon minced garlic	5 ml
2 teaspoons lemon pepper	10 ml
1 teaspoon dried basil	5 ml
1 tablespoon oil	15 ml
3 potatoes	

- Preheat oven to 325° (162° C). Combine garlic, lemon pepper and basil and press evenly into surface of beef. In large, heavy pan, heat oil over medium-high heat until hot. Brown roast. Add 1 cup (240 ml) water. Cover and bake for 3 hours. Quarter potatoes and cook another 45 minutes. Serves 6 to 8.

Artichoke-Spinach Casserole

1 (16 ounce) can artichoke hearts, drained	.5 kg
2 (16 ounce) packages frozen chopped spinach, cooked, drained well	2 (.5 kg)
2 (3 ounce) packages cream cheese	2 (84 g)
4 tablespoons butter, melted, divided	60 ml
⅛ teaspoon nutmeg	.5 ml
½ cup breadcrumbs	120 ml

- Arrange artichoke hearts in sprayed 9 x 13-inch (23 x 33 cm) baking dish. Blend cooked spinach and cheese with 2 tablespoons (30 ml) melted butter.

- Add nutmeg and a little salt and pepper. Pour on top of artichokes. Refrigerate at least 45 minutes. Blend crumbs with remaining butter and add to top before baking. Bake at 350° (176° C) for 25 minutes. Serves 6 to 8.

1
2
3
4
5
6
7
8
9
10
11
12
13
14
15
16
17
18
19
20
21
22
23
24
25
26
27
28
29
30

Baked Hamburger

1½ pounds lean ground beef	**.7 kg**
1 (6 ounce) package seasoned croutons	**168 g**
2 (10 ounce) cans cream of chicken soup	**2 (280 g)**
1 soup can of milk	

- Preheat oven to 350° (176° C). Pat ground beef into sprayed 9 x 13-inch (23 x 33 cm) baking dish. Mix croutons, soup and milk. Pour over meat and bake for 1 hour. Serves 6 to 8.

Ranch Mashed Potatoes

4 cups prepared, unsalted instant mashed potatoes	**1 L**
1 (1 ounce) packet ranch dressing mix	**28 g**
¼ cup (½ stick) butter	**60 ml**

- Combine all ingredients in saucepan. Heat and stir on low until potatoes are thoroughly hot. Serves 6 to 8.

Poppy-Spinach Salad

2 (10 ounce) packages fresh spinach	**2 (280 g)**
1 quart fresh strawberries, halved	**1 L**
½ cup slivered almonds, toasted	**120 ml**
Poppy seed dressing	

- Remove stems and tear spinach into smaller pieces and add strawberries and almonds. Refrigerate until ready to serve. Toss with poppy seed dressing. Serves 6 to 8.

Curried Scallops

2 pounds scallops	1 kg
½ cup (1 stick) butter	120 ml
6 green onions, finely diced	
1½ tablespoons curry powder	22 ml
⅓ cup dry white wine	80 ml
5 cups cooked rice	1.3 L

• Wash and dry scallops. Dust lightly with flour and a little salt and pepper. Heat butter in skillet and saute green onions for 3 minutes. Add scallops, cook quickly and turn frequently to brown, about 3 minutes. Sprinkle with curry powder. Add wine and mix well. Serve over rice. Serves 4 to 6.

Prairie Schooners

4 large potatoes, baked	
1 (15 ounce) can ranch-style beans	425 g
1 cup sour cream	240 ml
½ cup (1 stick butter), softened	120 ml
1 teaspoon chili powder	5 ml
2 tablespoons chopped green bell pepper	30 ml
2 tablespoons chopped onion	30 ml
1 tablespoon butter	15 ml
1 cup shredded cheddar cheese	240 ml

• Preheat oven to 425° (220° C). Slice top one-third of baked potato lengthwise. Scoop out potato leaving ¼-inch (.6 cm) around potato skin. Mash potato until free of lumps. Drain beans thoroughly and reserve juice. Mash beans.

• Whip sour cream, butter, mashed beans, a little salt, pepper and chili powder. Add bean juice as needed to moisten. Spoon mixture into potato shells. Saute bell pepper and onion in butter. Top each potato with cheese, onion and green pepper. Bake for 10 to 20 minutes. Serves 4 to 6.

Rump Roast Supreme

⅓ cup chopped onion	80 ml
⅓ cup chopped celery	80 ml
½ teaspoon garlic powder	2 ml
1 (3 pound) rump roast	1.3 kg
1 (14 ounce) can beef broth	396 g

• Preheat oven to 350° (176° C). Combine onion and celery and place in sprayed roasting pan. Combine garlic powder with 1 teaspoon (5 ml) pepper and rub over roast. Place fat side up over vegetables. Bake uncovered for 2½ to 3 hours. Let stand for 15 minutes before carving. Add beef broth, stir to remove brown bits in pan and heat. Strain and discard vegetables. Serve au jus with roast. Serves 6 to 8.

Fried Okra and Tomatoes

1 (10 ounce) package frozen cut okra, thawed	280 g
½ cup cornmeal	120 ml
3 slices bacon, cut into pieces	
½ small onion, chopped	
1½ medium tomatoes, chopped	
1 teaspoon minced fresh hot red chili pepper	5 ml

• Shake thawed okra in plastic bag with cornmeal and ¾ teaspoon (4 ml) salt. Fry bacon in skillet until crisp, remove and set aside. Add okra and onion to bacon drippings. Saute and stir frequently. Add tomatoes, chili pepper and bacon. Cook 15 minutes or until tomatoes are soft and add a little salt. Serves 6.

Simple Side Dish:
Easy Sour Cream Mashed Potatoes

• Prepare 1 (7.2 ounce/198 g) according to package directions.

Pork Stir-Fry

2 boneless pork loin chops, cut into ¼-inch strips	.6 cm
1 (14 ounce) bag frozen Oriental stir-fry	
vegetables with seasoning	396 g
1 tablespoon soy sauce	15 ml
2 teaspoons vegetable oil	10 ml
Fluffy white rice	

• Coat large skillet or wok with cooking spray. Heat to medium-high heat and add pork strips. Stir-fry 3 minutes or until no longer pink. Add vegetables, cover and cook 5 minutes. Add ¼ cup (60 ml) water, seasoning with Oriental vegetables, soy sauce and oil. Cook and stir until mixture is hot. Serve over rice. Serves 6 to 8.

Fruit Medley

1 (24 ounce) jar mango wedges, drained, chopped	680 g
2 medium kiwi fruits, peeled, thinly sliced	
2 medium bananas, thinly sliced	
1 teaspoon lemon juice	5 ml

• Toss ingredients in lemon juice and chill.
• Serves 6 to 8.

April

1 – April Fool's Day
15 – Federal Tax Day
22 – Earth Day
Last Friday – Arbor Day

1
2
3
4
5
6
7
8
9
10
11
12
13
14
15
16
17
18
19
20
21
22
23
24
25
26
27
28
29
30

Chicken Souffle

16 slices white bread
½ cup mayonnaise   **120 ml**
6 boneless, skinless chicken breast halves, cooked
1 cup shredded cheddar cheese, divided   **240 ml**
5 large eggs, beaten
2 cups milk   **480 ml**
1 (10 ounce) can cream of mushroom soup   **280 g**

- Butter bread slices on 1 side and remove crusts. Spray 9 x 13-inch (23 x 33 cm) baking dish and line 8 bread slices in dish. Spread mayonnaise on bread and chicken and ½ cup (120 ml) cheese. Top with remaining 8 slices bread.

- Mix eggs, milk and 1 teaspoon (5 ml) salt and pour over entire dish. Chill overnight or all day. When ready to bake, spread soup over top and press down with back of spoon.

- Bake covered at 350° (176° C) for 45 minutes. Uncover, sprinkle with remaining ½ cup (120 ml) cheddar cheese, return to oven and bake 15 minutes longer. Serves 6 to 8.

Orange-Beet Salad

2 oranges, peeled, sliced
1 (8 ounce) can sliced pickled beets, drained   **227 g**
Bibb lettuce leaves
1 small purple onion, thinly sliced
½ cup creamy Italian dressing   **120 ml**

- Arrange orange and beet slices on lettuce. Top with onion slices. Pour dressing over top and serve. Serves 4.

Oven Brisket

1 (5 - 6 pound) trimmed brisket	2.2 kg
1 (1 ounce) packet onion soup mix	28 g
1 (12 ounce) can cola	340 g
1 (10 ounce) bottle steak sauce	280 g

• Preheat oven to 325° (162° C). Place brisket, fat-side up, in roasting pan. Combine onion mix, cola and steak sauce and pour over brisket. Cover and bake for 4 to 5 hours or until tender. Remove brisket from pan, pour off drippings and chill both, separately, overnight. The next day, trim all fat from meat, slice and reheat. Skim fat off drippings, reheat and serve sauce over brisket. Serves 8 to 10.

Quick Potatoes

2 tablespoons butter	30 ml
½ onion, finely minced	
½ green bell pepper, diced	
2 (15 ounce) cans sliced new potatoes, drained	2 (425 g)

• Preheat oven to 350° (176° C). Melt butter in skillet. Add onion and bell pepper. Cook over medium heat until tender. Add drained potatoes and continue to saute for 5 minutes. Add a little pepper. Place in sprayed 9-inch (23 cm) pie pan and bake for 15 minutes. Serves 6 to 8.

Broccoli Salad

1 bunch fresh broccoli florets	
2 ounces feta cheese	57 g
½ head lettuce, torn in bite-size pieces	
½ cup mayonnaise	120 ml

• Combine ingredients and serve. Serves 6.

1
2
3
4
5
6
7
8
9
10
11
12
13
14
15
16
17
18
19
20
21
22
23
24
25
26
27
28
29
30

Sausalito Scampi

⅓ cup olive oil	80 ml
2 cloves garlic, minced	
6 boneless, skinless chicken breast halves, cut in 1-inch pieces	2.5 cm
1 pound shrimp, shelled, veined	.5 kg
1 lemon	
Fluffy white rice	

• Place oil in large skillet. Cook garlic and chicken and until brown and stir constantly. Push to one side. Add shrimp, cook and stir constantly, until pink. Season with 1 teaspoon (5 ml) salt and lemon juice and cook 1 more minute. Serve over rice. Serves 8 to 10.

Cauliflower Salad

1 head cauliflower, broken in florets	
1 (8 ounce) bottle Italian salad dressing	227 g
1 (4 ounce) can sliced mushrooms, drained	114 g
1 onion, chopped	
1 (15 ounce) can green peas, drained	425 g

• Mix all ingredients and marinate overnight. Serves 6 to 8.

Garlic Toast

1 loaf sliced French bread	
1 tablespoon garlic powder	15 ml
2 tablespoons dried parsley flakes	30 ml
½ cup (1 stick) butter, melted	120 ml
1 cup parmesan cheese	240 ml

• Preheat oven to 225° (107° C). Combine bread, garlic, parsley and butter and spread on bread slices. Place on cookie sheet and bake for 1 hour. Serves 6 to 8.

Stir-Fry Chicken And Veggies

1¼ cups instant rice	300 ml
¼ cup (½ stick) butter	60 ml
1½ pounds chicken tenderloin strips	.7 kg
1 (16 ounce) package frozen broccoli, cauliflower and carrots	.5 kg
2 sweet red bell peppers, seeded, julienned	
½ cup stir-fry sauce	120 ml

• Cook rice according to package directions and keep warm. In large non-stick skillet, melt butter and stir-fry chicken strips about 5 minutes or until light brown. Stir in vegetables and cook 8 minutes longer. Pour in stir-fry sauce and mix well. Cover and cook 2 minutes or until hot. Serves 4 to 6.

Fantastic Fruit Salad

2 (11 ounce) cans mandarin oranges	2 (312 g)
2 (15 ounce) cans pineapple chunks	2 (425 g)
1 (16 ounce) carton frozen strawberries, thawed	.5 kg
1 (20 ounce) can peach pie filling	567 g
1 (20 ounce) can apricot pie filling	567 g

• Drain oranges, pineapple and strawberries. Combine all ingredients and fold together gently. Spoon into glass serving bowl and refrigerate. Serves 4 to 6.

Simple Side Dish: Rice-On-The-Side

• Prepare 2 (4.3 ounce/114 g) boxes teriyaki rice and pasta and serve.

1
2
3
4
5
6
7
8
9
10
11
12
13
14
15
16
17
18
19
20
21
22
23
24
25
26
27
28
29
30

New Orleans French Toast

2 eggs	
½ cup milk	**120 ml**
4 pieces French bread	
Oil	
¼ cup packed brown sugar	**60 ml**
¼ cup finely chopped pecans	**60 ml**
1 tablespoon butter	**15 ml**

- Combine eggs and milk and soak bread in mixture. Fry bread in small amount of oil. Combine brown sugar, pecans and butter and warm in microwave. Spread praline mixture over fried bread slices and place on baking sheet. Toast under broiler until mixture bubbles. Serves 4.

Fruit Smoothies

2 - 3 bananas (ripe, overly ripe, or frozen)	
1 (15 ounce) can peaches, drained	**425 g**
1 cup orange juice	**240 ml**
1 (16 ounce) box frozen strawberries, thawed	**.5 kg**
2 tablespoons sugar	**30 ml**
Frozen vanilla yogurt	

- Put bananas, peaches and orange juice in blender on high. Add strawberries and sugar and continue to blend. Place scoop of frozen yogurt in glass and pour smoothie mixture over it. Serves 2 to 4.

Tip: Serve breakfast for dinner on Sunday nights and begin your own fun, family tradition.

Breakfast or Brunch

Adobe Chicken

2 cups cooked brown rice	480 ml
1 (10 ounce) can diced tomatoes and green chilies, drained	280 g
3 cups cooked, chopped chicken	710 ml
1 (8 ounce) package shredded Monterey Jack cheese, divided	227 g

• Preheat oven to 325° (162° C). Combine rice, tomatoes and green chilies, chicken and half Jack cheese. Spoon into sprayed 7 x 11-inch (18 x 28 cm) baking dish. Cook covered for 30 minutes. Uncover, sprinkle remaining cheese over casserole and return to oven for 5 minutes. Serves 4 to 6.

Carrot Salad

3 cups finely grated carrots	710 ml
1 (8 ounce) can crushed pineapple, drained	227 g
4 tablespoons flaked coconut	60 ml
1 tablespoon sugar	15 ml
⅓ cup mayonnaise	80 ml

• Combine all ingredients. Toss well. Refrigerate. Serves 4 to 6.

Simple Side Dish: **Potato Dinner Rolls**

• Heat 1 (16 ounce/.5 kg) package potato dinner rolls according to package directions.

Broccoli-Cheese Chicken

6 boneless, skinless chicken breast halves	
1 (10 ounce) can broccoli-cheese soup	280 g
1 (16 ounce) package frozen broccoli florets	.5 kg
½ cup milk	120 ml

- In skillet, with a little oil, cook chicken 15 minutes or until brown on both sides, remove and set aside. In same skillet, combine soup, broccoli, milk and a little pepper and heat to boiling. Return chicken to skillet and reduce heat to low. Cover and cook another 25 minutes until chicken is no longer pink and broccoli is tender. Serve over rice. Serves 4 to 6.

Wined-Fruit Medley

3 fresh ripe pears, peeled, chopped	
1 cup seedless grapes, halved	240 ml
2 bananas, sliced	
½ cup orange juice	120 ml
½ cup dry white wine	120 ml

- Toss pears, grapes and bananas together. Combine orange juice and wine. Pour over fruits and mix gently to coat fruit. Refrigerate. Serves 4 to 6.

Cheddar Puffs

½ cup (1 stick butter), softened	120 ml
1 cup shredded cheddar cheese	240 ml
1¼ cups flour	300 ml

- Preheat oven to 375° (190° C). Blend butter and cheese until smooth. Stir in flour and ¼ teaspoon (1 ml) salt. Knead lightly with hands. Roll, teaspoon (5 ml) at a time, into balls. Place on baking sheet. Bake for 14 to 15 minutes or until golden brown. Serves 4 to 6.

Peach-Pineapple Baked Ham

1 (3 - 4) pound boneless, smoked ham	1.3 kg
4 tablespoons dijon-style mustard, divided	60 ml
1 cup peach preserves	240 ml
1 cup pineapple preserves	240 ml

- Preheat oven to 325° (162° C). Spread 2 tablespoons (30 ml) mustard on ham. Place ham in sprayed, shallow baking pan and bake for 20 minutes. Combine remaining 2 tablespoons (30 ml) mustard and both preserves and heat in microwave oven for 20 seconds or in small saucepan on low heat for 2 to 3 minutes. Pour over ham and bake for about 15 minutes. Serves 8 to 10.

Parmesan-Bread Deluxe

1 loaf unsliced Italian bread	
½ cup refrigerated creamy Caesar dressing	120 ml
⅓ cup grated parmesan cheese	80 ml
3 tablespoons finely chopped green onions	45 ml

- Cut 24 (½ inch/1.2 cm) slices from bread. Reserve remaining bread for other use. In small bowl, combine dressing, cheese and onion. Spread 1 teaspoon (5 ml) dressing mixture on each bread slice. Place bread on baking sheet. Broil 4 inches (10 cm) from heat until golden brown. Serve warm. Serves 6 to 8.

365

1
2
3
4
5
6
7
8
9
10
11
12
13
14
15
16
17
18
19
20
21
22
23
24
25
26
27
28
29
30
31

Maple-Plum Glazed Turkey Breast

2 cups red plum jam	480 ml
1 cup maple syrup	240 ml
1 teaspoon dry mustard	5 ml
¼ cup lemon juice	60 ml
1 (5 pound) bone-in turkey breast	2.2 kg

• In saucepan, combine all ingredients except turkey. Bring to boiling point, turn heat down and simmer for about 20 minutes or until it thickens. Reserve 1 cup (240 ml) glaze. Place turkey breast in roasting pan and pour remaining glaze over turkey. Bake turkey according to package directions. Slice turkey and serve with reserved hot glaze. Serves 6 to 8.

Sauteed Snow Peas

1 tablespoon butter	15 ml
¾ pound fresh mushrooms, sliced	340 g
1 (8 ounce) can water chestnuts, sliced, drained	227 g
¾ pound fresh snow peas	340 g

• Melt butter over medium heat in skillet. Saute mushrooms and water chestnuts. Add snow peas and saute until peas turn bright green. Serves 6.

Yummy Potatoes

1 (1 ounce) packet dry onion soup mix	28 g
½ cup (1 stick) butter, melted	120 ml
8 medium new potatoes with peel, cubed	
Parsley flakes	

• Preheat oven to 350° (176° C). Combine 1 cup (240 ml) hot water, soup mix and butter in sprayed 2-quart (2 L) baking dish. Add potatoes, cover and bake about 1 hour. Uncover during last 20 minutes and sprinkle with parsley flakes. Serves 6.

Bacon-Wrapped Chicken

6 boneless, skinless chicken breast halves
1 (8 ounce) carton whipped cream cheese with onion
  and chives   227 g
Butter
6 bacon strips

- Preheat oven to 375° (190° C). Flatten chicken to
  ½-inch (1.2 cm) thick. Spread 3 tablespoons (45 ml)
  cream cheese over each. Dot with butter and a little
  salt and roll. Wrap each with bacon strip.
- Place seam-side down in sprayed 9 x 13-inch
  (23 x 33 cm) baking dish. Bake uncovered for 40 to
  45 minutes or until juices run clear. To brown, broil
  6 inches (15 cm) from heat for about 3 minutes or
  until bacon is crisp. Serves 4 to 6.

Stuffed-Cucumber Slices

3 cucumbers, peeled
2 (3 ounce) packages cream cheese, softened   2 (84 g)
¼ cup chopped stuffed green olives   60 ml

- Halve cucumbers lengthwise and scoop out seeds.
  Beat cream cheese with mixer until creamy. Add
  olives and ½ teaspoon (2 ml) salt. Fill hollows with
  cream cheese mixture, press halves together, wrap
  tightly in plastic wrap and chill. Cut crosswise in
  ⅓-inch (.8 cm) slices to serve. Serves 4 to 6.

1
2
3
4
5
6
7
8
9
10
11
12
13
14
15
16
17
18
19
20
21
22
23
24
25
26
27
28
29
30
31

Vegetable Pockets

1 cucumber, peeled	
1 green bell pepper, seeded	
1 large half-ripe tomato	
1 small onion, quartered	
1 carrot, peeled	
1 tablespoon unflavored gelatin	**15 ml**
1 cup mayonnaise	**240 ml**
Pita bread	

- Grind vegetables in blender, drain juices, heat and set vegetables aside. Pour 4 tablespoons (60 ml) hot juices into bowl, add gelatin and dissolve. Add mayonnaise and a little salt and pepper to gelatin mixture, mix well and pour over drained vegetables. Chill. Fill pitas. Makes 1½ cups (360 ml).

Zesty Chicken-Cream Soup

2 tablespoons butter	**30 ml**
½ onion, finely chopped	
1 carrot, grated	
1 (10 ounce) can cream of celery soup	**280 g**
1 (10 ounce) can cream of mushroom soup	**280 g**
1 (10 ounce) can cream of chicken soup	**280 g**
1 (14 ounce) can chicken broth	**396 g**
2 soup cans milk	
¼ teaspoon garlic powder	**1 ml**
1 (16 ounce) package cubed Mexican Velveeta® cheese	**.5 kg**
4 boneless, skinless chicken breasts, cooked, diced	

- In large roasting pan melt butter and saute onion and carrots for 10 minutes but do not brown. Add remaining ingredients and heat but do not boil. Reduce heat to medium-low and cook until cheese melts. Serve piping hot. Serves 6 to 8.

Silver Dollar Pancakes

2 eggs, beaten	
2 cups buttermilk*	480 ml
4 tablespoons oil	60 ml
2 cups flour	480 ml
2 tablespoons plus 2 teaspoons sugar	30 ml/10 ml
2 teaspoons baking powder	10 ml
1 teaspoon baking soda	5 ml

• Combine all ingredients plus ½ teaspoon (2 ml) salt. Beat just until smooth. Drop by tablespoons onto hot griddle. Cook and serve with butter and warmed maple syrup. Serves 4 to 6.

TIP: To make buttermilk, mix 1 cup (240 ml) with 1 tablespoon (15 ml) lemon juice or vinegar and let milk rest about 10 minutes.

Sweet Strawberries and Cream

2 pints fresh strawberries, sliced	1 kg
Sugar	
1 (8 ounce) carton whipping cream	227 g
1 cup chopped almonds	240 ml

• Divide sliced strawberries in serving bowls and sprinkle liberally with sugar. Beat whipping cream with 1 tablespoon (15 ml) sugar until peaks form. Sprinkle almonds over strawberries and top with whipped cream. Serves 4 to 6.

Simple Side Dish: **Quick Maple Bacon**

• Lay strips of bacon across rack on shallow pan. Bake at 325° (162° C) for 45 minutes.

Breakfast or Brunch

Lemon-Almond Chicken

2 (14 ounce) cans cut asparagus, well drained	2 (396 g)
4 boneless, skinless chicken breast halves, cut	
into ½-inch strips	1.2 cm
3 tablespoons butter	45 ml
1 (10 ounce) can cream of asparagus soup	280 g
⅔ cup mayonnaise	160 ml
¼ cup milk	60 ml
1 sweet red bell pepper, julienned	
2 tablespoons lemon juice	30 ml
1 teaspoon curry powder	5 ml
¼ teaspoon ground ginger	1 ml
½ cup sliced almonds, toasted	120 ml

- Preheat oven to 350° (176° C). Place asparagus in sprayed 7 x 11-inch (18 x 28 cm) baking dish and set aside. Sprinkle chicken with ½ teaspoon (2 ml) salt. In large skillet, saute chicken in butter for about 15 minutes. Spoon chicken strips over asparagus.

- In skillet, combine asparagus soup, mayonnaise, milk, sweet red bell pepper, lemon juice, curry powder, ginger and ¼ teaspoon (1 ml) pepper and heat just enough to mix well. Spoon over chicken and sprinkle almonds over top. Bake uncovered for 35 minutes. Serves 4 to 6.

French-Fry Cheese Melt

1 large bag frozen french fries	
1 (12 ounce) package shredded cheddar cheese	340 g

- Place fries on large sprayed baking sheet and bake according to package directions. Salt and pepper fries and bunch into individual servings. Sprinkle cheese on top. Return to oven and bake until cheese melts. Serves 4 to 6.

Creole Pepper Steak

2 cloves garlic, crushed	
1 teaspoon thyme	5 ml
1 teaspoon red pepper	5 ml
1 pound (1 inch/2.5 cm) thick beef top round steak	5 kg

• Combine garlic, thyme and red pepper. Press evenly into both sides of steak. Grill 12 to 14 minutes for rare to medium and turn once. Cut steak diagonally into thin slices to serve. Serves 4 to 6.

Creamy Mashed Potatoes

6 large potatoes	
1 (8 ounce) carton sour cream	227 g
1 (8 ounce) package cream cheese, softened	227 g

• Preheat oven to 325° (162° C). Peel, cut and boil potatoes. Drain. Add sour cream, cream cheese, ½ teaspoon (2 ml) pepper and 1 teaspoon (5 ml) salt. Whip until cream cheese melts. Pour into sprayed 3-quart (3 L) baking dish. Cover and bake at for 20 minutes. Serves 4 to 6.

Garlic Green Beans

3 (15 ounce) cans whole green beans, drained	3 (425 g)
⅔ cup oil	160 ml
½ cup vinegar	120 ml
½ cup sugar	120 ml
2 tablespoons minced garlic	30 ml

• Place green beans in container with lid. Mix oil, vinegar, sugar and garlic. Pour over beans and sprinkle with a little salt and pepper. Let stand overnight in refrigerator. Serves 4 to 6.

Oven-Fried Chicken

1 teaspoon Creole seasoning	5 ml
1 cup crushed corn flakes	240 ml
6 (5 ounce) boneless, skinless chicken breast halves	6 (143 g)
¼ cup buttermilk*	60 ml

• Preheat oven to 375° (190° C). Combine Creole seasoning and corn flake crumbs. Brush chicken with buttermilk and roll in crumb mixture. Place chicken in sprayed 9 x 13-inch (23 x 33 cm) baking dish and bake for 1 hour. Serves 4 to 6.

TIP: To make buttermilk, mix 1 cup (240 ml) with 1 tablespoon (15 ml) lemon juice or vinegar and let milk rest about 10 minutes.

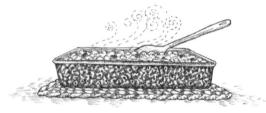

Asparagus Bake

4 (10 ounce) cans asparagus	4 (280 g)
3 eggs, hard-boiled, sliced	
⅓ cup milk	80 ml
1½ cups shredded cheddar cheese	360 ml
1¼ cups cheese cracker crumbs	300 ml

• Preheat oven to 350° (176° C). Place asparagus in sprayed 7 x 11-inch (18 x 28 cm) baking dish, layer eggs slices on top and pour milk over casserole. Sprinkle cheese on top and add cracker crumbs. Bake uncovered for 30 minutes. Serves 4 to 6.

Apple-Cinnamon French Bread

8 large eggs	
3½ cups milk	830 ml
1 cup sugar, divided	240 ml
1 tablespoon vanilla	15 ml
1 large loaf unsliced French bread	
3 teaspoons cinnamon	15 ml
1 teaspoon nutmeg	5 ml
4 - 5 medium cooking apples, peeled, sliced	
⅓ cup butter	80 ml

• Preheat oven to 350° (176° C). Beat eggs, milk,
½ cup (120 ml) sugar and vanilla for 30 seconds.
Slice bread 1½ inches (3 cm) thick and place sprayed
9 x 13-inch (23 x 33 cm) baking dish. Pour 1½ cups
(360 ml) mixed ingredients over bread. Place apples
on top. Pour remaining mix over apples. Sprinkle
remaining ½ cup (120 ml) sugar, cinnamon, nutmeg
and butter over top. Cover and place in refrigerator
overnight. Bake uncovered for 1 hour. Serves 4 to 6.

Stuffed Mushrooms

2 - 3 cartons large fresh mushrooms	
1 pound sage-flavored sausage	.5 kg
1 small onion, chopped	
1 (8 ounce) package cream cheese	227 g

• Preheat oven to 300° (148° C). Remove stems from
mushrooms. Brown sausage, onions and mushroom
stems. Drain sausage, add cream cheese and stir
until it melts. Stuff mushrooms with sausage mixture.
Place on cookie sheet and bake for 30 minutes.
Serves 4 to 6.

1
2
3
4
5
6
7
8
9
10
11
12
13
14
15
16
17
18
19
20
21
22
23
24
25
26
27
28
29
30
31

Broccoli-Wild Rice Soup

1 (6 ounce) package chicken-flavored wild rice mix	168 g
1 (10 ounce) package frozen chopped broccoli, thawed	280 g
2 teaspoons dried minced onion flakes	10 ml
1 (10 ounce) can cream of chicken soup	280 g
1 (8 ounce) package cream cheese, cubed	227 g

- In large saucepan, combine rice, rice seasoning packet and 6 cups (1.5 L) water. Bring to a boil, reduce heat, cover and simmer for 10 minutes, stirring once.
- Stir in broccoli and onion flakes and simmer 5 minutes. Stir in soup and cream cheese. Cook and stir until cheese melts. Serves 4 to 6.

Southwest Cornbread

1 cup flour	240 ml
1 cup yellow cornmeal	240 ml
4 teaspoons baking powder	20 ml
2 tablespoons sugar	30 ml
1½ cups milk	360 ml
1 egg, beaten	
2 tablespoons oil	30 ml

- Preheat oven to 450° (230° C). Sift dry ingredients and 1 teaspoon (5 ml) salt. Add milk and mix well. Beat in egg and oil. Pour batter into sprayed cast-iron skillet. Bake for 15 to 20 minutes or until golden brown. Serves 4 to 6.

Oven-Fried Ginger Chicken

1 cup flour	240 ml
1 teaspoon dried ginger	5 ml
½ teaspoon cinnamon	2 ml
½ cup (¼ stick) butter	120 ml
4 boneless, skinless chicken breast halves	
½ cup soy sauce	120 ml
Fluffy brown rice	

- Preheat oven to 350° (176° C). Mix flour, ginger, cinnamon, 1 teaspoon (5 ml) salt and ½ teaspoon (2 ml) pepper. Melt butter in sprayed 9 x 9-inch (23 x 23 cm) baking dish. Rinse chicken breasts and pat dry. Coat with flour mixture. Arrange meaty side down in prepared dish. Bake for 30 minutes. Turn chicken over and pour soy sauce over chicken. Bake for 20 to 25 minutes or until done. Serve over rice. Serves 4.

Green Beans With Walnuts

2 tablespoons olive oil	30 ml
1 teaspoon minced garlic	5 ml
¼ cup ground walnuts	60 ml
1 (8 ounce) can French-style green beans, drained	227 g

- Heat oil in skillet. Add garlic, walnuts and beans. Mix gently and toss beans until hot. Serves 4.

May

1 - Loyalty Day
2nd Sunday - Mother's Day
3rd Saturday - Armed Forces Day
Last Monday - Memorial Day

1
2
3
4
5
6
7
8
9
10
11
12
13
14
15
16
17
18
19
20
21
22
23
24
25
26
27
28
29
30
31

Beef And Mushroom Bake

2 (10 ounce) packages frozen spinach, thawed	2 (280 g)
1 pound lean ground beef	.5 kg
1 large onion, chopped	
½ pound fresh mushrooms, sliced	227 g
1 (8 ounce) carton sour cream	227 g
⅛ teaspoon ground nutmeg	.5 ml
1½ teaspoons Italian seasoning	7 ml
1 cup shredded cheddar cheese, divided	240 ml

• Preheat oven to 350° (176° C). Place spinach in wire strainer and press out all water. Set aside. Sprinkle 1 teaspoon (5 ml) salt over ground beef and cook in medium skillet. Add onions and mushrooms. Cook about 5 minutes.

• Remove from heat and stir in spinach, sour cream, ½ teaspoon (2 ml) salt, nutmeg, Italian seasoning and half cheddar cheese. Pour into sprayed, shallow 2-quart (2 L) baking dish. Sprinkle remaining cheese over top. Bake uncovered for 20 minutes. Serves 4 to 6.

Seven-Layer Salad

1 small head lettuce, chopped	
1 (8 ounce) can water chestnuts, chopped	227 g
1 red onion, chopped	
1 (10 ounce) box frozen peas, thawed	280 g
6 eggs, hard-boiled, sliced	
6 slices bacon, fried crisp, crumbled	
½ cup mayonnaise	120 ml
Shredded mozzarella cheese	

• Layer all ingredients in bowl in order listed. Seal with mayonnaise. Top with mozzarella cheese. Place uncovered in refrigerator for 24 hours. Serves 6.

Sour Cream Tacos

1 pound lean ground beef	.5 kg
1 large onion, diced	
2 teaspoons minced garlic	10 ml
1 (10 ounce) can tomato soup	280 g
2 jalapeno peppers, seeded, diced	
1 (8 ounce) package shredded Velveeta® cheese	227 g
1 (1 pint) carton sour cream	.5 kg
Corn chips	

- Preheat oven to 350° (176° C). Brown beef, onion and garlic in skillet. Add soup and peppers. Add cheese and sour cream, heat and stir constantly until they melt.
- Line sprayed 7 x 11-inch (18 x 28 cm) baking dish with large corn chips and pour mixture on top. Bake for 20 minutes. Serves 4 to 6.

Yummy Cucumbers

2 seedless cucumbers	
1 (8 ounce) carton sour cream	227 g
3 tablespoons wine vinegar	45 ml
1 tablespoon sugar	15 ml
1 small onion, chopped	

- Peel and cut cucumbers into thick slices. Mix cucumber and 1 tablespoon (15 ml) salt in bowl. Cover with 2 cups (480 ml) cold water. Let stand for 1 hour. Drain cucumbers. Mix sour cream, vinegar, sugar, onion and ½ tablespoon (7 ml) salt. Stir mixture into cucumbers. Cover and refrigerate several hours before serving. Serves 4 to 6.

Pizza Burgers

1 pound lean ground beef	.5 kg
1 cup spaghetti sauce	240 ml
1 cup shredded mozzarella cheese	240 ml
4 hamburger buns	

- Shape beef into 4 patties. Cook hamburgers as desired. Separate buns in half. Place bottom part of bun on baking sheet. Put 3 tablespoons (45 ml) spaghetti sauce on each bun.
- Place cooked patties on each bun half. Top each hamburger patty with 3 tablespoons (45 ml) cheese. Cover each hamburger with top half of bun. Bake at 350° (176° C) for 5 minutes. Serves 4.

Red Potato Medley

2 tablespoons butter	30 ml
3 cups cubed new (red) potatoes*	710 ml
1½ cups diagonally sliced carrots	360 ml
¾ cup chopped onion	180 ml
¼ cup minced fresh parsley	60 ml
1 garlic clove, minced	

- In large skillet over medium heat, melt butter, add potatoes and carrots and toss to coat. Add remaining ingredients with ¼ teaspoon (1 ml) each of salt and pepper. Mix well and reduce heat to medium-low. Cover and cook for 15 to 20 minutes or until vegetables are tender. Stir every 5 minutes. Serves 4 to 6.

*TIP: About 2½ pounds (1.2 kg) new potatoes equals 3 cups (710 ml) cubed potatoes.

Chicken Bombay

6 boneless, skinless chicken breast halves	
Flour	
½ cup cooking sherry	120 ml
2 tablespoons brown sugar	30 ml
1 tablespoon soy sauce	15 ml
2 tablespoons oil	30 ml
½ teaspoon ginger	2 ml
Fluffy white rice	

- Preheat oven to 375° (190° C). Sprinkle a little salt and pepper on chicken, dredge in flour and brown on all sides in skillet. Place in sprayed 9 x 13-inch (23 x 33 cm) baking dish. Combine remaining ingredients, except rice, and pour over chicken. Cover and bake for 30 to 45 minutes. Serve over rice. Serves 4 to 6.

Green Bean Bake

1 (10 ounce) can cream of mushroom soup	280 g
½ cup milk	120 ml
1 tablespoon soy sauce	15 ml
2 (10 ounce) packages frozen cut green beans, cooked, drained	2 (280 g)
1 (3 ounce) french-fried onions	84 g

- Preheat oven to 350° (176° C). Combine soup, milk, soy sauce and beans. Bake at for 25 minutes. Top with onions and bake for 5 minutes. Serves 4 to 6.

Speedy Breadsticks

1 (10 count) can biscuits
2 egg whites, slightly beaten
Garlic salt

- Preheat oven to 400° (204° C). Roll each biscuit into pencil shapes on cookie sheet. Brush with egg whites. Sprinkle with garlic salt and bake until brown.

1
2
3
4
5
6
7
8
9
10
11
12
13
14
15
16
17
18
19
20
21
22
23
24
25
26
27
28
29
30
31

Spaghetti Pizza

½ cup milk	120 ml
1 egg	
1 (16 ounce) package thin or angel hair pasta, cooked	.5 kg
1 (26 ounce) spaghetti sauce	737 g
1 pound ground beef	.5 kg
1 (12 ounce) package shredded mozzarella cheese	340 g

• Preheat oven to 350° (176° C). Mix milk and egg and toss with spaghetti.

• Spread pasta in sprayed 9 x 13-inch (23 x 33 cm) baking pan. Top with spaghetti sauce. Crumble beef on top. Sprinkle with cheese. Bake for 30 minutes. Serves 4 to 6.

Splendid Spinach Salad

8 cups fresh spinach	1.8 L
¾ cup chopped macadamia nuts	180 ml
1 cup fresh raspberries or strawberries	240 ml
3 kiwi fruits	

• Toss all ingredients together.

Dressing:

2 tablespoons raspberry vinegar	30 ml
2 tablespoons raspberry or strawberry jam	30 ml
⅓ cup oil	80 ml

• Mix dressing ingredients. Pour over salad ingredients and toss. Serves 4 to 6.

Tator Tot Casserole

1 pound lean ground beef	.5 kg
1 small onion, chopped	
1 (16 ounce) package frozen tator tots	.5 kg
1 (10 ounce) can cream of mushroom soup	280 g
1 (10 ounce) can cream of celery soup	280 g
1 soup can milk	
1 (3 ounce) can french-fried onion rings	84 g

• Preheat oven to 325° (162° C). Brown meat and onion in skillet, season with a little salt and pepper and drain. Put half meat mixture in sprayed 9 x 13-inch (23 x 33 cm) baking pan.

• Cover with tator tots and add remaining meat mixture. Combine soups with milk and heat. Pour mixture over meat. Cover with onion rings. Bake uncovered for 1 hour. Serves 6 to 8.

Hot Slaw

1 (2 pound) cabbage	1 kg
6 strips bacon	
¼ cup packed brown sugar	60 ml
½ teaspoon celery seed	2 ml
½ teaspoon dry mustard	2 ml
¼ cup vinegar	60 ml

• Shred cabbage. Dice bacon and cook until crisp. Remove bacon and save pan drippings. Add sugar, celery seed, mustard, ½ teaspoon (2 ml) salt and vinegar to skillet. When mixture is hot, pour over cabbage and turn to mix well. Add bacon bits and serve. Serves 6 to 8.

1
2
3
4
5
6
7
8
9
10
11
12
13
14
15
16
17
18
19
20
21
22
23
24
25
26
27
28
29
30
31

Chicken Tetrazzini

1 (10 ounce) can cream of mushroom soup	280 g
1 (10 ounce) can cream of chicken soup	280 g
1 cup milk	240 ml
4 cups cooked, shredded chicken	1 L
1 (12 ounce) package spaghetti, cooked	340 g
1 (16 ounce) package shredded sharp cheddar cheese	.5 kg
1 (4 ounce) can chopped pimento, drained	114 g
1 (5 ounce) package grated parmesan cheese	143 g

- Preheat oven to 350° (176° C). Mix all ingredients, except parmesan cheese.
- Transfer to sprayed 9 x 13-inch (23 x 33 cm) baking dish. Top with lots of parmesan cheese. Bake uncovered for 20 to 30 minutes. Serves 6 to 8.

Mandarin Orange Salad

2 (3 ounce) packages orange gelatin	2 (84 g)
2 cups frozen orange juice	480 ml
1 (1 pint) carton vanilla ice cream	.5 kg
2 (11 ounce) cans mandarin oranges, drained	2 (312 g)

- Dissolve gelatin in 1½ cups (360 ml) hot water. Add frozen orange juice and ice cream. Beat until they blend well. Add oranges and pour into mold or 7 x 11-inch (18 x 28 cm) glass pan. Refrigerate until set. Serves 6 to 8.

Creamy Butter Bread

1 cup (2 sticks) butter, softened	240 ml
2 cups flour	480 ml
1 (8 ounce) carton sour cream	227 g

- Preheat oven to 350° (176° C). Combine all ingredients and mix well. Drop by teaspoonfuls into sprayed miniature muffin cups. Bake for 20 minutes or until light brown. Serves 4 to 6.

Black-Eyed Pea Chowder

1 pound turkey bacon	.5 kg
1 teaspoon butter	5 ml
½ cup chopped onion	120 ml
1 cup chopped celery	240 ml
½ cup chopped bell pepper	120 ml
2 (15 ounce) cans black-eyed peas	2 (425 g)
1 (10 ounce) can beef broth	280 g
1 (15 ounce) can whole kernel corn with juice	425 g
2 (15 ounce) cans Mexican stewed tomatoes	2 (425 g)

- In skillet, brown turkey bacon. Chop into bite-size pieces and set aside. In large, heavy pan, melt butter and saute onion, celery and bell pepper until tender. Add turkey bacon and all remaining ingredients. Bring to a boil, reduce heat and simmer for 30 minutes. Serves 6 to 8.

Cornbread Crumble

1 (6 ounce) package jalapeno cornbread mix	168 g
1 (6 ounce) package plain cornbread mix	168 g
2 eggs, divided	
1⅓ cups milk	
1 onion, chopped	
1 green pepper, chopped	
2 ribs celery	
1 (1 pint) jar mayonnaise	.5 kg
Garlic salt	
3 cups chopped fresh tomatoes	710 ml
3 slices bacon, fried, crumbled	

- Prepare both cornbread mixes according to package directions using 1 egg and ⅔ cup milk for each mix. Cool and crumble. Add onions, peppers, celery and mayonnaise and stir. Sprinkle with garlic salt and stir in tomatoes. Just before serving, sprinkle bacon on top. Serves 6 to 8.

1 2 3 4 5 6 7 8 9 10 11 12 13 14 15 16 17 18 19 20 21 22 23 24 25 26 27 28 29 30 31

1
2
3
4
5
6
7
8
9
10
11
12
13
14
15
16
17
18
19
20
21
22
23
24
25
26
27
28
29
30
31

Simple Beef Stroganoff

1 pound round steak, cut into thin strips	**.5 kg**
½ cup sliced onion	**120 ml**
1 (10 ounce) can cream of mushroom soup	**280 g**
½ cup sour cream	**120 ml**
Cooked noodles	

• Brown meat and onion in skillet and drain. Cook onion in butter until tender. Add remaining ingredients and ½ cup (120 ml) water. Simmer 45 minutes or until tender. Serve over noodles. Serves 4 to 6.

Carrot Salad

3 (15 ounce) cans sliced carrots, drained	**3 (425 g)**
1 medium onion, chopped	
1 medium bell pepper, chopped	
1 jalapeno pepper, seeded, diced	
1 (10 ounce) can tomato soup	**280 g**
¾ cup sugar	**180 ml**
½ cup vinegar	**120 ml**
¼ cup oil	**60 ml**

• Combine carrots, onion and peppers with a little salt in large bowl. Cook soup, sugar, vinegar and oil for 3 minutes in saucepan. Pour soup mixture over vegetables and mix well. Cover and refrigerate overnight. Serves 4 to 6.

1 - Loyalty Day
2nd Sunday - Mother's Day
3rd Saturday - Armed Forces Day
Last Monday - Memorial Day

Irish-Italian Spaghetti

1 medium onion, chopped	
2 tablespoons oil	30 ml
1 pound lean ground beef	.5 kg
½ teaspoon chili powder	2 ml
1 teaspoon hot sauce	5 ml
1 (10 ounce) can cream of mushroom soup	280 g
1 (10 ounce) can tomato soup	280 g
1 (8 ounce) package spaghetti	227 g
Parmesan cheese	

- Brown onion in oil. Add meat with ½ teaspoon (2 ml) salt and other seasonings. Cover and simmer 10 minutes. Stir in soups. Cover and simmer for 45 minutes. Cook spaghetti in boiling salted water. Drain and add to sauce. Mix well. Top with parmesan cheese. Serves 4 to 6.

Yummy Cabbage Salad

1 medium cabbage, finely chopped	
2 red apples, cored, chopped	
5 tablespoons sugar	75 ml
1 (8 ounce) can crushed pineapple with juice	227 g
6 marshmallows, cut in small pieces	
½ cup chopped nuts	120 ml
1 tablespoon vinegar	15 ml
Lettuce	

- Place cabbage and apples in mixing bowl. Add sugar, pineapple and marshmallows. Let stand for 30 minutes. Just before serving, add nuts and vinegar and mix gently. Serve on crisp piece of lettuce. Serves 4 to 6.

May

Ravioli And More

1 pound lean ground beef	.5 kg
1 teaspoon garlic powder	5 ml
1 large onion, chopped	
2 zucchini squash, grated	
¼ cup (½ stick) butter	60 ml
1 (28 ounce) jar spaghetti sauce, divided	794 g
1 (25 ounce) package ravioli with portobello mushrooms, cooked, divided	708 g
1 (12 ounce) package shredded mozzarella cheese, divided	340 g

- Preheat oven to 350° (176° C). Brown ground beef in large skillet until no longer pink and drain. Add garlic powder and ½ teaspoon (2 ml) each of salt and pepper. In saucepan cook onion and zucchini in butter just until tender-crisp and stir in spaghetti sauce.

- In sprayed 9 x 13-inch (23 x 33 cm) baking dish, spread ½ cup (120 ml) sauce.   Layer half ravioli, half spaghetti sauce, half beef and half cheese. Repeat layers, but omit remaining cheese. Cover and bake for 35 minutes. Uncover and sprinkle remaining cheese. Let stand 10 minutes before serving. Serves 4 to 6.

Gazpacho Salad

1 (3 ounce) package lemon gelatin	84 g
1 tablespoon vinegar	15 ml
¼ teaspoon garlic salt	1 ml
Dash of hot sauce	
1 (15 ounce) can stewed tomatoes	425 g
1 (4 ounce) can chopped green chilies	114 g
1 cup peeled, chopped cucumbers	240 ml

- Dissolve gelatin in 1 cup (240 ml) boiling water. Add remaining ingredients plus ¼ teaspoon (1 ml) salt and pour into shallow salad bowl. Refrigerate. Serves 4 to 6.

Pork Chop Casserole

6 - 8 pork chops
3 potatoes, peeled, sliced
1 onion, sliced
1 (10 ounce) can cream of mushroom soup   280 g
½ cup milk   120 ml

- Preheat oven to 350° (176° C). Brown pork chops
  and set aside. Place potatoes in sprayed 9 x 13-inch
  (23 x 33 cm) pan. Add layer of onions. Combine
  soup and milk and cover with three-fourths mixture.
  Place browned pork chops on top. Spread remaining
  one-fourth soup mixture. Bake covered for 1 hour.
  Serves 6 to 8.

Savory Tomatoes, Beans and Squash

1 large onion, sliced
1 clove garlic, minced
2 tablespoons oil   30 ml
¼ teaspoon ground thyme   1 ml
¼ teaspoon sage   1 ml
2 (15 ounce) cans green beans with liquid   2 (425 g)
1 (15 ounce) can diced tomatoes   425 g
2 cups sliced zucchini squash   480 ml

- Cook onion, garlic and seasonings in oil in large skillet for
  3 minutes. Add 1 teaspoon (5 ml) salt and ¼ teaspoon
  (1 ml) pepper. Add remaining ingredients, cover and
  simmer 20 minutes or until zucchini is tender. Serves 6 to 8.

May
1
2
3
4
5
6
7
8
9
10
11
12
13
14
15
16
17
18
19
20
21
22
23
24
25
26
27
28
29
30
31

Brunch Casserole

1 (6 ounce) package herb croutons	168 g
1 pound ground sausage	.5 kg
6 eggs, beaten	
1 medium onion, chopped	
1 (10 ounce) can cream of chicken soup	280 g
1 (10 ounce) can cream of mushroom soup	280 g
1 cup milk	240 ml
1 (8 ounce) shredded Monterey Jack cheese	227 g

• Preheat oven to 325° (162° C). Sprinkle croutons in sprayed 9 x 13-inch (23 x 33 cm) pan. Brown sausage. Drain fat and crumble. Place meat over croutons. In mixing bowl, mix eggs, onion, soups, milk and a little salt and pepper. Pour over croutons and meat. Top with cheese. Cover and refrigerate overnight. Bake for 45 minutes. Serves 6 to 8.

Tasty Coffee Cake

1 cup sugar	240 ml
1 cup oil	240 ml
4 eggs	
2 cups flour	480 ml
1 teaspoon baking powder	5 ml
1 (20 ounce) favorite pie filling	567 g
Powdered sugar	

• Preheat oven to 350° (176° C). Cream sugar and oil. Add eggs and mix well. Combine flour and baking powder and add to mixture. Spread half batter in sprayed 9 x 13-inch (23 x 33 cm) baking pan. Top with pie filling. Spread remaining batter over pie filling. Bake for 30 minutes. Dust with powdered sugar. Serves 6 to 8.

Breakfast or Brunch

Creamy Chicken Bake

1 (8 ounce) package egg noodles	227 g
1 (16 ounce) package frozen broccoli florets, thawed	.5 kg
¼ cup (½ stick) butter, melted	60 ml
1 (8 ounce) package shredded cheddar cheese	227 g
1 (10 ounce) can cream of chicken soup	280 g
1 cup half-and-half cream	240 ml
¼ teaspoon dry mustard	1 ml
3 cups cooked, cubed chicken breasts	710 ml
⅔ cup slivered almonds, toasted	160 ml

- Preheat oven to 325° (162° C). Cook noodles according to package directions and drain; keep warm. Combine noodles and broccoli in large bowl. Add butter and cheese and stir until cheese melts. Stir in chicken soup, cream, mustard, chicken and a little salt and pepper.
- Spoon into sprayed 2½-quart (2.5L) baking dish. Bake covered for about 25 minutes. Remove from oven, sprinkle with slivered almonds and cook for 15 minutes longer. Serves 6 to 8.

Broccoli-Green Bean Salad

1 large bunch broccoli, cut into florets	
2 (15 ounce) cans cut green beans, drained	2 (425 g)
1 bunch fresh green onions, chopped	
2 (6 ounce) jars marinated artichoke hearts	
chopped, drained	2 (168 g)
1½ cups ranch dressing	360 ml

- Combine broccoli, green beans, onions and artichokes and mix well. Add dressing and toss. Refrigerate 24 hours before serving. Serves 6 to 8.

1
2
3
4
5
6
7
8
9
10
11
12
13
14
15
16
17
18
19
20
21
22
23
24
25
26
27
28
29
30
31

Ranch Chicken Salad

2 cups cooked, cubed chicken	480 ml
1 cup sliced celery	240 ml
1 (20 ounce) can pineapple chunks with juice	567 g
1 (1 ounce) packet dry buttermilk, ranch-style	
dressing mix	28 g
½ cup mayonnaise	120 ml

- Combine chicken, celery and pineapple in medium bowl. Separately, combine dressing mix, mayonnaise and ¼ cup (60 ml) pineapple juice. Add dressing to chicken mixture and toss to coat. Chill. Serves 4 to 6.

Cold Strawberry Soup

2¼ cups strawberries	540 ml
⅓ cup sugar	80 ml
½ cup sour cream	120 ml
½ cup whipping cream	120 ml
½ cup light red wine	120 ml

- Place strawberries and sugar in blender and puree. Pour into bowl, stir in creams and blend well. Add 1¼ cups (300 ml) water and wine. Stir and chill. Serves 4 to 6.

Crispy Herb Bread

1½ teaspoons basil	7 ml
1 teaspoon rosemary	5 ml
½ teaspoon thyme	2 ml
1 cup (2 sticks) butter, melted	240 ml
1 package hot dog buns	

- Preheat oven to 300° (148° C). Combine all ingredients except buns and let stand several hours at room temperature. Spread on buns and cut into strips. Bake for 15 to 20 minutes. Serves 6 to 8.

Cabbage And Potato Soup

4 cups coarsely shredded cabbage	1 L
2 medium potatoes, peeled, chopped	
1 cup chopped onion	240 ml
2 (15 ounce) cans diced tomatoes with juice	2 (425 g)
3 tablespoons lemon juice	45 ml
2 tablespoons plus 2 teaspoons sugar	30 ml/10 ml
¼ teaspoon dried thyme	1 ml

- In large pot, combine cabbage, potatoes, onions and 3 cups (710 ml) water. Cover and cook on medium heat for 15 minutes. Add remaining ingredients. Bring to a boil. Cover and reduce heat to low. Simmer 45 minutes to 1 hour or until potatoes are tender. Serves 4 to 6.

Pizza Bread

1 pound frozen pizza crust dough	.5 kg
2 teaspoons olive oil	10 ml
1 tablespoon thyme	15 ml
¾ teaspoon kosher salt	4 ml

- Preheat oven to 450° (230° C). Press dough onto sprayed cookie sheet. Pierce dough all over. Drizzle oil over dough. Sprinkle with thyme and salt. Bake until golden brown, about 10 minutes. Cut in wedges. Serves 4 to 6.

May

1 - Loyalty Day
2nd Sunday - Mother's Day
3rd Saturday - Armed Forces Day
Last Monday - Memorial Day

Freezer French Toast

4 eggs	
1 cup milk	240 ml
2 tablespoons sugar	30 ml
1 teaspoon vanilla	15 ml
¼ teaspoon nutmeg	1 ml
8 (¾-inch) thick slices day-old French bread	8 (1.8 cm)
Melted butter	

- In medium bowl, beat eggs, milk, sugar, vanilla and nutmeg. Put bread slices on sprayed 9 x 13-inch (23 x 33 cm) baking dish, pour egg mixture over bread and let stand for a few minutes. Turn slices over and let stand until all egg mixture absorbs.

- Freeze uncovered on sheet of foil until firm, put in air-tight package and return to freezer. To serve, put slices on lightly sprayed cookie sheet. Brush each slice with melted butter. Bake at 400° (204° C) for 8 minutes. Turn slices over, brush with melted butter and bake additional 10 minutes. Serves 4 to 6.

Green Chile Squares

2 cups chopped green chilies	480 ml
1 (8 ounce) package shredded sharp cheddar cheese	227 g
8 eggs, beaten	
½ cup half-and-half cream	120 ml

- Preheat oven to 350° (176° C). Place green chilies in sprayed 9 x 13-inch (23 x 33 cm) baking pan. Cover with cheese. Combine eggs, cream and a little salt and pepper. Pour over chilies and cheese.   Bake for 30 minutes. Let stand at room temperature for a few minutes before cutting into squares. Serves 6 to 8.

Breakfast or Brunch

Gourmet Pizza

2 large vidalia onions, thinly sliced	
1 (12 ounce) refrigerated pizza crust roll	340 g
10 medium sun-dried tomatoes without oil	
3 ounces gorgonzola cheese	84 g
10 pieces spinach, washed, dried	

- Coat large nonstick pan with cooking spray and warm over medium heat. Add onions and reduce heat to medium-low. Cook for 15 to 20 minutes, stirring frequently, until onions brown.
- Prepare pizza crust according to package directions. Mince tomatoes, crumble cheese and tear spinach into pieces; set aside. Spread caramelized onions on pizza crust and bake at 425° (220° C) for 12 minutes.
- Remove from oven and add tomatoes, spinach and cheese. Bake until cheese melts, about 3 more minutes. Serve with freshly ground pepper. Serves 4.

Nutty Green Salad

1 (10 ounce) mixed salad greens	280 g
1 medium zucchini, sliced	
1 (8 ounce) can sliced water chestnuts, drained	227 g
½ cup chopped walnuts	120 ml
⅓ cup Italian salad dressing	80 ml

- Toss greens, zucchini, water chestnuts and walnuts. When ready to serve, add salad dressing and toss. Serves 4.

Chicken Pot Pie

1 (15 ounce) package frozen piecrust	425 g
Flour	
1 (15 ounce) can mixed vegetables, drained	425 g
1 (10 ounce) can cream of potato soup	280 g
1 (10 ounce) can cream of chicken soup	280 g
2 (6.5 ounce) cans white-meat chicken, drained	2 (180 g)

- Preheat oven to 375° (190° C). Place bottom crust in pie pan. Mix rest of ingredients with a little pepper. Pour into crust and top with remaining crust. Prick vent holes in crust to allow steam to escape. Bake for 45 minutes or until golden brown. Serves 4.

Tomato-Cucumber-Onion Salad

1 seedless cucumber, peeled	Olive oil
3 medium tomatoes	Balsamic vinegar
½ red onion	

- Chop cucumber, tomatoes and onion. Drizzle with olive oil, balsamic vinegar and a little pepper. Refrigerate. Serves 4.

Cherry-Cinnamon Cobbler

1 (20 ounce) can cherry pie filling	567 g
1 (12 ounce) tube refrigerated cinnamon rolls	340 g

- Preheat oven to 400° (204° C). Spread pie filling into sprayed 8-inch (20 cm) baking dish. Set aside icing from cinnamon rolls. Arrange rolls around edge of baking dish. Bake for 15 minutes. Cover and bake 10 minutes longer. Spread icing over rolls and serve warm. Serves 4.

Make-Ahead
Ham and Cheese Sandwiches

1 cup (2 sticks) butter, softened	240 ml
3 tablespoons mustard	45 ml
1 small onion, finely grated	
1 tablespoon Worcestershire sauce	15 ml
1½ cups poppy seeds	360 ml
1 pound deli shaved ham	.5 kg
8 slices Swiss cheese	
8 buns	

• Preheat oven to 275° (135° C). Mix butter, mustard, onion, Worcestershire and poppy seeds. Spread on both sides of buns. Fill with ham and cheese. Wrap individually in foil. Bake for 20 minutes. Serves 6 to 8.

Terrific Taters

5 - 6 medium potatoes, peeled, sliced	
1 (8 ounce) carton sour cream	227 g
1 (1 ounce) packet ranch-style salad dressing mix	28 g
1½ cups shredded cheddar cheese	360 ml
3 slices bacon, fried, crumbled	

• Preheat oven to 350° (176° C). Boil potatoes until tender and drain. Place potatoes in 2-quart (2 L) baking dish. Combine sour cream, salad dressing mix and a little pepper. Toss with potatoes until they coat. Sprinkle with cheese. Bake for 20 minutes. Sprinkle bacon on top. Serves 4 to 6.

1
2
3
4
5
6
7
8
9
10
11
12
13
14
15
16
17
18
19
20
21
22
23
24
25
26
27
28
29
30

Tomato-Basil Soup

1 (15 ounce) can diced tomatoes	425 g
4 cups tomato juice	1 L
12 - 14 fresh basil leaves	
1 (8 ounce) carton whipping cream	227 g
¼ cup (½ stick) butter	60 ml

• Combine tomatoes and juice. Simmer for 30 minutes.
  Puree along with basil leaves in blender. Return to
  saucepan and add cream, butter, ¼ teaspoon (1 ml) each
  of salt and pepper. Heat thoroughly. Serves 4 to 6.

Cheese Strudel

1 cup (2 sticks) butter	240 ml
1 cup sour cream	240 ml
2½ cups flour	600 ml

• Mix ingredients and chill in refrigerator about 3 hours.

Filling:

2 (8 ounce) packages cream cheese, softened	2 (227 g)
½ cup sugar	120 ml
1 teaspoon vanilla	5 ml

• Preheat oven to 350° (176° C). Beat ingredients
  thoroughly and divide in half. Take half of dough
  mixture and roll into rectangle. Spread half filling
  down middle. Fold over sides toward middle and
  place on baking sheet.
• Repeat with second half of dough. Place on baking
  sheet and bake for 30 to 35 minutes. Slice in 1-inch
  (2.5 cm) serving pieces. Serves 4 to 6.

Baked Chicken Breasts

6 boneless, skinless chicken breast halves	
2 (10 ounce) cans cream of chicken soup	2 (280 g)
1 cup shredded Swiss cheese	240 ml
2 cups herb-seasoned stuffing mix	480 ml
½ cup (1 stick) butter	120 ml

• Preheat oven to 350° (176° C). Arrange chicken breasts in sprayed 9 x 13-inch (23 x 33 cm) baking dish. Combine soup with ¼ cup (60 ml) water in small mixing bowl. Pour over chicken breasts. Sprinkle with stuffing mix. Melt butter and drizzle over top of casserole. Bake for 60 to 75 minutes. Serves 4 to 6.

Fresh Broccoli Salad

2 bunches broccoli	
½ pound bacon, fried, crumbled	227 g
½ cup chopped sweet onion	120 ml
1 red bell pepper, seeded, chopped	
1 cup shredded sharp cheese	240 ml

Dressing:
1 cup mayonnaise	240 ml
2 tablespoons vinegar	30 ml
¼ cup sugar	60 ml

• Chop tender portions of broccoli into bite-size pieces. Mix bacon with broccoli, onion, bell pepper and cheese. Add dressing just before serving. Serves 4 to 6.

1
2
3
4
5
6
7
8
9
10
11
12
13
14
15
16
17
18
19
20
21
22
23
24
25
26
27
28
29
30

Spiced Pot Roast

2 cups sweet cider	480 ml
1 tablespoon brown sugar	15 ml
2 - 3 whole cloves	
¼ teaspoon ginger	1 ml
¼ teaspoon cinnamon	1 ml
3 - 4 pounds boneless beef rump roast	1.3 kg
2 tablespoons flour	30 ml
2 tablespoons oil	30 ml
1 onion, sliced	

- Preheat oven to 325° (162° C). In small bowl, mix cider, brown sugar, cloves, ginger and cinnamon. Pour over meat in roasting pan. Cover and refrigerate 24 hours. Remove meat from marinade and pat dry with paper towel.
- Combine flour, 2 teaspoons (10 ml) salt and ¼ teaspoon (1 ml) pepper. Dredge meat. Brown meat in oil on all sides in roasting pan. Add 1 cup (240 ml) marinade and onion. Cover tightly and cook for 2½ to 3 hours or until tender. Add water to cooking liquid to make 2 cups (480 ml). Thicken cooking liquid with flour for gravy, if desired. Serves 6 to 8.

Carrot-Rice Casserole

4 tablespoons butter	1 L
1 (16 ounce) package grated carrots	.5 kg
1 medium onion, chopped	
1⅓ cups shredded cheddar cheese	320 ml
2 cups cooked rice	480 ml
2 eggs, beaten	

- Preheat oven to 350° (176° C). Melt butter in 10-inch (25 cm) skillet. Add carrots and onions and saute. Stir in cheese, rice, eggs and a little salt. Spoon into sprayed 2-quart (2 L) baking dish. Bake for 18 to 20 minutes. Serves 6 to 8.

Smoked Turkey Puffs

1 pound smoked turkey, chopped	.5 kg
1½ cups finely shredded cheddar cheese	360 ml
12 eggs	
2 cups milk	480 ml
Dash Worcestershire sauce	

- Preheat oven to 350° (176° C). Spray 6 individual bowls or egg cups, 4 inches (10 cm) in diameter. Divide turkey equally in each bowl and add ¼ cup (60 ml) cheese to each. Place eggs, milk and Worcestershire sauce in blender. Blend until frothy.

- Pour egg mixture (about 1 cup/240 ml per bowl) over cheese. Bowls will be quite full. Add some freshly ground pepper. Bake for 30 to 35 minutes or until brown and puffed. Serves 4 to 6.

Honey-Peanut Butter Muffins

1 cup whole wheat flour	240 ml
1 cup flour	240 ml
1 cup chopped salted peanuts	240 ml
1 tablespoon baking powder	15 ml
1⅓ cups evaporated milk	320 ml
1 cup honey	240 ml
1 cup peanut butter	240 ml
1 egg	

- Preheat oven to 350° (176° C). Combine flours, peanuts, baking powder and ¼ teaspoon (1 ml) salt. Set aside. Combine milk, honey, peanut butter and egg. Add honey mixture all at once to dry ingredients and stir only until moist. Spoon into lightly sprayed muffin cups. Bake for 20 to 25 minutes. Serves 4 to 6.

Orange Roughy With Peppers

1 pound orange roughy filets	**.5 kg**
1 onion, sliced	
2 red bell peppers, cut into julienne strips	
1 teaspoon dried thyme leaves	**5 ml**

- Cut fish into 4 serving-size pieces. Heat a little oil in skillet, layer onion and bell peppers in oil and sprinkle with thyme and ¼ teaspoon (1 ml) pepper. Place fish over peppers. Cover and cook fish on medium heat for 15 to 20 minutes or until fish flakes easily. Serves 3 to 4.

Creamy Vegetable Casserole

1 (16 ounce) package frozen broccoli, carrots, cauliflower	**.5 kg**
1 (10 ounce) can cream of mushroom soup	**280 g**
1 (8 ounce) carton garden-vegetable cream cheese	**227 g**
1 cup seasoned croutons	**240 ml**

- Preheat oven to 375° (190° C). Cook vegetables according to package directions, drain and place in large bowl. Place soup and cream cheese in saucepan and heat just enough to mix easily. Pour soup mixture into vegetable mixture, stir well and pour into sprayed 2-quart (2 L) baking dish. Sprinkle with croutons and bake uncovered for 25 minutes or until bubbly.
- Serves 4.

Sunflower Salad

2 apples, cored, chopped	
1 cup halved, seedless green grapes	**240 ml**
½ cup chopped celery	**120 ml**
¾ cup chopped pecans	**180 ml**
⅓ cup mayonnaise	**80 ml**

- Combine all ingredients and chill. Serves 4.

Baked Cod Vinaigrette

1 pound cod fillets	.5 kg
3 tablespoons vinaigrette dressing	45 ml
1 tablespoon minced chives	15 ml

• Preheat oven to 450° (230° C). Arrange fillets in shallow baking dish and brush with salad dressing. Sprinkle with chives. Bake uncovered for 10 to 12 minutes or until fillets flake with fork. Serves 3 to 4.

Herb-Seasoned Vegetables

1 (14 ounce) can chicken broth with Italian herbs	396 g
½ teaspoon garlic powder	2 ml
1 (16 ounce) package frozen mixed vegetables	.5 kg
½ cup grated parmesan cheese	120 ml

• Heat broth, garlic and vegetables to a boil. Cover and cook over low heat for 5 minutes or until tender-crisp. Drain. Place in serving dish and sprinkle parmesan cheese over vegetables. Serves 3 to 4.

Simple Side Dish: **Snow-Capped Tomatoes**

• Place heaping spoons of cottage cheese on tomatoes.

1 - Children's Day
14 - Flag Day
3rd Sunday - Father's Day

1
2
3
4
5
6
7
8
9
10
11
12
13
14
15
16
17
18
19
20
21
22
23
24
25
26
27
28
29
30

Delectable Apricot Ribs

4 - 5 pounds baby back pork loin ribs	1.8 kg
1 (16 ounce) jar apricot preserves	.5 kg
⅓ cup soy sauce	80 ml
¼ cup packed light brown sugar	60 ml
2 teaspoons garlic powder	10 ml

- Place ribs in large, sprayed slow cooker. In bowl, combine preserves, soy sauce, brown sugar and garlic powder and spoon over ribs. Cover and cook on LOW for 6 to 7 hours. Serves 4 to 6.

Spinach-Artichoke Casserole

2 (10 ounce) packages frozen spinach, cooked	2 (280 g)
½ cup chopped onion	120 ml
½ cup (1 stick) butter	120 ml
1 (16 ounce) can marinated artichoke hearts, drained	.5 kg
1 (8 ounce) carton sour cream	227 g
½ cup grated parmesan cheese	120 ml

- Preheat oven to 350° (176° C). Drain spinach well and set aside. Saute onion in butter, add spinach and place in sprayed 2-quart (2 L) baking dish.
- Place artichokes on top of spinach. Spread with sour cream and sprinkle with parmesan cheese. Bake covered for 20 minutes. Serves 4 to 6.

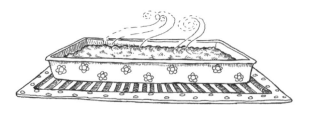

Slow-Cooker Breakfast

1 (32 ounce) package frozen hash browns	1 kg
1 pound cooked ham, cubed	.5 kg
1 onion, diced	
1 green bell pepper, seeded, diced	
1½ cups shredded cheese	360 ml
12 eggs	
1 cup skim milk	240 ml

- Layer some potatoes, ham, onion, green bell pepper, cheese in sprayed slow cooker. Repeat to make several layers. Beat eggs, milk, ½ teaspoon (2 ml) each of salt and pepper and pour over layers in slow cooker. Cover and cook on LOW for 10 to 12 hours overnight. Serves 6 to 8.

Blueberry Muffins

1½ cups flour	360 ml
½ cup sugar	120 ml
2 teaspoons baking powder	10 ml
¼ cup oil	60 ml
1 egg, slightly beaten	
½ cup milk	120 ml
¾ cup blueberries	180 ml

- Preheat oven to 350° (176° C). Sift dry ingredients with ½ teaspoon (2 ml) salt. Add oil, egg and milk. Stir until they mix well. Gently fold in blueberries. Pour into sprayed muffin cups. Bake for 20 to 25 minutes. Serves 4 to 6.

Breakfast or Brunch

Turkey Chili

3 pounds ground turkey	1.3 kg
½ teaspoon garlic powder	2 ml
3 tablespoons chili powder	45 ml
1 (8 ounce) can tomato sauce	227 g
Shredded cheese	

- In large saucepan combine turkey, garlic powder and 1 cup (240 ml) water. Cook over medium heat until mixture begins to fry. Add chili powder and tomato sauce and simmer until meat is tender. Garnish with cheese. Serves 6 to 8.

Spicy Saltines

1 cup oil	240 ml
1 teaspoon sesame seeds	5 ml
1 teaspoon dill weed	5 ml
1 teaspoon garlic powder	5 ml
1 teaspoon cayenne pepper	5 ml
4 sleeves saltine crackers	

- Combine oil, sesame seeds, dill weed, garlic powder, and cayenne pepper. Place in large container with crackers. Cover and gently toss, every 15 minutes for 1½ hours. Serves 6 to 8.

❀❀❀ June ❀❀❀

1 - Children's Day
14 - Flag Day
3rd Sunday - Father's Day

Chicken Crunch

4 - 6 boneless, skinless chicken breast halves	
½ cup Italian salad dressing	120 ml
½ cup sour cream	120 ml
2½ cups crushed corn flakes	600 ml

- Preheat oven to 375° (190° C). Place chicken in resealable plastic bag, add dressing and sour cream and chill for 1 hour. Remove chicken from marinade and discard marinade. Dredge chicken in corn flakes and place in sprayed 9 x 13-inch (23 x 33 cm) baking dish. Bake uncovered for 45 minutes. Serves 4 to 6.

Cheese-Spaghetti And Spinach

1 (7 ounce) box ready-cut spaghetti	198 g
2 tablespoons butter	30 ml
1 (8 ounce) carton sour cream	227 g
1 cup shredded cheddar cheese	240 ml
1 (8 ounce) package shredded Monterey Jack cheese, divided	227 g
1 (10 ounce) package frozen, chopped spinach, thawed, drained	280 g
1 (6 ounce) can cheddar french-fried onions	168 g

- Cook spaghetti according to package directions, drain and stir in butter until it melts.
- In large bowl, combine sour cream, cheddar cheese, half Monterey Jack cheese, spinach and half of onions. Fold into spaghetti and spoon into sprayed slow cooker.
- Cover and cook on LOW for 2 to 4 hours. When ready to serve, sprinkle remaining Jack cheese and fried onion rings over top. Serves 6 to 8.

1
2
3
4
5
6
7
8
9
10
11
12
13
14
15
16
17
18
19
20
21
22
23
24
25
26
27
28
29
30

Crab And Angel Hair Pasta

½ cup (1 stick) butter	120 ml
½ onion, finely chopped	
1 bell pepper, chopped	
1 teaspoon dried parsley flakes	5 ml
½ teaspoon celery salt	2 ml
1 teaspoon lemon pepper	5 ml
2 (15 ounce) cans diced tomato	2 (425 g)
1 (15 ounce) can Italian stewed tomatoes	425 g
1 pound crabmeat or lobster, flaked	.5 kg
1 pound angel hair pasta, cooked, drained	.5 kg
Freshly grated parmesan cheese	

• In large saucepan, melt butter and saute onion and bell pepper. Stir in all seasonings and tomatoes and bring to a boil. Add crabmeat and simmer for 2 minutes. Place warm pasta in serving dish and top with crab mixture. Serve with parmesan cheese. Serves 4 to 6.

Cheesy Potatoes

4 - 5 cups instant mashed potatoes, prepared	960 ml
1 (10 ounce) can cream of chicken soup	280 g
2 green onions, chopped	
1 cup shredded cheese	240 ml

• Preheat oven to 350° (176° C). Mix ingredients with a little salt and pepper and spoon into sprayed 2-quart (2 L) baking dish. Bake until cheese melts. Serves 4 to 6.

Simple Side Dish: **Favorite Relish Tray**

• Check your refrigerator for dill pickles, black olives, green olives, radishes, celery sticks and carrot sticks.

Potato-Beef Casserole

4 medium potatoes, peeled, sliced	
1¼ pounds lean ground beef, browned, drained	567 g
1 (10 ounce) can cream of mushroom soup	280 g
1 (10 ounce) can vegetable-beef soup	280 g

• Preheat oven to 350° (176° C). In large bowl, combine all ingredients plus ½ teaspoon (2 ml) each of salt and pepper. Transfer to sprayed 3-quart (3 L) baking dish. Bake covered for 1 hour 30 minutes or until potatoes are tender. Serves 4 to 6.

Squash Casserole

6 - 8 small squash, cooked, mashed	
2 beef bouillon cubes	
2 tablespoons butter	30 ml
1 tablespoon grated onion	15 ml
1 egg, well beaten	
1 (8 ounce) carton sour cream	227 g
½ cup breadcrumbs	120 ml
Paprika	

• Preheat oven to 350° (176° C). Mix all ingredients plus a little salt and pepper and place in baking dish. Sprinkle with paprika. Bake for 25 minutes or until set. Serves 4 to 6.

Simple Bread Idea: Hot Crescent Rolls

• Bake 1 to 2 (8 ounce/227 g) cans refrigerated crescent rolls according to package directions.

Noodles-Ham-Veggie Mix

1 (8 ounce) package medium egg noodles	227 g
1 (10 ounce) can cream of celery soup	280 g
1 (10 ounce) can cream of broccoli soup	280 g
1 teaspoon chicken bouillon granules	5 ml
1½ cups half-and-half cream	360 ml
1 (8 ounce) can whole kernel corn, drained	227 g
1 (16 ounce) package frozen broccoli, cauliflower and carrots, thawed	.5 kg
3 cups cooked cubed ham	710 ml
1 (8 ounce) package shredded cheddar-Jack cheese, divided	227 g

- Preheat oven to 350° (176° C). Cook noodles according to package directions and drain. In large bowl, combine soups, chicken bouillon, cream, corn, broccoli-carrot mixture, ham, ½ teaspoon (2 ml) each of salt and pepper and mix well. Fold in egg noodles and half of cheese.

- Spoon into sprayed 9 x 13-inch (23 x 33 cm) baking dish. Cover and bake for 45 minutes. Uncover and sprinkle remaining cheese over top of casserole. Return to oven and bake another 10 minutes or until cheese bubbles. Serves 6 to 8.

Emerald Salad

1 (3 ounce) package lime-flavored gelatin	84 g
¾ cup shredded cucumber	180 ml
2 teaspoons grated onion	10 ml
1 cup cottage cheese	240 ml
1 cup mayonnaise	240 ml
⅓ cup blanched almonds	80 ml

- Dissolve gelatin in ¾ cup (180 ml) boiling water. Cool. When slightly congealed, add remaining ingredients. Chill until set. Serves 6.

Spanish Hamburgers

1 pound lean ground beef	.5 kg
1 large onion, chopped	
1 (10 ounce) can tomato soup	280 g
1 teaspoon chili powder	5 ml
Hamburger buns	

- Brown hamburger and onion. Drain. Add soup and chili powder to hamburger mixture. Stir and simmer until hot. Serve over hamburger buns. Serves 4.

Roasted New Potatoes

2 tablespoons butter	30 ml
½ teaspoon marjoram	2 ml
4 medium new potatoes, quartered	
3 small onions, quartered	

- Preheat oven to 375° (190° C). Melt butter in 2-quart (2 L) baking dish and stir in marjoram. Add potatoes and onions and toss in melted mixture until they coat. Cover and bake for 1 hour. Serves 4.

Cherry Crunch

¼ cup (½ stick) butter	60 ml
1 (18 ounce) box white cake mix	510 g
2 (20 ounce) cans cherry pie filling	2 (567 g)

- Preheat oven to 350° (176° C). Melt butter and mix into cake mix. Put cherry pie filling into 9 x 13-inch (23 x 33 cm) pan. Crumble cake mixture over top. Bake for 25 minutes or until golden brown.
- Serves 6 to 8.

1
2
3
4
5
6
7
8
9
10
11
12
13
14
15
16
17
18
19
20
21
22
23
24
25
26
27
28
29
30

Hurry-Up Chicken Enchiladas

2½ - 3 cups cooked, shredded chicken breasts	600 ml
1 (10 ounce) can cream of chicken soup	280 g
2 cups chunky salsa, divided	480 ml
8 (6 inch) flour tortillas	8 (15 cm)
1 (10 ounce) can fiesta nacho cheese soup	280 g

- Combine chicken (or turkey), soup and ½ cup (120 ml) salsa in saucepan. Heat on low and stir constantly so mixture will not burn. Spread flour tortillas on counter and spoon about ⅓ cup (80 ml) chicken mixture on each tortilla. Roll tortilla around filling and place, seam-side down, in sprayed 9 x 13-inch (23 x 33 cm) baking dish.

- In saucepan, combine nacho cheese, remaining salsa and ¼ cup (60 ml) water and heat just enough to mix well. Pour over enchiladas. Cover with wax paper and microwave on HIGH, turning several times, for 4 to 5 minutes or until it bubbles. Serves 6 to 8.

Twist Sticks

½ cup sour cream	120 ml
½ (1 ounce) packet savory herb with garlic soup mix	½ (28 g)
1 (8 ounce) package refrigerator crescent rolls	227 g

- Preheat oven to 375° (190° C). Combine sour cream and soup mix. Spread out crescent rolls into 1 long piece of dough and press seams together. Spread mixture evenly onto dough. Cut dough into 1-inch (2.5 cm) strips and twist each strip loosely. Bake for 12 to 15 minutes. Serves 6 to 8.

Meal-In-One

1 pound lean ground beef	.5 kg
1 (15 ounce) can French-style green beans, drained	425 g
1 (18 ounce) package frozen tater tots, thawed	510 g
1 (10 ounce) can cream of mushroom soup	280 g

• Preheat oven to 350° (176° C). Brown ground beef and season with a little salt and pepper. In sprayed 10-inch (25 cm) deep-dish pie pan, layer ground beef, green beans and frozen tater tots. Spread soup over ingredients. Bake for 1 hour. Serves 4 to 6.

Raisin-Broccoli Salad

1 bunch fresh broccoli, cut in small bite-size florets	
½ purple onion, sliced, separated	
½ cup golden raisins	120 ml
1 cup slivered almonds, toasted	240 ml
½ cup chopped celery	120 ml
Bacon bits	

Dressing:

1 cup mayonnaise	240 ml
¼ cup sugar	60 ml
2 tablespoons vinegar	30 ml

• Make sure broccoli is well drained. In large bowl, combine broccoli, onion, raisins, almonds and celery. In separate bowl, combine all dressing ingredients plus 1 teaspoon (5 ml) salt and ½ teaspoon (2 ml) pepper, pour over vegetables and toss well. Refrigerate for several hours before serving. Sprinkle bacon bits over salad just before serving. Serves 4 to 6.

365

1
2
3
4
5
6
7
8
9
10
11
12
13
14
15
16
17
18
19
20
21
22
23
24
25
26
27
28
29
30

Yummy Barbecued-Grilled Chicken

6 boneless, skinless chicken breast halves or	
1 chicken, quartered	
3 cups ketchup	**710 ml**
½ cup packed brown sugar	**120 ml**
¼ cup Worcestershire sauce	**60 ml**
2 tablespoons vinegar	**30 ml**
1 teaspoon hot sauce	**5 ml**

- Wash and dry chicken breasts with paper towels. In saucepan, combine ketchup, brown sugar, Worcestershire sauce, vinegar, 2 teaspoons (10 ml) salt, ½ teaspoon (2 ml) pepper and hot sauce.

- Bring sauce to boil, reduce heat to low and cook for 15 minutes. Fire up grill and smoke over mesquite wood, if possible. Baste chicken frequently with barbecue sauce and turn chicken periodically. Cook chicken for 8 to 10 minutes per side. Serves 4 to 6.

Twice-Baked Potatoes

4 medium baked potatoes	
½ cup bacon bits	**120 ml**
½ cup (1 stick) butter	**120 ml**
½ cup sour cream	**120 ml**
1 cup shredded cheddar cheese	**240 ml**

- Preheat oven to 325° (162° C). Cut baked potatoes in half lengthwise. Scoop out flesh carefully. Place skins on baking sheet. In mixing bowl, mash potatoes and add all ingredients, except cheese. Mix well. Spoon mixture into skins and top with cheese. Bake for 15 minutes. Serves 4 to 6.

Strawberry Bread

3 cups flour	710 ml
1 teaspoon baking soda	5 ml
1 tablespoon cinnamon	15 ml
2 cups sugar	480 ml
3 eggs	
1 cup oil	240 ml
1 (10 ounce) package frozen sliced strawberries, thawed	280 g

• Preheat oven to 350° (176° C). Combine flour, baking soda, cinnamon and sugar with ½ teaspoon (2 ml) salt and mix well. Combine eggs, oil and strawberries. Add to dry ingredients and mix well. Pour into 2 sprayed, floured loaf pans. Bake for 1 hour. Serves 6 to 8.

Pecan Spread for Bread

2 (8 ounce) packages cream cheese, softened	2 (227 g)
1 (8 ounce) can crushed pineapple with juice	227 g
¾ cup chopped pecans	180 ml

• In mixing bowl, beat cream cheese. Drain pineapple, save juice and add pineapple to cream cheese. Stir by hand and add just enough juice to make mixture spreadable. Add pecans. Refrigerate. Spread on slices of strawberry bread.

Simple Side Dish: Easy Fresh Fruit

Cantaloupe	Clementine oranges
Honeydew melon	Red delicious apples

• Slice melons and put 1 serving each in plastic bags. Have oranges and apples ready with paper towels for each so everyone can grab a good snack on the way out the door.

1
2
3
4
5
6
7
8
9
10
11
12
13
14
15
16
17
18
19
20
21
22
23
24
25
26
27
28
29
30

1
2
3
4
5
6
7
8
9
10
11
12
13
14
15
16
17
18
19
20
21
22
23
24
25
26
27
28
29
30

Fiesta-Baked Potatoes

8 medium baking potatoes	
2 tablespoons butter	30 ml
1 (10 ounce) can fiesta nacho cheese soup	280 g
1 cup finely chopped ham	240 ml
Paprika	

- Bake potatoes at 350° (176° C) for 1 hour or until done. Cut potatoes in half lengthwise, scoop out flesh and leave thin shell. Use mixer to whip potato with butter and ½ teaspoon (2 ml) salt. Gradually add soup and ham and beat until light and fluffy. Spoon mixture into potato shells and sprinkle with paprika. Bake at 425° (220° C) for 15 minutes. Serves 4 to 6.

Sunny Spinach Salad

1 (10 ounce) package fresh spinach	280 g
1 medium red onion, thinly sliced	
¾ cup package chopped, dried apricots	180 ml
⅓ cup sunflower seeds	80 ml
Vinaigrette salad dressing	

- Combine ingredients. Serve with vinaigrette dressing. Serves 4 to 6.

Onion Biscuits and Butter

2 cups biscuit mix	480 ml
¼ cup milk	60 ml
1 (8 ounce) carton French onion dip	227 g

- Preheat oven to 375° (190° C). Combine all ingredients and mix well. Drop dough by tablespoonfuls in mounds onto sprayed baking sheet. Bake for 12 minutes. Serves 4 to 6.

Pork Chop Scallop

4 (½ inch) thick pork chops	4 (1.2 cm)
2 tablespoons butter	30 ml
1 (5 ounce) box scalloped potatoes	143 g
⅔ cup milk	160 ml

- In skillet brown pork chops in butter. Remove chops and set aside. Empty potatoes and packet of seasoning sauce mix into skillet. Stir in water and milk according to package directions. Heat to boil.

- Reduce heat and place chops on top. Cover and simmer 35 minutes or until potatoes are tender and chops cook thoroughly. Serves 4.

Not-Your-Banquet Beans

3 (15 ounce) cans cut green beans, drained	3 (425 g)
1 (8 ounce) can sliced water chestnuts, drained, chopped	227 g
½ cup slivered almonds	120 ml
½ cup chopped, roasted red bell peppers	120 ml
1 (12 ounce) package cubed Mexican Velveeta® cheese	340 g
1½ cups cracker crumbs	360 ml
¼ cup (½ stick) butter, melted	60 ml

- Preheat oven to 350° (176° C). Place green beans in sprayed 9 x 13-inch (23 x 33 cm) baking dish and cover with water chestnuts, almonds and red bell pepper. Spread cheese over green bean-almond mixture.

- Place casserole in microwave and heat just barely enough for cheese to begin to melt. (Watch closely.) Combine cracker crumbs and butter and sprinkle over casserole. Bake uncovered for 30 minutes. Serves 6 to 8.

1
2
3
4
5
6
7
8
9
10
11
12
13
14
15
16
17
18
19
20
21
22
23
24
25
26
27
28
29
30

Spaghetti And Meatballs

1 (18 ounce) package frozen meatballs, thawed	510 g
1 (28 ounce) jar spaghetti sauce	794 g
1 (8 ounce) package spaghetti	227 g
1 (5 ounce) package grated parmesan cheese	143 g

• In large microwave baking dish, heat meatballs and spaghetti sauce on HIGH for 10 to 12 minutes. Stir twice. Cook spaghetti according to package directions and drain well. Place onto serving plate and spoon meatball sauce over spaghetti. Top with cheese. Serves 4 to 6.

Fresh Green Salad

1 (10 ounce) package romaine lettuce, chopped	280 g
1 seedless cucumber, sliced	
1 yellow bell pepper, seeded, chopped	
½ cup dried sweetened cranberries	120 ml
1 (8 ounce) bottle balsamic-vinaigrette salad dressing	227 g

• In salad bowl, combine all ingredients except dressing. Serve with dressing. Serves 4 to 6.

Easy Rolls

1 (¼ ounce) package yeast	10 g
¼ cup sugar	60 ml
1 egg	
4 cups self-rising flour	1 L
¾ cup oil	180 ml

• Preheat oven to 375° (190° C). Mix yeast, 2 cups (480 ml) lukewarm water and sugar. Set aside for 5 minutes. Add egg and mix with whisk. Add flour and oil. Batter will be thin. Pour into covered container and place in refrigerator until ready to use. Spoon batter into sprayed muffin pan about half full. Bake for 7 to 8 minutes. Serves 4 to 6.

Quesadilla Pie

1 (4 ounce) can chopped green chilies	114 g
½ pound sausage, cooked	227 g
1 (8 ounce) package shredded cheddar cheese	227 g
3 eggs, well beaten	
1½ cups milk	360 ml
¾ cup biscuit mix	180 ml
Hot salsa	

- Preheat oven to 350° (176° C). Sprinkle green chilies, cooked sausage and cheddar cheese in sprayed 9-inch (23 cm) pie pan.
- In separate bowl, combine eggs, milk and biscuit mix. Pour mixture over chilies, sausage and cheese and bake for 30 to 40 minutes. Serve with salsa on top of each slice. Serves 4 to 6.

Fruity Waffles

1 (10 count) box frozen, prepared waffles, thawed	
1 cup sliced bananas	240 ml
1 cup blueberries	240 ml
1 cup maple syrup	240 ml

- Cut 1 waffle into 6 wedges and arrange in star shape on serving plate. Repeat with rest of waffles. Toss bananas and blueberries with maple syrup and spoon ½ cup (120 ml) mixture over waffle pieces on each plate.

Breakfast or Brunch

1
2
3
4
5
6
7
8
9
10
11
12
13
14
15
16
17
18
19
20
21
22
23
24
25
26
27
28
29
30

Southern-Stuffed Peppers

6 large green peppers	
½ pound chicken livers, chopped	227 g
6 slices bacon, diced	
1 cup chopped onion	240 ml
1 cup chopped celery	240 ml
1 clove garlic, crushed	
2 cups instant rice	480 ml
1 (15 ounce) can Italian stewed tomatoes	425 g

- Preheat oven to 375° (190° C). Wash peppers. Cut slice from stem end and remove seeds. Cook peppers about 5 minutes in small amount of boiling salted water. Remove from water and drain.

- Cook chicken livers, bacon, onion, celery and garlic until vegetables are tender. Add rice, 1 teaspoon (5 ml) salt and ¼ teaspoon (1 ml) pepper. Stuff peppers with this mixture. Arrange in baking dish. Pour stewed tomatoes in pan. Cover and bake for 20 to 25 minutes. Serves 4 to 6.

Sauteed Zucchini and Tomatoes

Butter	
1 large zucchini, julienned	
1 large tomato, chopped	
⅓ cup grated parmesan cheese	80 ml

- Melt small amount of butter in large skillet. Saute zucchini until it is soft but not brown. Add chopped tomato and a little salt and pepper. Stir until they are hot. Remove from heat, add parmesan cheese and stir well. Serves 4 to 6.

Southwest Grilled Burgers

1½ pounds lean ground beef	.7 kg
¾ cup hot chipotle salsa, divided	180 ml
¼ cup seasoned breadcrumbs	60 ml
6 hamburger buns	
6 slices pepper-Jack cheese	

• Heat grill. In large bowl, combine ground beef, 4 tablespoons (60 ml) salsa and seasoned breadcrumbs and mix well. Shape mixture into 6 (½ inch/1.2 cm) thick patties and grill patties about 14 minutes or broil in oven about 12 minutes. Turn once during cooking.

• Place buns cut-side down on grill and cook about 2 minutes or until buns toast lightly. Place 1 slice cheese on each cooked patty and cook just long enough for cheese to begin to melt. Move patties and cheese to bottom halves of buns, add 1 tablespoon (15 ml) salsa to each and top with bun. Serves 4 to 6.

Marinated Corn Salad

3 (15 ounce) cans whole kernel corn, drained	3 (425 g)
1 red bell pepper, chopped	
1 cup chopped walnuts	240 ml
¾ cup chopped celery	180 ml
1 (8 ounce) bottle Italian salad dressing	227 g

• In bowl with lid, combine corn, bell pepper, walnuts and celery. (For a special little zip, add several dashes hot sauce.) Pour salad dressing over vegetables. Refrigerate several hours before serving. Serves 4 to 6.

1
2
3
4
5
6
7
8
9
10
11
12
13
14
15
16
17
18
19
20
21
22
23
24
25
26
27
28
29
30

Party Sandwiches

1 (8 ounce) package cream cheese, softened	227 g
⅓ cup chopped stuffed olives with juice	80 ml
⅓ cup chopped pecans	80 ml
6 slices bacon, cooked, crumbled	

- Beat cream cheese with mixer until smooth and stir in olives, 2 tablespoons (30 ml) olive juice, pecans and bacon. Spread on party rye bread. Serves 4 to 6.

Million Dollar Pie

24 buttery round crackers, crumbled	
1 cup chopped pecans	240 ml
4 egg whites (absolutely no yolks at all)	
1 cup sugar	240 ml

- Preheat oven to 350° (176° C). Mix cracker crumbs with pecans. In separate mixing bowl, beat egg whites until stiff and slowly add sugar while mixing. Gently fold in crumbs and pecan mixture. Pour in pie plate and bake 20 minutes. Cool before serving. Serves 4 to 6.

Simple Side Dish: **Fast Italian-Pasta Salad**

- Prepare 1 (6.4 ounce/168 g) box pasta salad Italian according to package directions and add ½ cup (120 ml) zesty Italian salad dressing.

Sandwich Souffle

Butter, softened
8 slices white bread, crusts removed
4 slices ham
4 slices American cheese
2 cups milk   **480 ml**
2 eggs, beaten

- Preheat oven to 375° (190° C). Butter bread on both sides. Make 4 sandwiches with ham and cheese. Place sandwiches in buttered 8-inch (20 cm) square baking pan.
- Beat milk, eggs and a little salt and pepper. Pour over sandwiches and soak for 1 to 2 hours. Bake for 45 to 50 minutes. Serves 4.

Peanut Clusters

1 (12 ounce) package chocolate chips   **340 g**
1 (6 ounce) package peanut butter chips   **168 g**
1 tablespoon butter   **15 ml**
⅓ block paraffin
3 cups salted peanuts   **710 ml**

- Combine all ingredients in double boiler and heat until they melt. Drop by tablespoons onto wax paper. Serves 6 to 8.

Simple Side Dish: **Caesar-Pasta Salad**

- Prepare 1 (7.25 ounce/200 g) box Caesar Pasta Suddenly Salad® with 3 tablespoons oil (45 ml) according to package directions.

Corned Beef Supper

1 (4 - 5 pound) corned beef brisket	**1.8 kg**
4 large potatoes, peeled, quartered	
6 carrots, peeled, halved	
1 head cabbage	

- Place corned beef in roasting pan, cover with water and bring to boil. Reduce heat, simmer for 3 hours and add water if necessary. Add potatoes and carrots.
- Cut cabbage into eighths and lay over potatoes, carrots and brisket. Bring to boil, reduce heat and cook another 30 to 40 minutes or until vegetables are done. Slice corned beef across grain. Serves 6 to 8.

Southern Corn Muffins

1 cup white cornmeal	**240 ml**
½ cup milk	**120 ml**
2 teaspoons baking powder	**10 ml**
1 tablespoon butter	**15 ml**
1 egg, well beaten	

- Preheat oven to 450° (230° C). Combine cornmeal with 1 cup (240 ml) boiling water. Add rest of ingredients plus ½ teaspoon (2 ml) salt. Beat until they blend well. Pour into sprayed muffin cups. Bake for 20 minutes. Serves 4 to 6.

My Man's Salad

1 (20 ounce) can crushed pineapple with juice	**567 g**
1 (3 ounce) package pistachio instant pudding	**84 g**
½ cup chopped pecans	**120 ml**
½ cup miniature marshmallows	**120 ml**
1 (8 ounce) carton whipped topping	**227 g**

- Mix in order given. Pour into 9 x 13-inch (23 x 33 cm) pan. Refrigerate. Serves 4 to 6.

Salmon Patties

1 (7 ounce) can pink salmon with liquid	**198 g**
½ cup fine breadcrumbs	**120 ml**
2 egg whites	
2 tablespoons diced onion	**30 ml**
2 tablespoons chopped fresh parsley	**30 ml**
1 tablespoon lemon juice	**15 ml**
1 tablespoon oil	**15 ml**
Lemon wedges, optional	

- Place salmon in bowl, save liquid and mash with fork. Combine with breadcrumbs, egg whites, onion, parsley and lemon juice. Add ¼ teaspoon (1 ml) pepper.
- Add 2 or 3 tablespoons (30 ml to 45 ml) salmon liquid. Mix well and shape into patties. Fry patties in oil over medium heat until light brown on both sides. Serve with lemon wedges. Serves 4.

Corn-On-The-Cob

- Place ears of corn, in husk 1-inch (2.5 cm) apart in microwave dish. Cook on HIGH power. Turn corn over 1 time while cooking.

    1 ear - 2 to 3 minutes

    2 ears - 4 to 6 minutes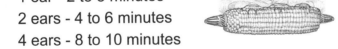

    4 ears - 8 to 10 minutes

- Let corn stand 5 to 10 minutes before removing husks and silk. Season each ear of corn with butter.

Easy Mexican Casserole

1 pound lean ground beef	.5 kg
1 (10 ounce) can enchilada sauce	280 g
1 (10 ounce) can cream of chicken soup	280 g
1 (10 ounce) can cream of mushroom soup	280 g
1 (13 ounce) package corn chips	370 g
1½ cups shredded cheddar cheese	360 ml

• Preheat oven to 350° (176° C). Brown meat and drain. Add enchilada sauce and both soups. Place three-fourths bag of chips into sprayed 9 x 13-inch (23 x 33 cm) baking dish. Pour meat mixture over chips. Top with cheese. Bake for 20 minutes. Serves 4 to 6.

Sopapillas

1¾ cups flour	420 ml
2 teaspoons baking powder	10 ml
2 tablespoons shortening	30 ml
Oil	
Honey	

• Mix flour and baking powder with 1 teaspoon (5 ml) salt. Cut in shortening. Add ⅔ cup (160 ml) cold water gradually. Mix and knead until smooth. Cover for 5 minutes. Roll into very thin rectangles. Cut in 3-inch (8 cm) squares and drop into very hot oil. Turn several times to puff evenly. Remove and drain. Serve with honey. Serves 4 to 6.

Simple Side Dish: **Spanish Rice**

• Prepare 2 (5.6 ounce/ 155 g) packages Spanish rice according to package directions.

Chili Relleno Casserole

1 pound lean ground beef	.5 kg
1 bell pepper, chopped	
1 onion, chopped	
1 (4 ounce) can chopped green chilies	114 g
1 teaspoon oregano	5 ml
1 teaspoon dried cilantro leaves	5 ml
¾ teaspoon garlic powder	4 ml
2 (4 ounce) cans whole green chilies	2 (114 g)
1½ cups shredded Monterey Jack cheese	360 ml
1½ cups shredded sharp cheddar cheese	360 ml
3 large eggs, beaten	
1 tablespoon flour	15 ml
1 cup half-and-half cream	240 ml

- Preheat oven to 350° (176° C). Brown meat with bell pepper and onion in skillet. Add chopped green chilies, oregano, cilantro, garlic powder and with a little salt and pepper. Seed whole chilies and spread in spread 9 x 13-inch (23 x 33 cm) baking dish.

- Cover with meat mixture and sprinkle with cheeses. Combine eggs and flour and beat with fork until they mix well. Add half-and-half cream, mix and pour slowly over top of meat in casserole. Bake uncovered for 35 minutes or until it is light brown. Serves 8.

Easy Guacamole Salad

4 avocados, softened	
1 (8 ounce) package cream cheese, softened	227 g
1 (10 ounce) can diced tomatoes and green chilies	280 g
1½ teaspoons garlic salt	7 ml
1 tablespoon lemon juice	15 ml

- Peel avocados and mash with fork. In mixing bowl, beat cream cheese until smooth. Add avocados, tomatoes and green chilies, garlic salt and lemon juice and mix well. Serve on lettuce leaf with tortilla chips. Serves 6 to 8.

1
2
3
4
5
6
7
8
9
10
11
12
13
14
15
16
17
18
19
20
21
22
23
24
25
26
27
28
29
30
31

1
2
3
4
5
6
7
8
9
10
11
12
13
14
15
16
17
18
19
20
21
22
23
24
25
26
27
28
29
30
31

Sloppy Joes

½ pound lean ground beef	227 g
1 (15 ounce) can stewed tomatoes	425 g
¼ cup ketchup	60 ml
¼ teaspoon oregano leaves	1 ml
5 hamburger buns	

• Brown ground beef and drain. Add tomatoes, ketchup and oregano and cook uncovered 20 minutes. Spoon onto hamburger buns. Serves 4 to 5.

Ranch-Style Beans

1 (16 ounce) package dried pinto beans	.5 kg
1 large onion, diced	
1 tablespoon oil	15 ml
2 cloves garlic	
2 teaspoons chili powder	10 ml
1 (15 ounce) can diced tomatoes	425 g

• Rinse beans well. Cover beans with 7 cups (1.6 L) water and let stand 6 to 8 hours or overnight. Bring beans and water to a boil. Add oil, onion, garlic, chili powder and 2 teaspoons (10 ml) salt. Cover, simmer 1½ hours and stir occasionally. Add tomatoes and cook 1 hour longer. Serves 4 to 5.

☆ July ☆

4 – Independence Day
4th Sunday – Parents' Day

Pork Chops And Apples

6 thick-cut pork chops   **Oil**
Flour   **3 baking apples**

- Preheat oven to 325° (162° C). Dip pork chops in flour, coat well and brown in skillet with a little oil. Place in sprayed 9 x 13-inch (23 x 33 cm) baking dish. Add ⅓ cup (80 ml) water and cook covered for 45 minutes. Peel, halve and seed apples. Place halves over each pork chop. Return to oven for 5 to 10 minutes. (DO NOT overcook apples.)
- Serves 4 to 6.

Cheese To The Rescue

1 large head cauliflower, cut into florets
1 sweet red bell pepper, sliced
½ cup chopped celery   **120 ml**
½ cup (1 stick) butter, divided   **120 ml**
1 (10 ounce) box frozen green peas, thawed   **280 g**
1 (8 ounce) package shredded Mexican 4-cheese
   blend, divided   **227 g**
⅓ cup flour   **80 ml**
1 pint half-and-half cream   **.5 kg**
½ cup milk   **120 ml**

- Preheat oven to 325° (162° C). Cook cauliflower in covered saucepan with small amount of water until tender-crisp. Don't overcook. Saute bell pepper and celery in small skillet in 3 tablespoons (45 ml) butter. Add bell pepper, celery and peas to drained cauliflower and toss with half cheese.
- Spoon into sprayed 3-quart (3 L) baking dish. Combine remaining butter and flour in another saucepan and mix well. On medium high heat, gradually add cream and milk. Cook, stirring constantly, until mixture thickens. Pour over vegetables. Cover and bake for 20 minutes. Uncover and sprinkle remaining cheese over top of casserole. Return to oven for 5 minutes. Serves 4 to 6.

1
2
3
4
5
6
7
8
9
10
11
12
13
14
15
16
17
18
19
20
21
22
23
24
25
26
27
28
29
30
31

Marinated Grilled Steak

1 lemon	
½ cup soy sauce	**120 ml**
3 tablespoons oil	**45 ml**
2 tablespoons Worcestershire sauce	**30 ml**
1 clove garlic, minced	
Chopped green onion	
2 pounds flank steak	**1 kg**

- Squeeze juice from lemon. Mix all ingredients
  except steak. Marinate steak with marinade and turn
  occasionally for 4 to 12 hours in refrigerator. Broil
  meat over hot coals as desired. Serves 6 to 8.

Country-Fried Mushrooms

1 pound fresh mushrooms	**.5 kg**
3 eggs	
1 - 1½ cups flour	**240 ml**
⅓ cup butter	**80 ml**

- Wash mushrooms. Gently pull stems from caps. Dry
  on towel. Beat eggs in small bowl. Dip mushrooms
  and stems in egg and roll in flour. Fry slowly in melted
  butter, stir gently and add a little salt and pepper.
  Brown on both sides, put lid on loosely and turn down
  heat. Cook until mushrooms are done, about 20
  minutes. Serves 6 to 8.

Simple Side Dish: **Vermicelli With Garlic**

- Prepare 1 (4.6 ounce/128 g) box garlic-olive oil
  vermicelli pasta and rice with 2 tablespoons (30 ml)
  butter according to package directions.

Tuna Toast

1 (10 ounce) can cream of chicken soup	280 g
1 (6 ounce) can white tuna in water, drained	168 g
3 slices frozen, thick Texas toast, toasted both sides	
3 fresh green onions, chopped	

- In saucepan over low heat, combine soup, tuna, dash of pepper and about ¼ cup (60 ml) milk or water. Stir until hot. Place each slice Texas toast on individual plates and spoon one-third tuna mixture on top of toast. Sprinkle chopped green onion over tuna mixture. Serves 3 to 4.

Corn Pudding

1 (8 ounce) package corn muffin mix	227 g
1 (15 ounce) can cream-style corn	425 g
½ cup sour cream	120 ml
3 eggs, slightly beaten	

- Preheat oven to 350° (176° C). Combine all ingredients and pour into sprayed 2-quart (2 L) baking dish. Bake uncovered for about 35 minutes. Serves 3 to 4.

Simple Side Dish: **Easy French Fries**

- Heat 1 (24 ounce/680 g) package crinkle-cut french fries according to package directions.

1
2
3
4
5
6
7
8
9
10
11
12
13
14
15
16
17
18
19
20
21
22
23
24
25
26
27
28
29
30
31

Cheese Enchiladas

12 corn tortillas	
1 (12 ounce) package shredded Mexican 4-cheese	
blend, divided	**340 g**
1 small onion, chopped	
2 (10 ounce) cans enchilada sauce	**2 (280 g)**

- Wrap 6 tortillas in slightly damp paper towel. Place between 2 plates and microwave on HIGH 45 seconds. On each tortilla, place about ⅓ cup (80 ml) cheese and 1 tablespoon (15 ml) onion and roll.

- On sprayed 9 x 13-inch (23 x 33 cm) baking dish, place tortillas seam-side down and repeat with remaining tortillas. Pour enchilada sauce on top and sprinkle with remaining cheese and onions. Cover and microwave on MEDIUM 5 to 6 minutes. Serves 4 to 6.

Spanish Rice

6 tablespoons (¾ stick) butter, melted	**90 ml**
1 onion, chopped	
2 cups cooked white rice	**480 ml**
1 (10 ounce) can tomatoes and green chilies	**280 g**

- Preheat oven to 375° (190° C). In bowl, combine butter, onion, rice, tomatoes and green chilies. Add a little salt and pepper. Spoon mixture into sprayed 3-quart (3 L) baking dish. Cover and cook for 25 minutes. Serves 4 to 6.

Special Spinach Salad

1 (10 ounce) package fresh spinach	280 g
1 (15 ounce) can bean sprouts, drained	425 g
8 slices bacon, cooked crisp	
1 (8 ounce) can water chestnuts, chopped	227 g

- Combine spinach and bean sprouts. When ready to serve, add crumbled bacon and water chestnuts. Toss with vinaigrette salad dressing or make with 3 parts olive oil and 1 part red wine vinegar. Serves 4.

Philly Potatoes

4½ cups instant mashed potatoes, prepared, hot	1.1
2 tablespoons freeze-dried chives	30
1 (8 ounce) package cream cheese, softened	22
1 egg, slightly beaten	

- Preheat oven to 350° (176° C). Mix all ingred and blend well. Place in sprayed 3-quart (3 L dish. Bake covered for 30 minutes. Uncove bake for additional 15 minutes. Serves 4 to

Super Simple Main Dish:
Lemon-Garlic Turkey Tenderl

- Cook 1 (2 pound/1 kg) lemon-garlic turke tenderloin according to package direction may be served hot or chilled.

1
2
3
4
5
6
7
8
9
10
11
12
13
14
15
16
17
18
19
20
21
22
23
24
25
26
27
28
29
30
31

Ham-It-Up Wild Rice

1 (6 ounce) package instant long grain-wild rice	168 g
1 (10 ounce) package frozen broccoli spears, thawed	280 g
1 (8 ounce) can whole kernel corn, drained	227 g
3 cups, fully cooked, cubed ham	710 ml
1 (10 ounce) can cream of mushroom soup	280 g
1 cup mayonnaise	240 ml
1 teaspoon mustard	5 ml
1 cup shredded cheddar cheese	240 ml
1 (3 ounce) can fried onion rings	84 g

• Preheat oven to 350° (176° C). Prepare rice according to package directions. Spoon into buttered 3-quart (3 L) baking dish. Top with broccoli, corn and ham. In saucepan, combine soup, mayonnaise, mustard and shredded cheese and mix well. Spread over top of rice-ham mixture. Cover and bake for about 20 minutes. Remove from oven and sprinkle onion rings over top. Return to oven, uncovered, and bake additional 15 minutes. Serves 6 to 8.

Crunchy Pecan Salad

1 (16 ounce) package frozen green peas, thawed	.5 kg
½ head cauliflower, cut into small florets	
1 cup chopped celery	240 ml
1 (8 ounce) can sliced water chestnuts, drained	227 g
1 (4 ounce) jar pimentos, drained	114 g
1½ cups mayonnaise	360 ml
¼ cup Italian dressing	60 ml
1 cup chopped pecans	240 ml
½ cup bacon bits	120 ml

• Combine peas, cauliflower, celery, water chestnuts, pimentos and about 1 teaspoon (5 ml) salt in large bowl. Mix mayonnaise and Italian dressing.

• Combine with salad, cover and refrigerate. When ready to serve, add pecans and toss well. Sprinkle bacon bits over top as garnish. Serves 6 to 8.

Stand-Up Shrimp Salad

1 (12 ounce) package frozen, cooked salad shrimp,
  thawed, well drained .... **340 g**
1 (32 ounce) carton deli potato salad .... **1 kg**
1 bunch fresh green onions with tops, chopped
1½ teaspoons dried thyme leaves .... **7 ml**

- In large bowl, combine shrimp and potato salad and mix well. Add most of onions and thyme leaves and toss lightly. Add a little pepper, if desired. Serve in salad bowl and garnish with remaining green onions. Serves 4 to 6.

Deluxe Egg-Salad Sandwiches

Softened cream cheese with chive
Fresh bean sprouts
Deli egg salad
Kaiser rolls
American cheese slices

- Spread Kaiser rolls with cream cheese and egg salad. Top with cheese slices and fresh bean sprouts.

4 - Independence Day
4ᵗʰ Sunday - Parents' Day

1
2
3
4
5
6
7
8
9
10
11
12
13
14
15
16
17
18
19
20
21
22
23
24
25
26
27
28
29
30
31

Asian Beef-Noodles

1¼ pounds lean ground beef	567 g
1 (16 ounce) package frozen oriental stir-fry mixture	.5 kg
2 (3 ounce) packages oriental-flavored ramen noodles	2 (84 g)
½ teaspoon ground ginger	2 ml
3 tablespoons thinly sliced green onions	45 ml

- In large skillet, brown ground beef and drain. Add ½ cup (120 ml) water, a little salt and pepper, simmer 10 minutes and transfer to separate bowl. In same skillet, combine 2 cups (480 ml) water, vegetables, broken up noodles, ginger and both seasoning packets. Bring to a boil and reduce heat.

- Cover, simmer 3 minutes or until noodles are tender and stir occasionally. Return beef to skillet and stir in green onions. Serve right from skillet. Serves 4 to 6.

Pine Nut Green Beans

1 (16 ounce) package frozen green beans	.5 kg
¼ cup (½ stick) butter	60 ml
¾ cup pine nuts	180 ml
¼ teaspoon garlic powder	1 ml

- Cook beans according to package directions and drain. Melt butter in skillet over medium heat, add pine nuts and cook, stirring frequently, until golden. Add pine nuts to green beans and add seasonings and a little salt. Serve hot. Serves 4 to 6 .

Simple Side Dish: **Fresh Fruit**

- Slice favorite fruit and serve cold.

Pinto Bean Pie

1 pound lean ground beef	.5 kg
1 onion, chopped	
2 (15 ounce) cans pinto beans with juice	2 (425 g)
1 (10 ounce) can tomatoes and green chilies	
with juice	280 g
1 (3 ounce) can french-fried onion rings	84 g

- Preheat oven to 350° (176° C). In skillet, brown beef and onion and drain. In sprayed 2-quart (2 L) baking dish, layer 1 can beans, beef-onion mixture and half can tomatoes and green chilies. Repeat layer. Top with onion rings and bake uncovered for 30 minutes. Serves 4 to 6.

Red Hot Onions

3 large purple onions	
2 tablespoons hot sauce	30 ml
3 tablespoons olive oil	45 ml
3 tablespoons red wine vinegar	45 ml

- Cut onions into thin slices. Pour 1 cup (240 ml) boiling water over onions, let stand for 1 minute and drain. Combine hot sauce, oil and vinegar and pour over onion rings in bowl with lid. Cover and chill for at least 3 hours. Drain to serve. Serves 4 to 6.

Simple Bread Idea: **Garlic-Cheese Bread**

- Heat 1 (10 ounce/280 g) package frozen 3-cheese garlic bread according to package directions.

Italian Salad

1 (8 ounce) package macaroni, cooked, drained	227 g
1 (3 ounce) package pepperoni, diced	84 g
1½ cups shredded provolone cheese	360 ml
3 green onions with tops, chopped	
1 (15 ounce) can garbanzo beans, drained	425 g
Italian dressing	

- Combine all ingredients except dressing and toss.
  Use desired amount of dressing. Chill 1 to 2 hours.
  Serves 4 to 6.

Tomatoes and Crabmeat

1 (6 ounce) can crabmeat, drained, flaked	168 g
2 - 3 large red tomatoes, sliced thick	

Russian Dressing:

½ cup oil	120 ml
¼ cup wine vinegar	60 ml
6 tablespoons sugar	90 ml
3 tablespoons ketchup	45 ml
Leaf lettuce	

- Mount crabmeat on each tomato slice. Combine
  dressing ingredients with 1 teaspoon (5 ml) salt.
  Drizzle dressing over each tomato-crabmeat assembly.
  Serve on bed of lettuce. Serves 4 to 6.

Bing Cherry Gelatin Salad

1 (3 ounce) package cherry gelatin	84 g
1 (3 ounce) package cream cheese	84 g
¼ cup chopped walnuts	60 ml
1 (15 ounce) can bing cherries with juice	425 g

(Continued on page 205.)

(Continued from page 204.)

- Dissolve cherry gelatin in 1 cup (240 ml) boiling water. Add enough water to cherry juice to make 1 cup (240 ml). Add to gelatin. Pour into ring mold. Chill until partially set. Mix cream cheese with walnuts. Roll into marble-sized balls. Drop cherries and cheese balls alternately into cherry gelatin. Refrigerate to set. Serves 4 to 6.

Italian Corn

1 (16 ounce) package frozen whole kernel corn	**.5 kg**
2 slices bacon, cooked, diced	
1 small onion, chopped	
1 (15 ounce) can Italian stewed tomatoes	**425 g**

- Place all ingredients in 2-quart (2 L) pan and cook until most of liquid in tomatoes cooks out. Serves 4 to 6.

Potato Pancakes

3 pounds white potatoes, peeled, grated	**1.3 kg**
1 onion, finely minced	
3 eggs, beaten	
½ cup seasoned breadcrumbs	**120 ml**

- In large bowl, combine potatoes, onions, eggs, breadcrumbs and a little salt and pepper and mix well. In skillet, drop by spoonfuls in hot oil and brown on both sides. Serves 4 to 6.

Super Main Dish: **Rotisserie Chicken**

- Keep 1 deli rotisserie chicken warm to serve. Slice into serving-size pieces.

Roasted Chicken with Red Peppers

1 (14 ounce) can chicken broth	396 g
1 (8 ounce) can whole kernel corn, drained	227 g
2 cups cooked, cubed chicken breasts	480 ml
1 cup roasted red bell peppers	240 ml
¼ cup pine nuts, toasted	60 ml

- In saucepan over medium-high heat, combine chicken broth, corn, chicken and roasted bell peppers. Cover and simmer about 3 minutes. Transfer to serving dish and sprinkle pine nuts over top. Serves 4 to 6.

Favorite Spinach

2 (10 ounce) packages frozen chopped spinach, thawed, well drained	2 (280 g)
1 (1 ounce) packet dry onion soup mix	28 g
1 (8 ounce) carton sour cream	227 g
⅔ cup shredded Monterey Jack cheese	160 ml

- Preheat oven to 350° (176° C). Combine spinach, onion soup mix and sour cream. Pour into sprayed 2-quart (2 L) baking dish. Bake at 350° for 20 minutes. Take out of oven, sprinkle cheese over top and place casserole back in oven for 5 minutes. Serves 4 to 6.

Super Bread Idea: **Toasted Italian Bread**

- Slice 1 loaf Italian bread and butter each slice and toast on baking sheet until light brown.

Southwest Salmon

1 - 1½ pounds salmon fillet or pieces, quartered	
3 tablespoons fresh lime juice	45 ml
½ teaspoon each cumin	2 ml
½ teaspoon chili powder	2 ml
2 tablespoons (¼ stick) butter, melted	30 ml

- Preheat oven to 400° (204° C). Place salmon, skin-side down in sprayed 9 x 13-inch (23 x 33 cm) baking dish. Rub lime juice over fillets and marinate at room temperature about 10 minutes. Pat salmon lightly with paper towel.

- In small bowl, combine cumin, chili powder and a little salt and pepper. Rub mixture on tops and sides of salmon. Roast salmon in baking pan between 5 to 7 minutes or until salmon is opaque and flakes easily. Do not overcook. Serves 4 to 6.

Spinach-Orange Salad

1 (10 ounce) package fresh baby spinach	280 g
2 (11 ounce) cans mandarin oranges, drained	2 (312 g)
½ small jacama, peeled, julienned	
⅓ cup slivered almonds, toasted	80 ml
1 (8 ounce) bottle balsamic salad dressing	227 g

- In salad bowl, combine all salad ingredients and toss with dressing. Serves 4 to 6.

4 - Independence Day
4th Sunday - Parents' Day

1
2
3
4
5
6
7
8
9
10
11
12
13
14
15
16
17
18
19
20
21
22
23
24
25
26
27
28
29
30
31

Barbecue Chicken Breasts

6 boneless, skinless chicken breast halves
1 (5.5 ounce) box barbecue-glazed chicken coating
   mix   **155 g**

•   Bake chicken breasts according to package instructions. Serves 4 to 6.

Cheddar-Broccoli Bake

1 (10 ounce) can cheddar cheese soup   **280 g**
½ cup milk   **120 ml**
1 (16 ounce) bag frozen broccoli florets, cooked   **.5 kg**
1 (3 ounce) can french-fried onion rings   **84 g**

•   Preheat oven to 350° (176° C). In 2-quart (2 L) baking dish, mix soup, milk and broccoli. Bake for 25 minutes. Stir and sprinkle onions over broccoli mixture. Bake additional 5 minutes or until onions are golden. Serves 4 to 6.

Simple Side Dish: **Bake Potato Zap**

•   Microwave baking potatoes and serve with butter and sour cream.

4 - Independence Day
4th Sunday - Parents' Day

Pork Picante

1 pound pork tenderloin, cubed	.5 kg
2 tablespoons taco seasoning	30 ml
1 cup chunky salsa	240 ml
⅓ cup peach preserves	80 ml

- Toss pork with taco seasoning and brown with a little oil in skillet. Stir in salsa and preserves. Bring to a boil. Lower heat and simmer 30 minutes. Pour over hot, cooked rice. Serves 4 to 6.

Corn-Green Chile Casserole

2 (10 ounce) packages frozen corn	2 (280 g)
2 tablespoons butter	30 ml
1 (8 ounce) package cream cheese	227 g
1 tablespoon sugar	15 ml
1 (4 ounce) can chopped green chilies	114 g

- Preheat oven to 350° (176° C). Cook corn according to package directions, drain and set aside. Melt butter in saucepan over low heat, add cream cheese and stir until it melts.
- Stir in corn, sugar and green chilies and spoon into sprayed 2-quart (2 L) baking dish. Cover and bake for 25 minutes. Serves 4 to 6.

Simple Side Dish: Spring Green Salad

- Toss 1 (10 ounce/280 g) package spring greens and 2 tomatoes, quartered with half bottle of 1 (8 ounce/227 g) bottle creamy ranch dressing.

Oven-Fried Turkey

1 - 1 ½ pounds turkey tenderloins, thawed	.5 kg
1 (5.5 ounce) package baked chicken coating mix	155 g

• Preheat oven to 400° (204° C). Place all tenderloins strips on several pieces of paper towels to partially dry them. Pour chicken coating mix into shallow bowl and press both sides of each piece of turkey into seasoned coating. Place in large sprayed baking pan, without pieces touching. Bake 20 minutes or until turkey is light brown. Serves 4 to 6 .

Poppy Seed Breadsticks

1½ cups shredded Monterey Jack cheese	360 ml
¼ cup poppy seeds	60 ml
2 tablespoons dry onion soup mix	30 ml
2 (11 ounce) cans breadstick dough	2 (312 g)

• Preheat oven to 375° (190° C). In large shallow bowl, combine cheese, poppy seeds and soup mix. Separate breadstick dough and stretch slightly until each stick is about 12 inches (32 cm) long. Cut dough in pieces 3 to 4 inches (8 to 10 cm) long. Dip strips in cheese mixture and turn to coat all sides. Place on sprayed baking pan and bake about 12 minutes or until breadsticks brown. Serves 6 to 8.

Simple Side Dish: Cheesy Au Gratin Potatoes

• Prepare 1 (5 ounce/ 143 g) box cheesy cheddar au gratin potatoes according to package directions.

Grilled Tuna with Mediterranean Salsa

6 (1 inch) thick fresh tuna steaks	6 (2.5 cm)
½ teaspoon minced garlic	2 ml

Mediterranean Salsa:

1 (4 ounce) can chopped ripe olives, drained	114 g
1 tomato, chopped	
⅓ cup olive oil	80 ml
⅓ cup crumbled feta cheese	80 ml
1 teaspoon dried basil	5 ml

- Sprinkle tuna steaks with minced garlic and ½ teaspoon (2 ml) each of salt and pepper. In small bowl, combine ripe olives, tomato, oil, feta cheese and basil. Brush salsa mixture over tuna steaks and refrigerate any leftover mixture.

- Grill tuna steaks over medium-high heat about 3 to 5 minutes. Gently turn tuna steaks and continue grilling 3 to 5 minutes. When serving, top each steak with remaining salsa. Serves 4 to 6 .

Cashew-Pea Salad

1 (16 ounce) package frozen baby green peas, thawed, drained	.5 kg
¾ cup chopped celery, chilled	180 ml
¼ cup chopped red bell pepper, chilled	60 ml
1 cup cashew pieces, chilled	240 ml
½ - ¾ cup mayonnaise	120 ml

- In bowl with lid, combine drained peas, celery, red bell pepper and cashews and toss. Add ½ cup (120 ml) mayonnaise and mix well. (If you want the salad creamier, add remaining ¼ cup (60 ml) mayonnaise.) Chill. Serves 4 to 6.

Ranch Chicken

½ cup grated parmesan cheese	120 ml
1½ cups corn flakes	360 ml
1 (1 ounce) packet ranch salad dressing mix	28 g
2 pounds chicken drumsticks	1 kg
½ cup (1 stick) butter, melted	120 ml

- Preheat oven to 350° (176° C). Combine cheese, corn flakes and dressing mix. Dip washed, dried chicken in butter and dredge in corn flake mixture. Bake uncovered for 50 minutes. Serves 4 to 6.

Cheesy Green Beans

¾ cup milk	180 ml
1 (8 ounce) package cream cheese	227 g
½ teaspoon garlic powder	2 ml
½ cup grated parmesan cheese	120 ml
2 (15 ounce) cans green beans	2 (425 g)

- In saucepan, combine milk, cream cheese, garlic and parmesan cheese and heat until cheeses melt. Heat green beans in pan, drain and cover with cream cheese mixture. Toss to coat evenly and serve hot. Serves 4 to 6 .

Butter Rolls

2 cups biscuit mix	480 ml
1 (8 ounce) carton sour cream	227 g
½ cup (1 stick) butter, melted	120 ml

- Preheat oven to 400° (204° C). Combine all ingredients and spoon, half full, into sprayed muffin cups. Bake for 14 minutes. Serves 4 to 6.

Potato-Beef Bake

1 pound lean ground beef	.5 kg
1 (10 ounce) can sloppy Joe sauce	280 g
1 (10 ounce) can fiesta nacho cheese soup	280 g
1 (32 ounce) package frozen hash brown potatoes, thawed	1 kg

- Preheat oven to 400° (204° C). In skillet, cook beef over medium heat until no longer pink and drain. Add sloppy Joe sauce and fiesta nacho cheese soup. Place hash browns in sprayed 9 x 13-inch (23 x 33 cm) baking dish. Top with beef mixture. Cover and bake for 25 minutes. Uncover and bake 10 minutes longer. Serves 4 to 6.

Wild West Corn

3 (15 ounce) cans whole kernel corn, drained	3 (425 g)
1 (10 ounce) can tomatoes and green chilies, drained	280 g
1 (8 ounce) package shredded Monterey Jack cheese	227 g
1 cup cheese cracker crumbs	240 ml

- Preheat oven to 350° (176° C). In large bowl, combine corn, tomatoes and cheese and mix well. Pour into sprayed 2½-quart (2.5 L) baking dish. Sprinkle cracker crumbs over casserole. Bake uncovered for 25 minutes. Serves 4 to 6.

Simple Bread Idea: **French Bread**

- Butter and heat 1 loaf French bread.

Sausage Quiche

1 (9 inch) frozen deep-dish pie shell	23 cm
1 (7 ounce) can whole green chilies, seeded	198 g
1 pound hot sausage, cooked, crumbled	.5 kg
4 eggs, slightly beaten	
1 (1 pint) carton half-and-half cream	.5 kg
½ cup grated parmesan cheese	120 ml
¾ cup shredded Swiss cheese	180 ml

- Preheat oven to 350° (176° C). Line pie shell with split, green chilies. Sprinkle sausage over chilies. Combine eggs, cream, both cheeses and about ¼ teaspoon (1 ml) each of salt and pepper. Slowly pour over sausage.

- Cover edge of pastry with thin strip of foil to prevent excessive browning. Bake for 35 minutes or until center sets and is golden brown. Allow quiche to stand at room temperature for 5 minutes before slicing to serve. Serves 4 to 6.

Hopping John

2 (15 ounce) cans jalapeno black-eyed peas, with liquid	2 (425 g)
¾ pound ham, chopped	340 g
1 cup chopped onion	240 ml
2 cups hot cooked rice	480 ml
½ cup chopped green onions	120 ml

- Combine peas, ham and onion in saucepan. Bring to boil, reduce heat and simmer 15 minutes. Stir in hot rice and green onions. Serves 4 to 6.

Turkey-Surprise Sandwich

1 (24 ounce) loaf oatnut bread or whole wheat bread	680 g
Mayonnaise	
1 pound deli-shaved smoked turkey slices	.5 kg
1 (8 ounce) package provolone cheese slices	227 g
2 - 3 avocados	
2 green apples	

- To make 6 sandwiches, place 6 slices bread on counter and spread very slight amount of mayonnaise on each slice. Place several pieces of turkey on each slice of bread and layer provolone cheese and several slices avocado with dash of salt.

- Now for the surprise! Peel and core apples and with your best knife, cut very, very thin slices of apple and place over avocado. Spread mayonnaise on 6 more slices bread and top sandwich with remaining bread. Serves 6 to 8.

Jalapeno Bites

1 (12 ounce) can jalapeno peppers, drained	340 g
1 (8 ounce) package shredded cheddar cheese	227 g
4 eggs, beaten	
¼ cup whole milk or cream	60 ml

- Preheat oven to 375° (190° C). Seed and chop peppers and place in 9-inch (23 cm) pie pan.   Sprinkle cheese over peppers. Combine eggs and milk and pour over cheese. Bake for about 22 minutes. Cut into small slices to serve. Serves 6 to 8.

Shrimp Newburg

1 (10 ounce) can cream of shrimp soup	280 g
1 teaspoon seafood seasoning	5 ml
1 (1 pound) package frozen cooked salad shrimp, thawed	.5 kg

- In saucepan, combine soup, ¼ cup (60 ml) water and seafood seasoning and bring to boil. Reduce heat and stir in shrimp. Heat thoroughly. Serves 4 to 6.

Broccoli Salad

5 - 6 cups broccoli florets without stems	1.3 L
1 sweet orange bell pepper, seeded, julienned	
1 (8 ounce) package cubed mozzarella cheese	227 g
Creamy Italian salad dressing	

- Combine all ingredients and 1 teaspoon (5 ml) salt and mix well. Toss with creamy Italian salad dressing and chill. (If you can't get it made that morning, place in sealed freezer bag for 15 minutes, but no longer). It needs to be chilled before serving. Serves 4 to 6.

Simple Side Dish: **Buttered White Rice**

- Cook 1 (3.5 ounce/100 g) package boil-in-bag long grain rice with 2 tablespoons (30 ml) butter according to package directions.

Chicken Quesadillas

1 (7 ounce) package frozen, cooked chicken strips, thawed	198 g
1 (10 ounce) can fiesta nacho cheese soup	280 g
1 (16 ounce) jar chunky salsa, slightly drained, divided	.5 kg
8 - 10 (8 inch) flour tortillas	8 - 10 (20 cm)

- Preheat oven to 400° (204° C). Cut chicken strips into much smaller pieces (almost shredded). In bowl, combine soup and half salsa and mix well.

- Lay tortillas out on flat surface and spoon about ¼ to ⅓ cup (60 ml to 80 ml) mixture on half of each tortilla to within ½-inch (1.2 cm) of edge. Sprinkle slivers of chicken over cheese mixture.

- Fold tortillas over moisten edges with little water and press edges of tortillas to seal. Place on 2 baking sheets and bake 5 to 6 minutes or until tortillas brown. Serves 4 to 6.

Calico Corn

2 ribs celery, sliced	
2 tablespoons butter	30 ml
3 (11 ounce) cans Mexicorn®, drained	3 (312 g)
1 (10 ounce) can fiesta nacho cheese soup	280 g
1 cup coarsely crushed buttery crackers	240 ml

- Preheat oven to 375° (190° C). Saute celery in butter. Pour corn and cheese soup in with celery and heat just enough to mix well. Pour into sprayed 7 x 11-inch (18 x 28 cm) baking dish. Sprinkle crushed crackers over casserole and bake uncovered 20 to 25 minutes or until crumbs brown lightly. Serves 4 to 6.

1
2
3
4
5
6
7
8
9
10
11
12
13
14
15
16
17
18
19
20
21
22
23
24
25
26
27
28
29
30
31

Swiss Chicken

4 boneless, skinless chicken breast halves	
4 slices Swiss cheese	
1 (10 ounce) can cream of chicken soup	280 g
¼ cup dry white wine	60 ml
½ cup herb-seasoned stuffing	120 ml
¼ cup (½ stick) butter, melted	60 ml

- Preheat oven to 350° (176° C). Arrange chicken in sprayed 9 x 13-inch (23 x 33 cm) pan. Top with cheese slices. Combine soup and wine in saucepan and heat just enough to mix well. Spoon evenly over chicken and sprinkle with stuffing mix. Drizzle butter over crumbs. Bake uncovered for 45 to 55 minutes. Serves 4.

Corn-Vegetable Medley

1 (10 ounce) can golden corn soup	280 g
½ cup milk	120 ml
2 cups fresh broccoli florets	480 ml
2 cups cauliflower florets	480 ml
1 cup shredded cheddar cheese	240 ml

- In saucepan over medium heat, heat soup and milk just to boiling and stir often. Stir in broccoli and cauliflower florets and return to boiling. Reduce heat to low and cover. Cook 20 minutes or until vegetables are tender and stir occasionally. Stir in cheese and heat until cheese melts. Serves 4.

Southwestern Steak

1 pound tenderized round steak	.5 kg
Flour	
1 (15 ounce) can Mexican stewed tomatoes	425 g
¾ cup salsa	180 ml
2 teaspoons beef bouillon granules	10 ml

• Preheat oven to 325° (162° C). Cut beef into serving-size pieces and dredge in flour. In skillet, brown steak in a little oil. Mix tomatoes, salsa and beef bouillon and pour over steak. Cover and bake for 1 hour. Serves 4.

Watergate Salad

1 (20 ounce) can crushed pineapple with juice	567 g
2 (3 ounce) packages pistachio instant pudding mix	2 (84 g)
¾ cup chopped pecans	180 ml
1 (12 ounce) carton whipped topping	340 g

• Mix pineapple with instant pudding mix until it thickens slightly. Add pecans. Mix well and fold in whipped topping. Pour into pretty crystal bowl and refrigerate. Serves 4 to 6.

Simple Side Dish: **Au Gratin Potatoes**

• Prepare 1 (6 ounce/168 g) box loaded au gratin potatoes according to package directions.

1
2
3
4
5
6
7
8
9
10
11
12
13
14
15
16
17
18
19
20
21
22
23
24
25
26
27
28
29
30
31

Ham And Potatoes Olé

1 (24 ounce) package frozen hash browns with onion and peppers, thawed	680 g
3 cups cooked, cubed ham	710 ml
1 (10 ounce) can cream of chicken soup	280 g
1 (10 ounce) can fiesta nacho cheese soup	280 g
1 cup hot salsa	240 ml
1 (8 ounce) package shredded cheddar-Jack cheese	227 g

• Preheat oven to 350° (176° C). Combine potatoes, ham, both soups and salsa in saucepan and heat just enough to mix well. Spoon into sprayed 9 x 13-inch (23 x 33 cm) baking dish. Cover and cook for 40 minutes. Remove from oven, sprinkle cheese over casserole and bake uncover additional 5 minutes. Serves 6 to 8.

Tumbleweed Crackers

1 cup canola oil	240 ml
2 teaspoons red pepper flakes	10 ml
1 (1 ounce) packet ranch dressing mix	28 g
1 teaspoon dill weed	5 ml
1 teaspoon garlic powder	5 ml
1 teaspoon cayenne pepper	5 ml
4 sleeves saltine crackers	

• Mix oil and red pepper flakes. Let stand for 1 hour. Add ranch dressing mix and remaining spices and stir. Put crackers into gallon container with lid. Pour mixture onto crackers. Place lid on container. Tumble gently every 15 minutes for 1½ hours. Serves 6 to 8.

Chicken A La Reuben

4 boneless, skinless chicken breast halves
4 slices Swiss cheese
1 (15 ounce) can sauerkraut, drained   **425 g**
1 (8 ounce) bottle Catalina salad dressing   **227 g**

- Preheat oven to 350° (176° C). Arrange chicken breasts in sprayed 9 x 13-inch (23 x 33 cm) baking pan. Place cheese over chicken and then sauerkraut. Cover with Catalina dressing. Bake covered for 30 minutes. Uncover and cook another 15 minutes. Serves 4.

Crunchy Green Beans

3 (15 ounce) cans whole green beans, drained   **3 (425 g)**
2 (10 ounce) cans cream of mushroom soup   **2 (280 g)**
2 (8 ounce) cans water chestnuts, chopped   **2 (227 g)**
1 (3 ounce) can french-fried onion rings   **84 g**

- Preheat oven to 350° (176° C). Combine green beans, mushroom soup, water chestnuts, ½ teaspoon (2 ml) salt and a little pepper. Pour mixture into sprayed 2-quart (2 L) baking dish. Bake covered for 30 minutes. Remove casserole from oven, sprinkle onion rings over top and bake 10 more minutes longer. Serves 4.

Super Bread Idea: **Cheese-Garlic Biscuits**

- Prepare 1 (7.7 ounce/210 g) package frozen cheese-garlic biscuits according to package directions.

1
2
3
4
5
6
7
8
9
10
11
12
13
14
15
16
17
18
19
20
21
22
23
24
25
26
27
28
29
30
31

Mexican Casserole

1 (13 ounce) bag corn chips, divided	370 g
2 pounds lean ground beef	1 kg
1 (15 ounce) can Mexican stewed tomatoes	425 g
1 (8 ounce) package shredded Mexican 4-cheese blend	227 g

- Preheat oven to 350° (176° C). Partially crush half bag chips and place in sprayed 9 x 13-inch (23 x 33 cm) baking dish. Brown ground beef and drain. Add stewed tomatoes and cheese and mix well. Pour into baking dish and sprinkle finely crushed chips over top. Bake uncovered for 40 minutes. Serves 6 to 8.

Super Simple Side Dish: Fast Quesadillas

- Prepare 1 (20 ounce/567 g) box frozen mini quesadillas according to package directions.

Super Simple Side Dish: Fast Mexican Rice

- Prepare 1 (6 ounce/168 g) box Mexican rice and pasta according to package directions.

☆ July ☆

4 – Independence Day
4th Sunday – Parents' Day

Onion-Beef Bake

3 pounds lean ground beef	**1.3 kg**
1 (1 ounce) packet dry onion soup mix	**28 g**
2 (10 ounce) cans French onion soup	**2 (280 g)**

- Preheat oven to 350° (176° C). Combine beef, soup mix and ½ cup (120 ml) water. Stir well and shape into patties about ½-inch (1.2 cm) thick. Cook in large skillet and brown on both sides. Transfer patties to sprayed 9 x 13-inch (23 x 33 cm) baking dish. Pour soup over patties. Cover and bake for about 35 minutes. Serves 6 to 8.

Crunchy Fruit Salad

2 red apples with peels, chopped	
⅓ cup sunflower seeds	**80 ml**
½ cup green grapes	**120 ml**
⅓ cup vanilla yogurt	**80 ml**

- In bowl, combine apples, sunflower seeds, grapes and yogurt. Stir to coat salad. Refrigerate until serving. Serves 4 to 6.

Simple Side Dish:
Fast Fancy Mashed Potatoes

- Prepare 1 (7 ounce/198 g) box sour cream and chives mashed potatoes according to package directions.

1
2
3
4
5
6
7
8
9
10
11
12
13
14
15
16
17
18
19
20
21
22
23
24
25
26
27
28
29
30
31

Seafood Delight

2 (6 ounce) cans small, veined shrimp, drained	**2 (168 g)**
1 (6 ounce) can crabmeat, drained, flaked	**168 g**
2 (10 ounce) cans corn chowder	**2 (280 g)**
2 cups seasoned breadcrumbs, divided	**480 ml**

- Preheat oven to 375° (190° C). In bowl, combine shrimp, crabmeat, chowder and ¾ cup (180 ml) breadcrumbs. Spoon into sprayed, glass pie pan. Sprinkle remaining breadcrumbs over top of casserole and bake 25 minutes. Serves 4 to 6.

Cheese Drops

2 cups baking mix	**480 ml**
⅔ cup milk	**160 ml**
⅔ cup shredded sharp cheddar cheese	**160 ml**
¼ cup (½ stick) butter, melted	**60 ml**

- Preheat oven to 375° (190° C). Mix biscuit mix, milk and cheese. Drop 1 heaping tablespoon (15 ml) dough onto sprayed baking pan and bake for 10 minutes or until slightly brown. While warm, brush tops of biscuits with melted butter. Serves 4 to 6.

Simple Side Dish: **Easy Potato Salad**

- Chill 1 (24 ounce/680 g) carton refrigerated potato salad and serve.

Casserole Supper

1 pound lean ground beef	.5 kg
¼ cup white rice	60 ml
1 (10 ounce) can French onion soup	280 g
1 (3 ounce) can french-fried onion rings	84 g

• Preheat oven to 325° (162° C). Brown ground beef, drain and place in sprayed 7 x 11-inch (18 x 28 cm) baking dish. Mix rice, onion soup and ½ cup (120 ml) water and pour into baking dish. Cover and bake for 40 minutes. Uncover, sprinkle onion rings over top and return to oven for 10 minutes. Serves 4.

Fried Zucchini

3 large zucchini, grated	
3 eggs	
⅓ (12 ounce) box round buttery crackers, crushed	⅓ (340 g)
½ cup grated parmesan cheese	120 ml

• Combine zucchini, eggs and cracker crumbs and mix well. Add cheese and a little salt and pepper. Drop by spoonfuls into skillet with a little oil. Fry for about 15 minutes and brown on each side. Serves 4.

Garlic-Flavored Biscuits

5 cups biscuit mix	1.3 L
1 cup shredded cheddar cheese	240 ml
1 (14 ounce) can chicken broth with roasted garlic	396 g

• Preheat oven to 425° (220° C). Mix all ingredients and drop by tablespoons onto sprayed baking pan. Bake for 10 minutes. Serves 4 to 6.

1
2
3
4
5
6
7
8
9
10
11
12
13
14
15
16
17
18
19
20
21
22
23
24
25
26
27
28
29
30
31

Bueno Taco Casserole

2 pounds lean ground beef	1 kg
1½ cups taco sauce	360 ml
2 (15 ounce) cans Spanish rice	2 (425 g)
1 (8 ounce) package shredded Mexican 4-cheese blend, divided	227 g

- Preheat oven to 350° (176° C). In skillet, brown ground beef and drain. Add taco sauce, Spanish rice and half cheese. Spoon into sprayed 3-quart (3 L) baking dish. Cover and bake for 35 minutes. Uncover, sprinkle remaining cheese on top and return to oven for 5 minutes. Serves 6 to 8.

Grapefruit-Avocado Salad

2 (15 ounce) cans grapefruit sections, drained	2 (425 g)
2 ripe avocados, peeled, sliced	
½ cup slivered almonds, chopped	120 ml
Poppy seed salad dressing	
Lettuce	

- Combine grapefruit, avocados and almonds. Toss with half bottle poppy seed dressing. Serve on bed of lettuce. Serves 6 to 8.

Simple Side Dish: **Fast Chili Beans**

- Heat 2 (15 ounce/425 g) cans chili beans according to can directions.

Lemonade Chicken

6 boneless, skinless chicken breast halves
1 (6 ounce) can frozen lemonade, thawed
⅓ cup soy sauce
1 teaspoon garlic powder

- Preheat oven to 350°. Place chicken in sprayed 9 x 13-inch baking dish. Combine lemonade, soy sauce and garlic powder and pour over chicken. Cover with foil and bake for 45 minutes. Uncover, pour juices over chicken and cook additional 10 minutes. Serves 4 to 6.

Carrot Salad

3 cups finely grated carrots	**710 ml**
1 (8 ounce) can crushed pineapple, drained	**227 g**
4 tablespoons flaked coconut	**60 ml**
1 tablespoon sugar	**15 ml**
⅓ cup mayonnaise	**80 ml**

- Combine all ingredients. Toss with mayonnaise and mix well. Refrigerate. Serves 4 to 6.

Simple Bread Idea: **Potato Dinner Rolls**

- Heat 1 (16 ounce/.5 kg) package bakery potato dinner rolls at 350° (176° C) until hot and serve with butter.

1
2
3
4
5
6
7
8
9
10
11
12
13
14
15
16
17
18
19
20
21
22
23
24
25
26
27
28
29
30
31

Peach-Pineapple Baked Ham

1 (3 - 4) pound boneless smoked ham	1.3 kg
4 tablespoons dijon-style mustard, divided	60 ml
1 cup peach preserves	240 ml
1 cup pineapple preserves	240 ml

- Preheat oven to 325° (162° C). Spread 2 tablespoons (30 ml) mustard on ham. Place ham in sprayed, shallow baking pan and bake for 20 minutes. Combine remaining 2 tablespoons (30 ml) mustard and both preserves and heat in microwave oven for 20 seconds (or in small saucepan at low heat for 2 to 3 minutes). Pour over ham and bake for about 15 minutes. Serves 6 to 8.

Parmesan-Bread Deluxe

1 loaf unsliced Italian bread	
½ cup refrigerated creamy Caesar dressing	120 ml
⅓ cup grated parmesan cheese	80 ml
3 tablespoons diced green onions	45 ml

- Cut 24 (½ inch/1.2 cm) thick slices from bread. In small bowl, combine dressing, cheese and onion. Spread 1 teaspoon (5 ml) dressing mixture on each bread slice. Place bread on baking sheet. Broil 4 inches (10 cm) from heat until golden brown. Serve warm. Serves 4 to 6.

Simple Side Dish: Garlic-Butter Rice

- Cook 2 (6 ounce/168 g) package garlic and butter-flavored rice according to package directions.

Bacon-Wrapped Chicken

6 boneless, skinless chicken breast halves
1 (8 ounce) carton whipped cream cheese
    with onion and chives, softened   **227 g**
Butter
6 bacon strips

• Preheat oven to 375° (190° C). Flatten chicken to
  (½ inch/1.2 cm) thickness. Spread 3 tablespoons
  (45 ml) cream cheese over each. Dot with butter
  and a little salt and roll. Wrap each with bacon strip.
  Place seam-side down in sprayed 9 x 13-inch (23
  x 33 cm) baking dish. Bake uncovered for 40 to 45
  minutes or until juices run clear. To brown, broil 6
  inches (15 cm) from heat for about 3 minutes or until
  bacon is crisp. Serves 4 to 6.

Stuffed-Cucumber Slices

3 cucumbers, peeled
2 (3 ounce) packages cream cheese, softened   **2 (84 g)**
¼ cup stuffed green olives   **60 ml**

• Halve cucumbers lengthwise and scoop out seeds.
  Beat cream cheese with mixer until creamy.
  Add olives and ½ teaspoon (2 ml) salt. Fill
  hollows with cream cheese mixture, press halves
  together, wrap tightly in plastic wrap and chill.
  Cut crosswise in (⅓ inch/.8 cm) slices to serve.
  Serves 4 to 6.

Simple Side Dish: **Roasted-Garlic Potatoes**

• Cook 1 (7 ounce/198 g) box roasted garlic-potato mix
  according to package directions.

1
2
3
4
5
6
7
8
9
10
11
12
13
14
15
16
17
18
19
20
21
22
23
24
25
26
27
28
29
30
31

1
2
3
4
5
6
7
8
9
10
11
12
13
14
15
16
17
18
19
20
21
22
23
24
25
26
27
28
29
30
31

Tangy Pork Chops

4 - 6 pork chops
¼ cup Worcestershire sauce   **60 ml**
¼ cup ketchup   **60 ml**
½ cup honey   **120 ml**

- Preheat oven to 325° (162° C). In skillet, brown
  pork chops. Place in shallow baking dish. Combine
  Worcestershire, ketchup and honey. Pour over pork
  chops. Cover and bake for 45 minutes. Serves 4 to 6.

Marinated Brussels Sprouts Medley

2 (10 ounce) boxes frozen brussels sprouts, thawed 2 (280 g)
1 cup Italian dressing   **240 ml**
1 cup chopped green bell pepper   **240 ml**
½ cup chopped onion   **120 ml**

- Pierce box of brussels sprouts and cook in microwave
  for 7 minutes. Mix Italian dressing, bell pepper and
  onion. Pour over brussels sprouts and marinate at
  least 24 hours. Drain to serve. Serves 4 to 6.

Simple Side Dish: **Bacon-Scalloped Potatoes**

- Prepare 1 (7 ounce/198 g) box bacon-scalloped
  potatoes according to package directions.

Honey-Mustard Chicken

⅓ cup dijon-style mustard	80 ml
¾ cup honey	180 ml
2 tablespoons dried dill	30 ml
1 (2½ pound) chicken, quartered	1.2 kg

- Preheat oven to 350° (176° C). Combine mustard, honey and dill. Arrange chicken quarters in sprayed 9 x 13-inch (23 x 33 cm) baking dish. Pour mustard mixture over chicken.
- Turn chicken over and make sure mustard mixture covers chicken. Bake covered for 35 minutes. Uncover and bake additional 10 minutes. Serves 6 to 8.

Potatoes Supreme

1 (32 ounce) package frozen hash brown potatoes, thawed	1 kg
1 onion, chopped	
2 (10 ounce) cans cream of chicken soup	2 (280 g)
1 (8 ounce) carton sour cream	227 g

- Preheat oven to 350° (176° C). In large bowl, combine potatoes, onion, soup and sour cream. Pour into sprayed 9 x 13-inch (23 x 33 cm) baking dish. Bake covered for 1 hour. Serves 6 to 8.

Simple Side Dish: Corn In Butter Sauce

- Cook 1 (19 ounce/538 g) package frozen niblet corn in butter sauce according to package directions.

1
2
3
4
5
6
7
8
9
10
11
12
13
14
15
16
17
18
19
20
21
22
23
24
25
26
27
28
29
30
31

Skillet Shrimp

2 teaspoons olive oil	10 ml
2 pounds shrimp, peeled, veined	1 kg
⅔ cup prepared herb-garlic marinade	
with lemon juice	160 ml
¼ cup diced green onions with tops	60 ml

- In large nonstick skillet, heat oil and add shrimp and marinade. Cook, stirring often, until shrimp turns pink. Stir in green onions. Serve over hot, cooked rice. Serves 4 to 6.

Sliced Tomatoes And Celery Sticks

3 - 4 vine-ripened tomatoes, sliced	
1 stalk celery, ribs cut into 3-inch (8 cm) pieces	
1 (16 ounce) carton pimento cheese	.5 kg

- Slice tomatoes on serving plate. Stuff 1 heaping tablespoon (15 ml) pimento cheese on ribs of celery and place on serving plate with tomatoes. Serves 4.

Ranch French Bread

½ cup (1 stick) butter, softened	120 ml
1 tablespoon ranch dressing mix	15 ml
1 loaf French bread	

- Preheat oven to 350° (176° C). Cut loaf in half horizontally. Blend butter and dressing mix. Spread butter mixture on bread. Wrap bread in foil. Bake for 15 minutes. Serves 4 to 6.

Supper-Salad Supreme

2 (15 ounce) cans great northern beans, rinsed, drained	2 (425 g)
1 pound cooked, ham, cubed	.5 kg
2 bunches fresh broccoli, cut into florets	
1 red bell pepper, julienned	
1 orange bell pepper, julienned	
¾ pound Swiss cheese, cubed	340 g
Garlic-vinaigrette salad dressing	

- In large bowl, combine beans, ham, broccoli florets, bell peppers and Swiss cheese. Toss with garlic vinaigrette salad dressing. Serves 4 to 6.

Millionaire Sandwiches

¾ pound bacon, cooked, crumbled	340 g
1 (4 ounce) can chopped ripe olives, drained	114 g
½ cup chopped pecans	120 ml
1½ cups mayonnaise	360 ml
White or whole wheat bread	

- In bowl, combine all ingredients and blend well. Spread on white or whole wheat bread with crusts trimmed. Cut sandwiches into 3 strips. Serves 4.

Peanut Butter Sundae

1 cup light corn syrup	240 ml
1 cup chunky peanut butter	240 ml
¼ cup milk	60 ml
Ice cream or pound cake	

- In mixing bowl, stir corn syrup, peanut butter and milk until they blend well. Serve over ice cream or pound cake. Store in refrigerator.

1
2
3
4
5
6
7
8
9
10
11
12
13
14
15
16
17
18
19
20
21
22
23
24
25
26
27
28
29
30
31

Shrimp Alfredo

2 (12 ounce) bunches fresh asparagus spears, trimmed	**2 (340 g)**
1 sweet red bell pepper, julienned	
1 (12 ounce) package frozen, shelled, veined, shrimp, tails removed, thawed	**340 g**
1 (16 ounce) jar alfredo sauce	**.5 kg**

- Cut asparagus in 1½-inch (3 cm) pieces. Combine asparagus and bell pepper in skillet with ¼ cup (60 ml) water. Bring to a boil, reduce heat, cover and simmer about 5 minutes.
- Add shrimp, cook and stir about 4 minutes or until shrimp turns pink. Stir in alfredo sauce and pepper. Simmer for 3 to 4 minutes or until mixture heats through. Serve over Buttered Linguine. (See recipe below.) Serves 4 to 6.

Buttered Linguine

1 (8 ounce) package linguine	**227 g**
1 green bell pepper, seeded, chopped	
¼ cup (½ stick) butter	**60 ml**
2 tablespoons chopped fresh chives	**30 ml**

- Cook linguine according to package directions. Drain, cover and keep warm. In skillet, saute bell pepper in butter until tender-crisp. Add bell pepper and chives to linguine and mix well. Spoon linguine mixture into serving bowl and pour shrimp alfredo over pasta. Garnish shrimp with fresh, shredded parmesan cheese, if desired. Serves 4 to 6.

Tenderloin With Orange Sauce

2 (1 pound) pork tenderloins, cut in thick slices   2 (.5 kg)

Orange Sauce:
1 cup orange juice   240 ml
3 tablespoons soy sauce   45 ml
2 tablespoons honey-mustard dressing   30 ml
1 tablespoon minced fresh ginger
**   or ½ teaspoon dried ginger   15 ml/2 ml**

• In large skillet over medium heat, brown pork slices in a little oil for 4 to 5 minutes. While pork browns, combine sauce ingredients in small bowl and pour sauce over pork slices in skillet. Bring to a boil, reduce heat and simmer uncovered about 10 minutes. Serve tenderloin slices with sauce from pan. Serve over Crunchy Rice. (See recipe below.) Serves 4 to 6.

Crunchy Rice

1½ cups instant rice   360 ml
Butter
1 (10 ounce) package frozen green peas, thawed   280 g

• Cook rice according to package directions. Add half package frozen green peas and 1 tablespoon (15 ml) butter. Heat on low until rice gets hot again. To serve, place rice on platter and top with pork slices and sauce from pan from recipe above. Serves 4.

August dates column (1–31)

Snappy Ham

1 (¾ inch) thick center-cut ham slice	**1.8 cm**
1 (16 ounce) can whole cranberries	**.5 kg**
1 cup chopped pecans	**240 ml**
1 (12 ounce) jar apricot preserves	**340 g**

- Cook ham according to package directions and place on serving plate. In saucepan over medium heat, combine cranberries, pecans and apricot preserves, heat and stir until ingredients mix well. Spoon relish into gravy bowl or other small bowl and serve hot or chilled. Serves 4.

Breadsticks

1 (8 ounce) package shredded Monterey Jack cheese	**227 g**
¼ cup poppy seeds	**60 ml**
2 tablespoons onion soup mix	**30 ml**
2 (11 ounce) cans breadstick dough	**2 (312 g)**

- Preheat oven to 375° (190° C). In large shallow bowl, combine cheese, poppy seeds and soup mix. Separate breadstick dough and stretch slightly until each stick is about 12 inches (32 cm) long. Cover with cheese mixture and bake for 12 minutes. Serves 6 to 8.

Simple Side Dish: **Glazed Carrots**

- Heat 1 (24 ounce/680 g) package frozen glazed carrots according to package directions.

Hi-Ho Meat, Potatoes And Gravy

1¼ pounds lean ground beef	567 g
⅓ cup seasoned breadcrumbs	80 ml
1 egg, beaten	
⅓ cup finely minced onion	80 ml
1 (22 ounce) carton refrigerated mashed potatoes, heated	624 g

- In large bowl, combine all ingredients except potatoes and shape into 6 patties. Spray large skillet with cooking spray and cook patties over medium heat for 3 to 4 minutes on each side. Transfer patties to glass dish to serve. Keep warm. Serves 4.

Gravy:

2 (12 ounce) jars beef gravy	2 (340 g)
¼ teaspoon dried thyme	1 ml
1 (4 ounce) can sliced mushrooms, drained	114 g

- Heat gravy, thyme and mushrooms in same skillet where patties cooked. To serve, pour gravy and mushrooms over patties and mashed potatoes.

Fancy Fruit

2 (20 ounce) cans peach pie filling, chilled	2 (567 g)
1 (15 ounce) can pear slices, halved, chilled	425 g
1 (16 ounce) package frozen, sweetened strawberries, thawed	.5 kg
1 (20 ounce) cans pineapple tidbits, drained, chilled	567 g

- Combine all fruits in crystal bowl and serve.
- Serves 6 to 8.

1
2
3
4
5
6
7
8
9
10
11
12
13
14
15
16
17
18
19
20
21
22
23
24
25
26
27
28
29
30
31

Luscious Papaya-Chicken Salad

1 (10 ounce) package romaine lettuce leaves	280 g
2 ripe papayas, peeled, seeded, cubed	
1 large red bell pepper, seeded, sliced	
2 cups cooked, cubed chicken breast	480 ml
½ cup chopped pecans, toasted	120 ml

• In large salad bowl, combine lettuce, papayas and bell pepper.

Dressing:

¼ cup lime juice	60 ml
¼ cup honey	60 ml
2 teaspoons minced garlic	10 ml
3 tablespoons extra-virgin olive oil	45 ml

• In small bowl, whisk lime juice, honey, garlic and a little salt. Slowly add olive oil in thin stream and whisk dressing until they blend well. Pour dressing over salad, add cubed chicken and toss. To serve, sprinkle pecans over top of salad. Serves 4.

Ranch-Style French Bread

1 loaf French bread	
½ cup (1 stick) butter, softened	120 ml
1 tablespoon dry ranch dressing mix	15 ml

• Preheat oven to 350° (176° C). Cut loaf in half horizontally. Blend butter and dressing mix. Spread butter mixture on bread. Wrap bread in foil. Bake for 15 minutes. Serves 4 to 6.

Ham Quesadillas

2 cups shredded ham	480 ml
½ cup chunky salsa	120 ml
2 teaspoons chili powder	10 ml
¾ cup whole kernel corn	180 ml
1 (8 ounce) package shredded Mexican 4-cheese blend	227 g
8 large whole-wheat tortillas	

- In large bowl, combine shredded ham, salsa, chili powder and corn. Spread mixture over 4 tortillas to within ½-inch (1.2 cm) of edge and sprinkle cheese on top.
- Top with remaining tortillas and cook (1 quesadilla at a time) on medium-high heat, in large non-stick skillet about 5 minutes and turn after 2 minutes or until light golden brown. Cut in wedges to serve with pinto beans and guacamole. Serves 6 to 8.

Simple Side Dish: Easy Jalapeno Beans

- Heat 2 (15 ounce/425 g) cans pinto beans with jalapeno according to can directions.

Simple Side Dish: Fast Guacamole Salad

- Place lettuce on individual salad plate and spoon 2 heaping tablespoons (30 ml) guacamole from 2 (16 ounce/.5 kg) cartons prepared guacamole on each.

1
2
3
4
5
6
7
8
9
10
11
12
13
14
15
16
17
18
19
20
21
22
23
24
25
26
27
28
29
30
31

Chipper-Fish

½ cup Caesar salad dressing	120 ml
1½ - 2 pounds sole or orange roughy fillets	.7 kg
1½ cups seasoned breadcrumbs	360 ml
1 cup potato chips, crushed	240 ml

- Preheat oven to 375° (190° C). Pour dressing in shallow bowl and breadcrumbs in second shallow bowl. Dip fish in dressing and breadcrumbs and coat lightly. Place coated fish in large, sprayed baking dish. Sprinkle fish lightly with crushed potato chips and bake 20 to 25 minutes or until fish flakes easily with fork. Serves 4 to 6.

Spinach Salad

½ cup slivered almonds	120 ml
1 (8 ounce) package fresh baby spinach	227 g
2 eggs, hard-boiled, sliced	
1 sweet red bell pepper, julienned	
Raspberry vinaigrette dressing	

- Toast almonds on baking sheet at 275° (135° C) for 10 minutes. In salad bowl, combine all ingredients except dressing. Just before serving, pour about one-third bottle raspberry-vinaigrette dressing over salad and toss. Serves 4 to 6.

Simple Side Dish: **Fast Fried Potatoes**

- Heat 1 (22 ounce/624 g) package frozen waffle-fries according to package directions.

Delicious Pork Chops

¾ cup biscuit mix	180 ml
1 teaspoon paprika	5 ml
¾ cup Italian salad dressing	180 ml
1 cup garlic-herb-seasoned breadcrumbs	240 ml]
Oil	
6 (½ inch) thick boneless pork chops	6 (1.2 cm)

- Mix biscuit mix and paprika in shallow bowl. Pour dressing in second bowl and breadcrumbs in third bowl. Dip pork chops in biscuit mixture, in salad dressing and breadcrumbs.

- In skillet, heat about 3 tablespoons (45 ml) oil and cook pork chops 5 to 8 minutes or until both sides brown lightly. Reduce heat to low, cover and cook about 15 minutes longer. Drain on paper towels. Serves 4 to 6.

Broccoli Salad

5 cups broccoli florets, stemmed, chilled	1.3 L
1 sweet red bell pepper, julienned, chilled	
1 cup diagonally sliced celery, chilled	240 ml
1 (8 ounce) package cubed Monterey Jack cheese	227 g
1 zucchini, sliced	
Creamy Italian salad dressing	

- In salad bowl, combine all salad ingredients and toss with creamy Italian salad dressing. Refrigerate or freeze about 15 minutes (no longer). Salad is best served cold. Serves 4 to 6.

1
2
3
4
5
6
7
8
9
10
11
12
13
14
15
16
17
18
19
20
21
22
23
24
25
26
27
28
29
30
31

Chicken-Bacon Sandwiches

1 (12 ounce) can chicken breast meat, drained	340 g
⅓ cup mayonnaise	80 ml
1 tablespoon dijon-style mustard	15 ml
1 rib celery, finely chopped	
3 tablespoons minced green onions	45 ml
¼ cup cooked, crumbled bacon	60 ml
Shredded lettuce	
White or whole wheat bread	

• In medium bowl, combine chicken, mayonnaise, mustard, celery, green onions, bacon and a little salt and pepper. Spread chicken mixture on whole wheat or white bread and top with shredded lettuce. Serves 4 to 6.

Peachy Fruit Salad

2 (20 ounce) cans peach pie filling	2 (567 g)
1 (20 ounce) can pineapple chunks, drained	567 g
1 (11 ounce) can mandarin oranges, drained	312 g
1 (8 ounce) jar maraschino cherries, drained	227 g
1 cup miniature marshmallows	240 ml

• Combine all ingredients in large bowl, fold together gently and refrigerate. (Bananas may be added if you like.) Serve in pretty crystal bowl. Serves 4 to 6.

Honey-Glazed Chicken

¾ cup flour	180 ml
½ teaspoon cayenne pepper	2 ml
1 broiler-fryer chicken, quartered	
¼ cup (½ stick) butter, divided	60 ml
⅓ cup packed brown sugar	80 ml
⅓ cup honey	80 ml
1 teaspoon lemon juice	5 ml
1 tablespoon light soy sauce	15 ml

- Preheat oven to 350° (176° C). In shallow bowl, combine flour and cayenne pepper. Dredge chicken quarters (cut wing tips off) in flour mixture. Place 2 tablespoons (30 ml) butter in large, heavy skillet and brown chicken on both sides.
- Transfer to sprayed 9 x 13-inch (23 x 33 cm) baking dish. In same skillet, place remaining butter, brown sugar, honey, lemon juice and soy sauce and bring to boiling. Pour mixture over chicken. Bake uncovered for 35 to 40 minutes and baste several times with pan drippings. Serves 4 to 6.

Simple Side Dish: Real Easy Pasta Salad

- Prepare 1 (7.5 ounce/210 g) box ranch-bacon pasta salad according to package directions.

Simple Bread Idea: French Bread

- Butter 1 loaf French bread and serve hot.

1
2
3
4
5
6
7
8
9
10
11
12
13
14
15
16
17
18
19
20
21
22
23
24
25
26
27
28
29
30
31

Flounder Au Gratin

½ cup fine dry breadcrumbs	120 ml
¼ cup grated parmesan cheese	60 ml
1 pound flounder fillets	.5 kg
⅓ cup mayonnaise	80 ml

• Preheat oven to 350° (176° C). In shallow dish, combine crumbs and cheese. Brush both sides of fish with mayonnaise and coat with crumb mixture. Arrange fish in single layer in sprayed shallow pan and bake for 20 to 25 minutes or until fish flakes easily with fork. Serves 4.

Cheese Bread

1 (16 ounce) package shredded, sharp cheddar cheese	.5 kg
1 cup mayonnaise	240 ml
1 (1 ounce) packet ranch dressing mix	28 g
10 (1 inch) slices French bread	10 (2.5 cm)

• Combine cheese, mayonnaise and dressing mix. Spread on bread slices and heat in oven until brown. Serves 4 to 6.

Simple Side Dish: Easy Buttered Rice

• Prepare 1 (6 ounce/168 g) box parmesan-butter rice according to package directions.

Orange-Honey Pork Chops

6 thick butterfly-cut pork chops	
1½ cups orange juice	360 ml
½ cup honey	120 ml
2 teaspoons mustard	10 ml
2 cups instant brown rice, cooked	480 ml

- In large skillet over medium-high heat, pour about 2 tablespoons (30 ml) oil and brown pork chops on both sides. In bowl, combine orange juice, honey and mustard and pour over pork chops.
- Heat liquid and pork chops in skillet to boiling, reduce heat and simmer about 20 minutes. Cook rice according to package directions. (Rice should be ready when pork chops are done.) Serves 4 to 6.

Herb-Seasoned Vegetables

1 (14 ounce) can seasoned chicken broth with Italian herbs	396 g
½ teaspoon garlic powder	2 ml
1 (16 ounce) package frozen vegetables (broccoli, cauliflower, etc.)	.5 kg
½ cup grated parmesan cheese	120 ml

- Heat broth, garlic and vegetables to a boil. Cover and cook over low heat for 5 minutes or until tender-crisp. Drain. Place in serving dish and sprinkle parmesan cheese over vegetables. Serves 4 to 6.

1
2
3
4
5
6
7
8
9
10
11
12
13
14
15
16
17
18
19
20
21
22
23
24
25
26
27
28
29
30
31

Short-Order Fresh Tuna

4 (¾ inch) thick tuna steaks	4 (1.8 cm)
1 small onion, thinly sliced	
1 cup orange juice	240 ml
¼ teaspoon dried dill weed	1 ml
2 tablespoons butter	30 ml

- Sprinkle both sides of tuna steaks with 1 teaspoon (5 ml) salt. Place in sprayed skillet, cover and cook on both sides on medium heat for 3 to 4 minutes or until tuna is slightly pink in center.

- Remove tuna from skillet and keep warm. Add onion slices, cook 4 to 5 minutes and stir in orange juice, dill and butter. Continue cooking another 4 to 5 minutes or until sauce thickens. Serve sauce over tuna. Serves 4.

Nutty Green Salad

6 cups torn mixed salad greens	1.5 L
1 medium zucchini, sliced	
1 (8 ounce) can sliced water chestnuts, drained	227 g
½ cup peanuts	120 ml
⅓ cup Italian salad dressing	80 ml

- Toss greens, zucchini, water chestnuts and peanuts. When ready to serve, add salad dressing and toss. Serves 4 to 6.

Simple Side Dish: **Easy Rice Au Gratin**

- Cook 1 (6 ounce/168 g) box broccoli rice au gratin according to package directions.

Guacamole-Ham Wrap

¾ cup prepared guacamole	180 ml
4 (8 inch) spinach tortillas	4 (20 cm)
¾ cup salsa	180 ml
½ (8 ounce) package shredded 4-cheese blend	½ (227 g)
¾ pound ham, cut in thin strips	340 g
Shredded lettuce	

- Spread guacamole over half of each tortilla and layer salsa, cheese, ham strips and lettuce to within 2 inches (5 cm) of edges. Roll tightly. Serves 4.

Broccoli-Noodle Salad

1 cup slivered almonds	240 ml
1 cup sunflower seeds	240 ml
2 (3 ounce) packages chicken-flavored ramen noodles	2 (84 g)
1 (10 ounce) package broccoli slaw	280 g
1 (8 ounce) bottle Italian salad dressing	227 g

- Toast almonds and sunflower seeds in oven at 275° (135° C) for about 10 minutes. Break up ramen noodles and mix with slaw, almonds, sunflower seeds and seasoning packet.
- Toss with Italian salad dressing and refrigerate several hours before serving. Serves 4.

1
2
3
4
5
6
7
8
9
10
11
12
13
14
15
16
17
18
19
20
21
22
23
24
25
26
27
28
29
30
31

Mac 'N Cheese Casserole

4 eggs
1½ cups milk .... **360 ml**
1 (12 ounce) package macaroni, cooked .... **340 g**
1 (8 ounce) package shredded cheddar cheese .. **227 g**
2 cups cubed ham .... **480 ml**
¾ cup seasoned breadcrumbs .... **180 ml**

- Preheat oven to 350°
  (176° C). In large bowl,
  lightly beat eggs and
  milk with a little salt
  and pepper. Stir in
  macaroni, cheese and
  cubed ham. Spoon into
  buttered 7 x 11-inch (18 x 28 cm) baking dish, sprinkle
  breadcrumbs on top and bake uncovered for 30
  minutes. Serves 4 to 6.

Simple Side Dish: **Spinach Souffle Zap**

2 (12 ounce) packages frozen spinach souffle,
   thawed .... **2 (340 g)**

- While spaghetti and chicken cook, remove tray
  from both outer cartons and remove film covers.
  Microwave on HIGH 15 to 16 minutes and stir both
  trays after 10 minutes. Souffle is done when it
  bubbles around edges and knife inserted in center
  comes out clean.

Simple Salad Idea: **Sliced Tomatoes**

- Place a spoonful of cottage cheese on tomato slices
  and serve cold.

Parmesan-Crusted Chicken

1 egg white, beaten	
1½ cups breadcrumbs	360 ml
1 teaspoon dried parsley	5 ml
½ cup grated parmesan cheese	120 ml
4 small boneless, skinless chicken breast halves	

- Preheat oven to 425° (220° C). Combine beaten egg white and 1 tablespoon (15 ml) water. In shallow bowl, combine breadcrumbs, parsley, cheese and a little salt and pepper.
- Dip each piece of chicken in egg whites and dredge in crumb mixture. Place in heavy skillet with a little oil and saute chicken until golden on both sides, about 5 minutes. Transfer to sprayed baking dish and bake uncovered for 15 minutes.

Sage-Butter Sauce:

¼ cup minced shallots	60 ml
½ cup dry white wine	120 ml
½ cup whipping cream	120 ml
½ cup chicken broth	120 ml
¼ cup (½ stick) butter, cubed	60 ml
¾ teaspoon dried sage	4 ml

For sauce, saute shallots in a little oil in saucepan. Add wine, cream and chicken broth. Simmer until reduced by half. Stir in butter and sage. Serve over parmesan chicken. Serves 4.

Simple Side Dish: Easy Cheesy Rice

- Prepare 1 (4.6 ounce/128 g) box broccoli and cheese rice mix according to box directions.

1
2
3
4
5
6
7
8
9
10
11
12
13
14
15
16
17
18
19
20
21
22
23
24
25
26
27
28
29
30
31

Lemon-Pepper Pork Chops

6 butterfly pork chops	
¾ teaspoon garlic salt	4 ml
¾ teaspoon lemon pepper	4 ml
½ cup chopped pecans	120 ml
3 tablespoons lemon juice	45 ml
1 (9 ounce) package microwave-ready rice	255 g

- Sprinkle both sides of pork chops with garlic-pepper mixture. In large skillet, heat a little oil over medium-high heat. Add chops and cook about 5 minutes on each side until chops brown lightly. Reduce heat, add several tablespoons water, cover and simmer 10 minutes.

- Transfer pork chops to serving plate to keep warm. Top with pecans. Stir lemon juice into pan drippings, heat and stir constantly until they blend. Spoon drippings on pork chops and serve over rice. Serves 4 to 6.

Spinach Salad

½ cup slivered almonds	120 ml
1 (8 ounce) package fresh baby spinach	227 g
2 eggs, hard-boiled, sliced	
1 sweet red bell pepper, julienned	
Raspberry-vinaigrette dressing	

- Toast almonds on baking sheet at 275° (135° C) oven for 10 minutes. In salad bowl, combine all salad ingredients. Just before serving, pour about one-third bottle raspberry-vinaigrette dressing over salad. Serves 4 to 6.

Bratwurst Heroes

1 (6 - 8 count) package cooked bratwurst sausages
Hot dog buns
1 cup refrigerated marinara sauce   240 ml
1 (8 ounce) jar roasted bell peppers   227 g
6 - 8 slices pepper-Jack cheese

- Heat bratwurst on grill until hot and turn frequently.
  When brats are just about done, toast buns cut side
  down on grill. In saucepan, heat marinara sauce and
  place brats on toasted buns. Layer bell peppers,
  marinara sauce and cheese over bratwurst. Serves 6
  to 8.

Simple Side Dish: **Easy Three-Bean Salad**

- Serve 2 (15 ounce) cans 3-bean salad chilled or room
  temperature.

Simple Side Dish:
Favorite Relish Tray

- Check your refrigerator for dill pickles, black olives,
  green olives, green onions, radishes, celery sticks and
  carrot sticks.

1
2
3
4
5
6
7
8
9
10
11
12
13
14
15
16
17
18
19
20
21
22
23
24
25
26
27
28
29
30
31

Pasta-Turkey Salad Supper

1 (12 ounce) package tri-color spiral pasta	340 g
1 (4 ounce) can sliced ripe olives, drained	114 g
1 cup fresh broccoli florets	240 ml
1 cup fresh cauliflower	240 ml
2 small yellow squash, sliced	
1 cup halved, cherry tomatoes	240 ml
1 (8 ounce) bottle cheddar-parmesan ranch dressing	227 g
1½ pound hickory-smoked, cracked-pepper,	
turkey breast, sliced	.7 kg

• Cook pasta according to package directions. Drain
  and rinse in cold water. Place in large salad bowl
  and add olives, broccoli, cauliflower, sliced squash
  and tomatoes. Toss with dressing. Place thin slices
  of turkey breast, arranged in rows, over salad. Serve
  immediately. Serves 4.

Salad Muffins

⅓ cup sugar	80 ml
⅓ cup oil	80 ml
¾ cup milk	180 ml
2 eggs	
2 cups biscuit mix	480 ml

• Preheat oven to 400° (204° C). In mixing bowl,
  combine sugar, oil and milk. Beat in eggs and biscuit
  mix and mix well. (Mixture will be a little lumpy.) Pour
  into sprayed muffin cups two-thirds full. Bake for
  about 10 minutes or until light brown. Serves 4 to 6.

Pantry Chili Pie

2 (20 ounce) cans chili without beans	2 (567 g)
1 (13 ounce) package original corn chips	370 g
1 onion, finely chopped	
1 (12 ounce) package shredded cheddar cheese	340 g

- Preheat oven to 350° (176° C). In saucepan, heat and stir chili over low heat. In sprayed 9 x13-inch (23 x 33 cm) glass baking dish, layer half corn chips, half chili, half onions and half cheese. Repeat layers except cheese.

- Cover and bake 20 minutes, top with remaining cheese and return to oven just until cheese melts. Serve from baking dish. Serves 6 to 8.

Cottage Dip with Veggies

1 (16 ounce) carton small curd cottage cheese, drained	.5 kg
1 (1 ounce) packet dry onion soup mix	28 g
Mayonnaise	
Garlic powder	

Veggies:
Broccoli florets
Carrot sticks
Celery sticks
Cauliflower

- Blend all dip ingredients well and serve with veggies.

1
2
3
4
5
6
7
8
9
10
11
12
13
14
15
16
17
18
19
20
21
22
23
24
25
26
27
28
29
30
31

Beer-Battered Fish

1 pound flounder fillets	**.5 kg**
Oil	
1 cup biscuit mix	**240 ml**
1 (12 ounce) can beer	**340 g**

- In large saucepan or fish cooker, heat fillets in 1 to 2 inches (2.5 to 5 cm) oil. In mixing bowl, combine biscuit mix and just enough beer to make a batter (not too thin). Use tongs to dip 1 fillet at a time in batter. Place battered fillets in hot oil and cook. Drain on paper towels and fry remaining fillets. Serves 3 to 4.

Romaine Salad

1 (10 ounce) package romaine lettuce, torn	**280 g**
2 cups broccoli florets	**480 ml**
1 (1 pint) carton large fresh strawberries, quartered	**.5 kg**
½ red onion, coarsely chopped	
Raspberry-vinaigrette dressing	

- In salad bowl, toss all ingredients except dressing. When ready to serve, use raspberry-vinaigrette salad dressing (not fat-free dressing). Serves 4.

Simple Side Dish:
Easy Scalloped Potatoes

- Cook 1 (5 ounce/143 g) box cheesy scalloped potatoes with ⅔ cup (160 ml) milk and 1 tablespoon (15 ml) butter according to package directions.

Pasta, Ham and Veggies

1 (8 ounce) package bow-tie farfalle pasta	227 g
1 (10 ounce) package frozen broccoli florets, thawed	280 g
1 (10 ounce) package green peas, thawed	280 g
1 (16 ounce) jar alfredo sauce	.5 kg
1 pound cooked ham, cubed	.5 kg

• In large saucepan, cook pasta according to package directions. Add broccoli and peas during last 3 minutes of cooking time. Drain well. Add alfredo sauce and ham. Cook and stir gently over very low heat to keep ingredients from sticking to pan. Spoon into serving bowl. Serves 4.

Snappy, Spicy Tomato Soup

2 (10 ounce) cans tomato soup	2 (280 g)
1 (10 ounce) can tomato-bisque soup	280 g
1 (10 ounce) can tomatoes and green chilies	280 g
½ cup sour cream	120 ml

• In saucepan over medium heat, combine tomato soups, tomatoes and green chilies and ¾ cup (180 ml) water and heat until hot. When ready to serve (make sure soup is still very hot), stir in sour cream and pour into cups. Serves 4.

Simple Bread Idea: **Hot Garlic Bread**

• Heat 1 (12 ounce/340 g) package frozen garlic bread according to package directions.

1
2
3
4
5
6
7
8
9
10
11
12
13
14
15
16
17
18
19
20
21
22
23
24
25
26
27
28
29
30

Tuna Twisters

1 (7 ounce) can tuna, drained	198 g
⅓ cup sweet pickle relish, drained	80 ml
½ cup chipotle mayonnaise	120 ml
1 (8 ounce) package shredded mozzarella cheese	227 g
6 - 8 flour tortillas	

- Place tuna in bowl and break up chunks with fork to shred. Add pickle relish and mayonnaise and mix well. Lay all tortillas out flat and spread tuna mixture over tortillas. Top with about ⅓ cup (80 ml) shredded cheese.
- Mash down ingredients to make rolling tortillas easier. Roll tortilla. Place tortillas seam-side down on microwave-safe tray and microwave on HIGH about 15 to 20 seconds or until cheese melts. Serves 4 to 6.

Potato Salad Extra

1 (24 ounce) carton deli potato salad	680 g
3 fresh green onions, chopped	
1 (4 ounce) jar chopped pimento, drained	114 g
1 (10 ounce) jar stuffed green olives, chopped	280 g

- In serving bowl, combine potato salad, onions, pimentos and olives. Serves 4 to 6.

Simple Side Dish: **Easy Onion Rings**

- Heat 1 (20 ounce/567 g) package frozen, fried onion rings according to package directions.

1
2
3
4
5
6

Apricot-Glazed Chicken

½ cup teriyaki baste-and-glaze sauce	120 ml
⅔ teaspoon dried ginger	3 ml
1 cup apricot preserves	240 ml
8 boneless, skinless chicken breast halves, thawed	

- In small bowl, combine teriyaki glaze, ginger and apricot preserves. Mix well and set aside. Salt and pepper all chicken breast halves and place on grill over medium heat.

- Grill 18 to 22 minutes (depending on size of chicken breasts) or until chicken is fork-tender. Turn chicken once on grill. When chicken has 5 to 10 minutes remaining in cooking time, brush liberally with teriyaki-apricot mixture. Serves 6 to 8.

7
8
9
10
11
12
13
14
15

Mixed Green Salad

1 (10 ounce) package mixed salad greens	280 g
2 tomatoes, chopped	
1 (8 ounce) bottle creamy ranch salad dressing	227 g
1 (6 ounce) box seasoned croutons	168 g

- Combine chilled salad greens and chopped tomatoes. When ready to serve, toss with just enough dressing to moisten greens. Top with seasoned croutons. Serves 4 to 6.

16
17
18
19
20
21
22
23
24
25

Simple Side Dish:
Easy Twice-Baked Potatoes

- Heat 1 (16 ounce/5 kg) package frozen twice-baked potatoes according to package directions.

26
27
28
29
30

1
2
3
4
5
6
7
8
9
10
11
12
13
14
15
16
17
18
19
20
21
22
23
24
25
26
27
28
29
30

Walnut-Cream Sandwiches

2 (8 ounce) packages cream cheese, softened	2 (227 g)
½ cup mayonnaise	120 ml
1 teaspoon dijon-style mustard	5 ml
6 slices bacon, cooked, crumbled	
¾ cup finely chopped walnuts	180 ml

• In mixing bowl, beat cream cheese, mayonnaise and mustard until creamy. Fold in bacon and chopped walnuts and mix well. Spread on pumpernickel or rye bread and slice in thirds. Serves 4 to 6.

Tomato-French Onion Soup

1 (10 ounce) can fiesta nacho cheese soup	280 g
2 (10 ounce) cans French onion soup	2 (280 g)
Croutons	
Grated parmesan cheese	

• In saucepan, combine soups and 2 soup cans water and heat thoroughly. Serve in bowls topped with croutons and sprinkle with cheese. Serves 4 to 6.

September

1st Monday – Labor Day
Sunday after – Grandparents Day
11 – Patriot Day
17 – Citizenship Day

Beef, Beans and Greens

⅓ **pound cooked deli roast beef, julienned**	**150 g**
1 (15 ounce) can 3-bean salad, chilled, drained	**425 g**
1 (8 ounce) package cubed mozzarella cheese	**227 g**
1 (10 ounce) bag mixed salad greens	
with Italian dressing	**280 g**

- In large salad bowl, lightly toss beef, 3-bean salad and cheese. Pour in just enough dressing to moisten greens. Serves 4.

Caramel-Apple Delight

3 (2 ounce) Snickers® candy bars, frozen	**3 (57 g)**
2 apples, chilled, chopped	
1 (12 ounce) carton whipped topping	**340 g**
1 (3 ounce) package dry, instant vanilla pudding	**84 g**

- Smash frozen candy bars in wrappers with hammer. Combine all ingredients in crystal salad bowl and stir very well. Refrigerate. Serves 4.

Simple Side Dish:
Fast Pimento Cheese Sandwiches

- Spread 1 (16 ounce/.5 kg) carton pimento cheese on 1 loaf dark rye bread slices and serve.

1
2
3
4
5
6
7
8
9
10
11
12
13
14
15
16
17
18
19
20
21
22
23
24
25
26
27
28
29
30

Spicy Catfish Amandine

6 - 8 catfish fillets	
¼ cup (½ stick) butter, melted	**60 ml**
1½ teaspoons Creole seasoning	**7 ml**
½ cup sliced almonds, toasted	**120 ml**

- Preheat oven to 350° (176° C). Dip each fillet in butter and arrange fillets in sprayed 9 x 13-inch (23 x 33 cm) baking dish. Sprinkle with Creole seasoning and almonds. Bake for 20 to 25 minutes or until fish flakes easily when tested with fork. Serves 6 to 8.

Cheese-Topped Tomatoes

Shredded lettuce	
2 - 3 vine-ripened tomatoes	
1 (8 ounce) package shredded mozzarella cheese	**227 g**

- Place shredded lettuce on individual salad plates. Slice tomatoes and place 2 or 3 slices on each plate. Cover tomatoes with mozzarella cheese. Serves 6 to 8.

Simple Side Dish: **Easy Tater Puffs**

- Heat 1 (32 ounce/1 kg) package frozen tater puffs according to package directions.

September

1st Monday - Labor Day
Sunday after - Grandparents Day
11 - Patriot Day
17 - Citizenship Day

Turkey-Croissants

1 (8 ounce) package cream cheese, softened	227 g
¼ cup orange marmalade	60 ml
1 pound thinly sliced deli turkey	.5 kg
6 large croissants, split	

- Beat cream cheese and orange marmalade in mixing bowl with mixer, spread evenly on cut sides of croissants and turkey slices. Place top on croissant. Serves 4.

Spicy Tomato Soup

2 (10 ounce) cans tomato soup	2 (280 g)
1 (16 ounce) can Mexican stewed tomatoes	.5 kg
Sour cream	
½ pound bacon, fried, drained, crumbled	227 g

- In saucepan, combine soup and stewed tomatoes and heat. To serve, place dollop of sour cream on each bowl of soup and sprinkle crumbled bacon over sour cream. Serves 4.

Cheese-Topped Pear Slices

Shredded lettuce	
1 - 2 (15 ounce) cans pear halves, drained	1 - 2 (425 g)
Small curd cottage cheese	
Honey-mustard dressing	

- On individual salad plates, place shredded lettuce and 2 pear halves. Top each pear half with heaping tablespoon (15 ml) cottage cheese and pour small amount dressing over cottage cheese. Serves 4.

1
2
3
4
5
6
7
8
9
10
11
12
13
14
15
16
17
18
19
20
21
22
23
24
25
26
27
28
29
30

Spinach-Pecan Salad

1 (10 ounce) package baby spinach	280 g
2 eggs, hard-boiled, sliced	
½ cup chopped pecans, toasted	120 ml
1 (8 ounce) package pre-cooked bacon, crumbled	227 g
¼ cup crumbled blue cheese	60 ml
Italian salad dressing	

- In salad bowl, combine spinach, sliced eggs, pecans, bacon and blue cheese and toss. Drizzle with Italian salad dressing. Serves 4.

Zucchini Patties

1½ cups grated zucchini	360 ml
1 egg, beaten	
2 tablespoons flour	30 ml
⅓ cup finely minced onion	80 ml

- Mix all ingredients and heat skillet with about 3 tablespoons (45 ml) oil. Drop zucchini mixture by tablespoons into skillet at medium-high heat. Turn and brown both sides. Remove and drain on paper towels. Serves 4.

Salad Muffins

⅓ cup sugar	80 ml
⅓ cup oil	80 ml
¾ cup milk	180 ml
2 eggs	
2 cups biscuit mix	480 ml

- Preheat oven to 400° (204° C). In mixing bowl, combine sugar, oil and milk. Beat in eggs and biscuit mix. Mix well; mixture will be a little lumpy. Pour into sprayed muffin cups two-thirds full. Bake for about 10 minutes or until light brown. Serves 4 to 6.

Oven-Fried Catfish

4 - 6 catfish fillets	
1½ cups buttermilk*	360 ml
1 cup seasoned breadcrumbs	240 ml
2 cups crushed corn flakes	480 ml

- Preheat oven to 400° (204° C). Dry catfish fillets with paper towels. Place buttermilk in plastic freezer bag, add catfish fillets and turn to coat fish well. Seal and marinate about 20 to 30 minutes. Remove fillets from buttermilk and discard buttermilk.

- Sprinkle fillets with 2 teaspoons (10 ml) each of salt and pepper. Place breadcrumbs and crushed corn flakes in shallow bowl, dredge fillets in mixture and press mixture gently onto each fillet. Place on sprayed baking sheet and bake 35 minutes or until fish flakes easily. Serve immediately. Serves 4 to 6.

TIP: To make buttermilk, mix 1 cup (240 ml) milk with 1 tablespoon (15 ml) lemon juice or vinegar and let milk rest about 10 minutes.

Green Pea Salad

1 (16 ounce) bag frozen green peas, thawed	.5 kg
1 bunch fresh green onions with tops, chopped	
½ cup chopped celery	120 ml
½ cup sweet pickle relish, drained	120 ml
Mayonnaise	

- Mix peas, onions, celery and relish. Stir in enough mayonnaise to hold salad together and chill.
- Serves 4 to 6.

1
2
3
4
5
6
7
8
9
10
11
12
13
14
15
16
17
18
19
20
21
22
23
24
25
26
27
28
29
30

Creamy Mushroom Chicken

4 boneless, skinless chicken breast halves	
1 (10 ounce) can cream of mushroom soup	280 g
1 (4 ounce) can sliced mushrooms, drained	114 g
½ cup milk	120 ml

- Sprinkle chicken liberally with a little salt and pepper. In skillet over high heat with a little oil, brown chicken on both sides. While chicken browns, combine mushroom soup, mushrooms and milk in saucepan and heat just enough to mix well. Pour over chicken breasts, reduce heat to low and simmer covered for 15 minutes. Serves 4.

Seasoned Squash and Onions

8 yellow squash, sliced	
2 onions, chopped	
¼ cup (½ stick) butter	60 ml
1 cup grated American cheese	240 ml

- Cook squash and onion in small amount of water until tender and drain. Add butter and cheese, toss and serve hot. Serves 4 to 6.

Creamy Biscuits

2½ cups biscuit mix	600 ml
1 (8 ounce) carton whipping cream	227 g

- Preheat oven to 375° (190° C). Mix biscuit mix and cream. Place on floured board. Kneed several times. Pat out to ½-inch (1.2 cm) thickness. Cut with biscuit cutter or 2-inch (5 cm) glass and place biscuits on non-stick baking sheet. Bake for 12 to 15 minutes or until light brown. Serves 4 to 6.

Roasted Chicken and Vegetables

1 (10 ounce) can cream of mushroom soup	280 g
2 teaspoons dried oregano leaves	10 ml
8 - 10 new red potatoes, halved	
1 (16 ounce) package fresh baby carrots	.5 kg
4 large boneless, skinless chicken breast halves	

• Preheat oven to 375° (190° C). In sprayed 9 x 13-inch (23 x 33 cm) baking pan, combine soup, oregano leaves, potatoes and carrots. Place chicken breast halves over vegetables and season with a little salt and pepper. Bake uncovered for 55 minutes or until chicken is no longer pink. Serves 4 to 6.

Frozen Dessert Salad

1 (8 ounce) package cream cheese, softened	227 g
1 cup powdered sugar	240 ml
1 (10 ounce) box frozen strawberries, thawed	280 g
1 (15 ounce) can crushed pineapple, drained	425 g
1 (8 ounce) carton whipped topping	227 g

• In mixing bowl, beat cream cheese and sugar. Fold in remaining ingredients. (This will be even better if you stir in ¾ cup (180 ml) chopped pecans.) Pour into sprayed 9 x 9-inch (23 x 23 cm) baking pan and freeze. Cut into squares to serve. Serves 4 to 6.

September

1st Monday – Labor Day
Sunday after – Grandparents Day
11 – Patriot Day
17 – Citizenship Day

1
2
3
4
5
6
7
8
9
10
11
12
13
14
15
16
17
18
19
20
21
22
23
24
25
26
27
28
29
30

Cheese Ravioli and Zucchini

1 (25 ounce) package fresh cheese-filled ravioli	708 g
4 small zucchini, sliced	
2 ribs celery, sliced diagonally	
1 (16 ounce) jar marinara sauce	.5 kg

- Cook ravioli according to package directions and drain. Return to saucepan and keep warm. (If you prefer, you can use frozen chicken ravioli.) Place zucchini and celery in another saucepan and pour marinara sauce over vegetables.

- Cook and stir over medium-high heat about 8 minutes or until vegetables are tender-crisp. Spoon marinara-vegetable mixture over ravioli and toss gently. Pour into serving bowl and garnish with shredded parmesan, if desired. Serves 4 to 6.

Green Salad

1 (10 ounce) package chopped romaine lettuce	280 g
1 seedless cucumber, sliced	
½ cup dried sweetened cranberries	120 ml
1 (8 ounce) bottle balsamic-vinaigrette salad dressing	227 g

- In salad bowl, combine romaine, cucumber and cranberries. Serve dressing on the side. Serves 4 to 6.

Stuffed Pork Chops

4 (¾ inch) thick boneless center-cut pork chops   4 (1.8 cm)

Stuffing:
2 slices rye bread, diced	
⅓ cup chopped onion	**80 ml**
⅓ cup chopped celery	**80 ml**
⅓ cup dried, diced apples	**80 ml**
½ cup chicken broth	**120 ml**
½ teaspoon dried thyme	**2 ml**

- Preheat oven to 400° (204° C). Make 1-inch (2.5 cm) wide slit on side of pork chop and insert knife blade to other side, but not through pork chop. Sweep knife back and forth and carefully cut pocket opening larger.
- In bowl, combine rye bread pieces, onion, celery, apples, broth and thyme and mix well. Stuff chops with stuffing mixture and press to use all stuffing mixture. Place chops in heavy skillet with a little oil and saute each chop about 3 minutes on each side. Transfer to non-stick baking dish and bake uncovered for 10 minutes. Serves 4.

Whipped Sweet Potatoes

2 (15 ounce) cans sweet potatoes	**2 (425 g)**
¼ cup (½ stick) butter, melted	**60 ml**
¼ cup orange juice	**60 ml**
1 cup miniature marshmallows	**240 ml**

- Preheat oven to 350° (176 C). Combine sweet potatoes, butter, orange juice and ½ teaspoon (2 ml) salt in mixing bowl. Beat until fluffy. Fold in marshmallows. Spoon into sprayed 2-quart (2 L) baking dish. Bake uncovered for 25 minutes. Serves 4.

1
2
3
4
5
6
7
8
9
10
11
12
13
14
15
16
17
18
19
20
21
22
23
24
25
26
27
28
29
30

Pasta Salad Bowl

1 (16 ounce) package bow-tie pasta	.5 kg
1 (16 ounce) package frozen green peas, thawed	.5 kg
½ cup sliced scallions	120 ml
1 seedless cucumber, thinly sliced	
1 pound deli ham, cut in strips	.5 kg

• Cook pasta according to package directions. Drain and cool under cold running water and drain again. Transfer to serving bowl and add peas, scallions, cucumber slices and ham strips.

Dressing:

⅔ cup mayonnaise	160 ml
¼ cup cider vinegar	60 ml
1 teaspoon sugar	5 ml
2 teaspoons dried dill	10 ml

• In small bowl, combine all dressing ingredients and spoon over salad. Toss to mix and coat well. Refrigerate. Serves 6 to 8.

Party Sandwiches

1 (8 ounce) package cream cheese, softened	227 g
⅓ cup chopped stuffed olives	80 ml
2 tablespoons olive juice	30 ml
⅓ cup chopped pecans	80 ml
6 slices bacon, cooked, crumbled	
Party rye bread	

• Beat cream cheese with mixer until smooth and stir in olives, olive juice, pecans and bacon. Spread on party rye bread. Serves 6 to 8.

Moist and Crunchy Baked Chicken

½ cup (1 stick) butter, melted	120 ml
2 tablespoons mayonnaise	30 ml
2 tablespoons white wine Worcestershire sauce	30 ml
1 (6 ounce) can french-fried onions, crushed	168 g
6 boneless, skinless chicken breasts halves	

- Preheat oven to 375° (190° C). In shallow bowl, combine melted butter, mayonnaise and Worcestershire. Place crushed onions in another shallow bowl. Dry chicken breasts with paper towels and dip into butter mixture. Dredge each chicken breast in crushed onions.
- Place in sprayed 11 x 15-inch (30 x 38 cm) baking pan and arrange so that pieces do not touch. Bake 25 minutes or until chicken juices run clear. Serves 4 to 6.

Sunny Lime Pie

2 (6 ounce) cartons key lime pie yogurt	2 (168 g)
1 (3 ounce) package dry lime gelatin	84 g
1 (8 ounce) carton whipped topping	227 g
1 (6 ounce) graham cracker piecrust	168 g

- In bowl, combine yogurt and lime gelatin and mix well. Fold in whipped topping, spread in piecrust and freeze. Take out of freezer 20 minutes before slicing. Serves 4 to 6.

Simple Side Dish: Easy Mashed Potatoes

- Cook 1 (6.5 ounce/180 g) box mashed potato mix according to package directions.

1
2
3
4
5
6
7
8
9
10
11
12
13
14
15
16
17
18
19
20
21
22
23
24
25
26
27
28
29
30

Cracked-Pepper Turkey Breast

1 (2½ - 3 pound) cracked-pepper turkey breast	**1.2 kg**
1 (16 ounce) jar hot chipotle salsa	**.5 kg**
1 (8 ounce) package shredded 4-cheese blend	**227 g**

- Slice enough turkey for each person. Spoon 1 heaping tablespoon (15 ml) chipotle salsa over each slice and sprinkle a little cheese over top. Serves 6 to 8.

Pasta Salad

1 (7.5 ounce) box Suddenly Pasta Salad®	**210 g**
½ cup mayonnaise	**120 ml**
2 ribs celery, chopped	
½ sweet red bell pepper, chopped	

- Boil pasta in 3 quarts (3 L) water for about 15 minutes, drain and rinse in cold water. Stir in seasoning mix, mayonnaise, celery and bell pepper and refrigerate. Serves 4 to 6.

Simple Side Dish: **Fast Corn In Butter Sauce**

- Heat 1 (19 ounce/538 g) package frozen niblet corn in butter sauce according to package directions.

◇ September ✏

1st Monday – Labor Day
Sunday after – Grandparents Day
11 – Patriot Day
17 – Citizenship Day

Family Filet Mignon

1½ pounds very lean ground beef	.7 kg
1 (1 ounce) packet dry onion soup mix	28 g
1 teaspoon minced garlic	2 ml
6 slices bacon	

- In bowl, combine beef, onion soup mix and garlic and mix well.   Form into 6 thick patties that are flat on top. Wrap slice of bacon around outside of each patty and secure with toothpick. Place in shallow baking pan and broil about 10 minutes on each side. Serves 4 to 6.

Steamed Broccoli with Cheese

2 (16 ounce) packages frozen broccoli florets, thawed	2 (.5 kg)
1 (10 ounce) can cheddar cheese soup	280 g
1 (3 ounce) can french-fried onion rings	84 g

- Steam broccoli according to package directions and drain well. Sprinkle with a little salt and pepper. In small saucepan over low heat, stir and heat soup until hot. When ready to serve, place broccoli in serving bowl, spoon cheese soup over broccoli and top with onion rings. Serves 4 to 6.

Simple Side Dish: **New Parmesan Couscous**

- Cook 1 (6 ounce/168 g) package parmesan couscous mix according to package directions.

1
2
3
4
5
6
7
8
9
10
11
12
13
14
15
16
17
18
19
20
21
22
23
24
25
26
27
28
29
30

Taco Chicken Over Spanish Rice

1¼ cups flour	300 ml
2 (1 ounce) packets taco seasoning	2 (28 g)
2 large eggs, beaten	
8 boneless, skinless chicken breast halves	
2 (15 ounce) cans Spanish rice	2 (425 g)
1 cup shredded Mexican 4-cheese blend	240 ml

- Preheat oven to 350° (176° C). Place flour and taco seasoning in large shallow bowl. Place eggs and 3 tablespoons (45 ml) water in another shallow bowl and beat together. Dip each chicken breast in egg mixture. Dredge in flour-taco mixture and press to apply lots of flour mixture.

- Place in sprayed 10 x 15-inch (25 x 38 cm) baking pan and arrange so that chicken pieces do not touch. Bake 55 to 60 minutes or until juices run clear. About 10 minutes before chicken is done, place Spanish rice in saucepan and stir in cheese. Heat, stirring constantly, just until cheese melts. Spoon onto serving platter and place chicken pieces over hot rice. Serves 6 to 8.

Greens and Avocado Toss

1 (10 ounce) package tossed green salad	280 g
2 avocados, peeled, sliced	
1 seedless cucumber, sliced	
Honey-mustard salad dressing	

- Combine greens, avocados and cucumber slices and toss with dressing. Serves 4 to 6.

Cauliflower-Bacon Salad

1 large head cauliflower, cut into florets	
1 red and 1 green bell pepper, chopped	
1½ cups cubed mozzarella cheese	360 ml
1 (8 ounce) package pre-cooked, crumbled bacon	227 g
1 bunch fresh green onions, sliced	

Dressing:

1 cup mayonnaise	240 ml
1 tablespoon sugar	15 ml
1 tablespoon lemon juice	15 ml

- In plastic bowl with lid, combine cauliflower, bell peppers, cheese, crumbled bacon and green onions. In small bowl, combine mayonnaise, sugar, lemon juice and 1 teaspoon (5 ml) salt and stir to blend well. Spoon dressing over salad and toss to coat. Cover and refrigerate several hours before serving. Serves 4 to 6.

Simple Side Dish: **Easy Fried Shrimp**

- Fry 1 (16 ounce/.5 kg) package frozen breaded shrimp in hot oil according to package directions.

Simple Side Dish: **Easy Key Lime Pie**

- Let 1 (36 ounce/1 kg) frozen key lime pie stand for about 10 minutes before slicing.

1
2
3
4
5
6
7
8
9
10
11
12
13
14
15
16
17
18
19
20
21
22
23
24
25
26
27
28
29
30

Philly Meatball Sandwiches

1 tablespoon oil	15 ml
1 (16 ounce) package frozen chopped onions and	
bell peppers	.5 kg
½ (18 ounce) package frozen, cooked meatballs	½ (510 g)
6 hoagie rolls, toasted	
1 (8 ounce) package shredded cheddar cheese	227 g

• In skillet with oil on medium heat, cook and stir onions and bell peppers for 5 minutes. Add meatballs, cover and cook, stirring occasionally, about 12 minutes or until meatballs are thoroughly hot. Spoon mixture into toasted rolls and sprinkle cheese over meatballs. Serve hot. Serves 4 to 6.

Seasoned Cucumber Slices

2 seedless cucumbers, sliced	
1 (8 ounce) carton sour cream	227 g
2 tablespoons lemon juice	30 ml
2 tablespoons sugar	30 ml

• Combine all ingredients and a little salt, toss and chill. Serves 4 to 6.

Simple Side Dish: **Easy Caesar Pasta Salad**

• Prepare 1 (7 ounce/198 g) box Suddenly Caesar Pasta Salad® according to package directions.

Pimento Cheese-Stuffed Fried Chicken

4 skinless, boneless chicken breast halves	
½ cup milk	120 ml
1 large egg, beaten	
2 cups seasoned breadcrumbs	480 ml
1 (16 ounce) carton prepared pimento cheese	.5 kg

- Preheat oven to 350° (176° C). Dry chicken breasts with paper towels and sprinkle well with salt and pepper. Combine milk and beaten egg in shallow bowl and mix well. Place breadcrumbs in second shallow bowl.

- Dip chicken in milk mixture and dredge in breadcrumbs. In large skillet over medium-high heat, pour oil to ⅛-inch (.4 cm) depth and cook chicken about 10 to 12 minutes on each side. Transfer to baking sheet.

- Hold chicken with tongs and cut slit in 1 side of each chicken breast to form pocket. Spoon about ¼ cup (60 ml) pimento cheese into each pocket and bake about 3 minutes or until cheese melts. Serves 4 to 6.

Chive-Potato Souffle

3 eggs, separated	
2 cups cooked instant mashed potatoes	480 ml
½ cup sour cream	120 ml
2 heaping tablespoons chopped chives	30 ml

- Preheat oven to 350° (176° C). Beat egg whites until stiff and set aside. Beat yolks until smooth and add to potatoes. Fold beaten egg whites, sour cream, chives and 1 teaspoon (5 ml) salt into potato-egg yolk mixture and pour into sprayed 2-quart baking dish. Bake for 45 minutes. Serves 4.

1
2
3
4
5
6
7
8
9
10
11
12
13
14
15
16
17
18
19
20
21
22
23
24
25
26
27
28
29
30

Spinach-Chicken Salad

1 (10 ounce) package baby spinach	280 g
1 seedless cucumber, sliced	
1 red delicious apple with peel, thinly sliced	
1 bunch fresh green onions, sliced	
3 cups coarsely shredded rotisserie chicken meat	710 ml

- In salad bowl, combine spinach, cucumber, apple slices, green onions and chicken. Toss to mix well.

Dressing:

⅓ cup red wine vinegar	80 ml
3 tablespoons olive oil	45 ml
1 tablespoon dijon-style mustard	15 ml
½ teaspoon dried thyme	2 ml
1 teaspoon sugar	5 ml

- In saucepan, combine all dressing ingredients and heat just until thoroughly hot. Pour over salad and toss until salad coats evenly. Serve immediately. Serves 4.

Eggplant Fritters

1 medium eggplant	
1 egg, beaten	
3 tablespoons flour	45 ml
½ teaspoon baking powder	2 ml
Oil	

- Peel and slice eggplant, steam until tender and drain. Mash eggplant until smooth. Add egg, flour, ½ teaspoon (2 ml) salt and baking powder and mix well. Form into patties and deep fry in hot oil. Serves 4.

Spaghetti Toss

1 (10 ounce) package thin spaghetti	280 g
1 (10 ounce) package frozen sugar snap peas	280 g
2 tablespoons butter	30 ml
3 cups rotisserie-cooked chicken	710 ml
1 (11 ounce) can mandarin oranges, drained	312 g
⅔ cup stir-fry sauce	160 ml

- Cook spaghetti according to package directions. Stir in sugar snap peas and cook 1 additional minute. Drain and stir in butter until butter melts. Spoon into bowl. Cut chicken into strips and add to spaghetti with oranges and stir-fry sauce. Serves 4 to 6.

Swiss Salad

1 large head romaine lettuce	
1 bunch fresh green onions with tops, chopped	
1 (8 ounce) package shredded Swiss cheese	227 g
½ cup sunflower seeds	120 ml

Dressing:

⅔ cup salad oil	160 ml
⅓ cup red wine vinegar	80 ml

- Tear lettuce into bite-size pieces. Add onions, cheese, sunflower seeds and toss. Mix all ingredients plus 1 tablespoon (15 ml) salt for dressing and refrigerate. Serves 4 to 6.

1
2
3
4
5
6
7
8
9
10
11
12
13
14
15
16
17
18
19
20
21
22
23
24
25
26
27
28
29
30

Creamy Tarragon Chicken

1½ cups flour	360 ml
6 boneless, skinless chicken breast halves	
2 tablespoons oil	30 ml
1 (14 ounce) can chicken broth	396 g
1 cup milk	240 ml
2 teaspoons dried tarragon	10 ml
1 (4 ounce) can sliced mushrooms, drained	114 g
2 (8 ounce) packages roasted-chicken rice	2 (227 g)

- Mix flour and a little salt and pepper on wax paper and coat chicken. Save extra flour. Heat oil in large skillet over medium-high heat and cook chicken breasts, turning once, about 10 minutes or until light brown. Transfer to plate.

- In same skillet, stir in 2 tablespoons (30 ml) flour-salt mixture. Whisk in chicken broth, milk and tarragon and heat, stirring constantly, until bubbly. Add mushrooms and return chicken to skillet. Cover and simmer for 10 to 15 minutes or until sauce thickens.

- Microwave rice in package according to package directions and place on serving platter. Spoon chicken and sauce over rice. Serves 4 to 6.

Stained-Glass Fruit Salad

2 (20 ounce) cans peach pie filling	2 (567 g)
3 bananas, sliced	
1 (16 ounce) package frozen unsweetened strawberries, drained	.5 kg
1 (20 ounce) can pineapple tidbits, drained	567 g

- Drain all fruits except peach pie filling. Mix all fruits, chill and place in pretty crystal bowl. Refrigerate overnight. Serves 6 to 8.

Chicken and the Works

6 boneless, skinless chicken breast halves	
Paprika	
2 (10 ounce) cans cream of chicken soup	**2 (280 g)**
2 cups instant white rice	**480 ml**
1 (10 ounce) package frozen green peas, thawed	**280 g**

- Sprinkle chicken with a little pepper and paprika and brown in large, 12-inch (32 cm) skillet with a little oil. Reduce heat, cover and simmer about 15 minutes. Transfer chicken to plate and keep warm.

- Add soup, 2 cups (480 ml) water and mix well. Heat to boiling and stir in rice and green peas. Top with chicken breasts, cover and simmer over low heat about 10 minutes. Serves 4 to 6.

Tossed Green Salad

1 (10 ounce) package fancy salad greens mix	**280 g**
1 seedless cucumber, sliced	
1 bunch fresh green onions, sliced	
Seasoned croutons	
Blue cheese dressing	

- In salad bowl, combine greens, cucumber, green onions and toss with blue cheese dressing. Add croutons, if you like. Serves 4 to 6.

Simple Bread Idea: **Onion Rolls**

- Heat 1 (16 ounce/.5 kg) package bakery dinner rolls and serve with butter.

Sirloin In Rich Mushroom Sauce

1 pound boneless beef sirloin, cut in strips	.5 kg
1 (14 ounce) can beef broth	396 g
2 teaspoons minced garlic	10 ml
1 (10 ounce) can cream of mushroom soup	280 g
1 (8 ounce) can sliced mushrooms	227 g
1 (8 ounce) package angel hair pasta	227 g

- Brown steak strips in large non-stick skillet with 2 tablespoons (30 ml) oil over medium-high heat. (Sirloin will cook tender in less cooking time than cheaper cuts of meat.) Add beef broth, garlic, generous amount of pepper and ½ soup can of water.
- Heat to boiling, reduce heat and simmer 15 minutes. Spoon mushroom soup, mushrooms and 1 cup (240 ml) water in saucepan and heat just enough to mix well. Pour over steak and simmer 15 minutes. Serve over angel hair pasta. Serves 4 to 6.

Almond Green Beans

⅓ cup slivered almonds	80 ml
¼ cup (½ stick) butter	60 ml
1 teaspoon garlic salt	5 ml
2 tablespoons lemon juice	30 ml
1 (16 ounce) package frozen green beans	.5 kg

- In saucepan, saute almonds in butter. Add garlic salt and lemon juice and cook until almonds turn golden brown. Add green beans to almond-butter mixture and add ⅓ cup (80 ml) water. Cook for about 10 minutes until beans are tender-crisp. Serves 4 to 6.

Crunchy Chip Chicken

1½ cups crushed sour cream potato chips	360 ml
1 tablespoon dried parsley	15 ml
1 egg, beaten	
1 tablespoon Worcestershire sauce	15 ml
4 large boneless, skinless chicken breast halves	
¼ cup oil	60 ml

- In shallow bowl, combine potato chips and parsley. In another shallow bowl, combine beaten egg, Worcestershire and 1 tablespoon (15 ml) water. Dip chicken pieces in egg mixture, then dredge chicken in potato chip mixture.
- Heat oil in heavy skillet and fry chicken pieces for about 10 minutes. Turn each piece over and cook another 10 minutes until golden brown or until juices are no longer pink. Serves 4 to 6.

Macaroni, Cheese and Tomatoes

2 cups elbow macaroni	480 ml
1 (15 ounce) can stewed tomatoes with liquid	425 g
1 (8 ounce) package shredded cheddar cheese	227 g
2 tablespoons sugar	30 ml
1 (6 ounce) package cheese slices	168 g

- Preheat oven to 350° (176° C). Cook macaroni according to package directions and drain. In large mixing bowl, combine macaroni, tomatoes, shredded cheese, sugar, ¼ cup (60 ml) water and a little salt and mix well. Pour into sprayed 9 x 13-inch (23 x 33 cm) baking dish and place cheese slices on top. Bake for 30 minutes or until bubbly. Serves 4 to 6.

1
2
3
4
5
6

Salisbury Steak and Gravy

1½ pounds extra-lean ground beef	.7 kg
1 egg, beaten	
½ cup chili sauce	120 ml
¾ cup seasoned breadcrumbs	180 ml

7
8
9
10

- In medium bowl, combine all steak ingredients and mix well. Shape into 6 to 8 patties ¾-inch (1.8 cm) thick. In large skillet with a little oil, brown patties about 5 minutes on each side. Set aside in warm oven.

11
12
13
14

Brown Gravy:

2 (14 ounce) cans beef broth	2 (396 g)
¼ cup dry red wine	60 ml
2 tablespoons cornstarch	30 ml
1 (8 ounce) can sliced mushrooms, drained	227 g

15
16
17
18

- Add beef broth, wine and cornstarch to skillet and stir until cornstarch mixture dissolves. Cook and stir over high heat until mixture thickens. Add mushrooms and cook until hot and gravy bubbles. Spoon gravy over steaks to serve. Serves 4 to 6.

19
20

Crunchy Green Beans

21
22
23
24

3 (15 ounce) cans cut green beans, drained	3 (425 g)
2 (10 ounce) cans cream of mushroom soup	2 (280 g)
2 (8 ounce) cans water chestnuts, drained, chopped	2 (227 g)
1 (6 ounce) can french-fried onion rings	168 g

25
26
27
28

- Preheat oven to 350° (176° C). Combine green beans, soup and water chestnuts and spoon into sprayed 9 x 13-inch (23 x 33 cm) baking dish. Sprinkle onion rings over casserole and bake 20 minutes or until hot. Serves 6 to 8.

29
30

Lemony Chicken And Noodles

1 (8 ounce) package wide egg noodles	227 g
1 (10 ounce) package frozen sugar snap peas, thawed	280 g
1 (14 ounce) can chicken broth	396 g
1 teaspoon fresh grated lemon peel	5 ml
2 cups cubed, skinless rotisserie chicken meat	480 ml
½ cup whipping cream	120 ml

- In large saucepan with boiling water, cook noodles according to package directions, but add snap peas to noodles 1 minute before noodles are done. Drain and return to saucepan. Add chicken broth, lemon peel, chicken pieces and ½ teaspoon (2 ml) each of salt and pepper. Heat, stirring constantly, until thoroughly hot. Over low heat, gently stir in cream. Serve hot. Serves 4 to 6.

Calypso Coleslaw

1 (16 ounce) package shredded cabbage	.5 kg
1 bunch green onions with tops, sliced	
2 cups cubed cheddar or mozzarella cheese	480 ml
¼ cup sliced ripe olives	60 ml
1 (15 ounce) can whole kernel corn with peppers, drained	425 g

- Combine all slaw ingredients and add few sprinkles of salt.

Dressing:

1 cup mayonnaise	240 ml
2 tablespoons sugar	30 ml
1 tablespoon mustard	15 ml
2 tablespoons vinegar	30 ml

- Combine dressing ingredients and mix well. Toss dressing and slaw, cover and refrigerate. Serves 4.

1
2
3
4
5
6
7
8
9
10
11
12
13
14
15
16
17
18
19
20
21
22
23
24
25
26
27
28
29
30

Spaghetti and Meatballs

1 (18 ounce) package frozen meatballs, thawed	510 g
1 (28 ounce) jar spaghetti sauce	794 g
1 (8 ounce) package spaghetti	227 g
1 (5 ounce) package grated parmesan cheese	143 g

- In large microwave baking dish, heat meatballs on HIGH for 10 to 12 minutes. Stir twice. Cook spaghetti according to package directions and drain well. Pour onto serving plate and spoon meatball sauce over spaghetti. Top with cheese. Serves 4.

Spring Greens

1 (10 ounce) package spring-mix salad greens	280 g
1 seedless cucumber, sliced	
1 bunch red radishes, sliced	
1 orange bell pepper, chopped	
1 (16 ounce) jar refrigerated honey-mustard	
salad dressing	.5 kg

- In salad bowl, toss greens, cucumber, radishes and bell pepper. Add dressing as needed. Serves 4.

Toasted French Bread

1 loaf sliced French bread
Butter
Garlic powder

- Butter each slice of bread and sprinkle a little garlic powder on each slice. Place under broiler and toast until light brown. Serves 4 to 6.

Speedy Gonzales Special

1½ pounds lean ground beef	.7 kg
1 (1.5 ounce) packet taco seasoning mix	45 g
½ teaspoon cayenne pepper, optional	2 ml
1 (4.5 ounce, 12 count) package tostada shells	128 g

- Preheat oven to 300° (148° C). In skillet, brown and crumble ground beef. Add 1 cup (240 ml) water, taco seasoning and cayenne pepper and heat to boiling. Reduce heat and simmer about 12 minutes. While beef cooks, heat 6 to 8 tostada shells on baking sheet at 300° (148° C).

Topping:

1 (10 ounce) package shredded lettuce	280 g
2 - 3 vine-ripened tomatoes, chopped, drained	
1 (8 ounce) package shredded cheddar cheese	227 g
1 (16 ounce) bottle chunky salsa	.5 kg

- In serving bowl, combine about 2 cups (480 ml) shredded lettuce, chopped tomatoes and cheese and toss. When ready to serve, place about 2 heaping tablespoons (30 ml) beef on each shell and spread out. Top with heaping spoonfuls lettuce-cheese mixture. Let each person add salsa. Serve immediately. Serves 4 to 6.

Sunshine Salad

3 (11 ounce) cans Mexicorn®, drained chilled	3 (312 g)
1 (15 ounce) can green peas, drained, chilled	425 g
1 (15 ounce) can wax beans, rinsed, drained, chilled	425 g
1 (8 ounce) bottle Italian dressing, chilled	227 g

- In bowl with lid, combine corn, peas and beans. Stir in Italian dressing and toss. Refrigerate. Serves 6 to 8.

1
2
3
4
5
6
7
8
9
10
11
12
13
14
15
16
17
18
19
20
21
22
23
24
25
26
27
28
29
30
31

Beef Patties
in Creamy Onion Sauce

1½ pounds lean ground beef	.7 kg
½ cup chunky salsa	120 ml
1⅓ cups buttery cracker crumbs	320 ml
2 (10 ounce) cans cream of onion soup	2 (280 g)
Biscuits	

- In large bowl, combine beef, salsa and cracker crumbs and form into 6 to 7 patties. In sprayed skillet over medium heat, brown patties. Reduce heat and add ¼ cup (240 ml) water. Cover and simmer 15 minutes.

- In same skillet, combine onion soup, 1 teaspoon (5 ml) pepper and ½ cup (120 ml) water or milk. Heat and mix well. Pour onion sauce over beef patties and simmer another 5 minutes. Serve over hot biscuits. Serves 4 to 6.

Green Bean Casserole

2 (15 ounce) cans cut green beans, drained	2 (425 g)
1 (10 ounce) can cream of mushroom soup	280 g
1 cup shredded cheddar cheese	240 ml
1 (3 ounce) can french-fried onion rings	84 g

- Preheat oven to 375° (190° C). Combine green beans, soup and cheese and spoon into sprayed 7 x 11-inch (18 x 28 cm) baking dish. Top with onion rings and bake 20 minutes. Serves 4 to 6.

Vegetable-Stuffed Potatoes

2 (10 ounce) cans fiesta nacho cheese soup   **2 (280 g)**
1 (16 ounce) package frozen mixed stew
    vegetables, cooked, drained   **.5 kg**
8 baking potatoes, washed

- In large saucepan, heat fiesta nacho cheese soup, add cooked vegetables and mix well. Prick potatoes with fork and cook in microwave until insides are tender. Slightly mash flesh in each potato and spoon hearty amount of soup-vegetable mixture onto each split potato. If necessary, warm filled potatoes in microwave 1 to 2 minutes. Serves 6 to 8.

Simple Main Dish:
Seasoned Turkey Breast Slices

- Slice 1 (2 pound/1 kg) hickory smoked cracker-pepper turkey breast and serve hot or cold.

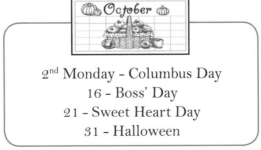

2nd Monday – Columbus Day
16 – Boss' Day
21 – Sweet Heart Day
31 – Halloween

1
2
3
4
5
6
7
8
9
10
11
12
13
14
15
16
17
18
19
20
21
22
23
24
25
26
27
28
29
30
31

1
2
3
4
5
6
7
8
9
10
11
12
13
14
15
16
17
18
19
20
21
22
23
24
25
26
27
28
29
30
31

Hawaiian Pork

2 (1 pound) pork tenderloins, sliced	2 (.5 kg)
1 (20 ounce) can pineapple tidbits with juice	567 g
1 (8 ounce) bottle sweet-and-sour sauce	227 g
1 teaspoon ginger	5 ml
1 tablespoon cornstarch	15 ml

- Season pork slices with a little salt and pepper and place in large skillet with about 2 tablespoons (30 ml) oil. Over medium-high heat, brown slices on both sides and cook about 5 minutes. Add pineapple chunks, sweet and sour sauce and ginger and stir well.

- In small bowl, combine cornstarch and ½ cup (120 ml) water, mix well and add to pork-pineapple mixture. Heat to boiling, reduce heat and simmer 25 minutes; stir several times. Serve over cooked instant rice.

- Serves 4 to 6.

Hawaiian Slaw

1 (16 ounce) package shredded coleslaw mix, chilled	.5 kg
1 (8 ounce) can crushed pineapple, drained, chilled	227 g
1 (8 ounce) bottle coleslaw dressing, chilled	227 g
¼ cup flaked coconut, optional	60 ml

- In salad bowl, toss slaw mix, drained pineapple, dressing and a little coconut. Serves 4.

Walnut Roughy

1½ pounds fresh or frozen orange roughy	.7 kg
½ cup mayonnaise	120 ml
3 tablespoons grated parmesan cheese	45 ml
1 teaspoon dried basil	5 ml
⅓ cup chopped walnuts	80 ml

• Preheat oven to 425° (220° C). Cut orange roughy into serving-size pieces and place in sprayed baking pan. Do not let pieces touch. In bowl, combine mayonnaise, parmesan cheese and dried basil and spread over fish. Sprinkle with chopped walnuts. Bake uncovered 14 to 15 minutes or until fish flakes easily. Serves 4.

Baked New Potatoes

1 pound new potatoes with peels	.5 kg
1 clove garlic, minced	
1 large onion, coarsely chopped	
½ cup (1 stick) butter	120 ml

• Preheat oven to 350° (176° C). Par-boil new potatoes. Drain and quarter. In large skillet, saute onion and garlic with butter until onions are translucent. Add potatoes and toss to coat. Place in sprayed 9 x 13-inch (23 x 33 cm) baking dish. Add 1 teaspoon (5 ml) salt. Bake, basting occasionally, for 25 to 30 minutes until potatoes are fork tender. Serves 4 to 6.

Simple Bread Idea: **Stuffed Breadsticks**

• Heat 2 (12.5 ounce/350 g) boxes frozen stuffed breadsticks according to package directions.

1
2
3
4
5
6
7
8
9
10
11
12
13
14
15
16
17
18
19
20
21
22
23
24
25
26
27
28
29
30
31

Grilled Swordfish Steaks
with Mango Salsa

4 (6 - 8 ounce) swordfish steaks   **4 (168 g)**
Extra-virgin olive oil
1 lime, halved
Garlic salt

- Rinse and dry swordfish steaks. Rub olive oil over surface, drizzle juice of half lime and sprinkle with garlic salt. Grill steaks over medium heat for about 3 to 5 minutes per side. Do not overcook.

Mango Salsa:
2 ripe mangoes, peeled, finely chopped
1 jalapeno, seeded, finely chopped
4 green onions with tops, finely chopped
1 yellow bell pepper, seeded, finely chopped

- Mix all ingredients in bowl and squeeze remaining half lime over salsa. Chill while steaks cook. Serves 4.

Creamy Baked Potatoes

4 baking potatoes
Butter, softend
Sour cream
1 (8 ounce) package shredded cheddar cheese   **227 g**

- Wash potatoes and stick fork in each. Wrap in paper towels and microwave on HIGH for about 8 to 10 minutes and turn once. Split potatoes, scoop flesh in bowl, but leave ½-inch (1.2 cm) on skins. Mash potatoes, mix with butter, sour cream and cheese and place mixture in potato shells. Place in oven at 275° (135° C) to keep warm. Serves 4.

Cheese-N-Weiner Crescents

8 large wieners
4 slices American cheese, cut into 6 strips
1 (8 count) can refrigerated crescent dinner rolls

- Preheat oven to 375° (190° C). Slit wieners within ½-inch (1.2 cm) of edge and insert 3 strips cheese in each slit. Separate crescent dough into 8 triangles and roll wieners inside dough. Place rolls cheese side down on baking sheet and bake 12 to 15 minutes or until golden brown. Serves 4 to 6.

Juicy Apples

1 (8 ounce) package cream cheese, softened	**227 g**
1 (7 ounce) jar marshmallow cream	**198 g**
¼ teaspoon ground ginger	**1 ml**
¼ teaspoon ground cinnamon	**1 ml**
2 delicious apples, cut in wedges	

- With mixer, blend cream cheese, marshmallow cream, ginger and cinnamon. Use apple wedges for dipping. Serves 4.

Simple Side Dish: **Easy Baked Beans**

- Heat 2 (15 ounce/425 g) cans baked beans according to can directions.

1
2
3
4
5
6
7
8
9
10
11
12
13
14
15
16
17
18
19
20
21
22
23
24
25
26
27
28
29
30
31

Jam-Glazed Pork Tenderloins

4 pork tenderloins (about 2 pounds)	1 kg

Jam Glaze:

1¼ cups grape or plum jam	300 ml
¼ cup oil	60 ml
2 teaspoons chopped fresh rosemary leaves	10 ml
1 small onion, finely chopped	

• In saucepan over low heat, combine jam, oil, rosemary leaves and chopped onion. Heat and stir just until ingredients mix well. Place pork in resealable plastic bag and pour half jam mixture over pork. Seal, marinate 15 minutes and turn once. Remove pork from marinade and grill over unheated side of grill about 20 minutes. Turn, brush with reserved basting marinade and continue to cook until pork is no longer pink. Discard any remaining marinade. When ready to serve, heat reserved jam mixture and serve over sliced pork. Serves 6 to 8.

Spinach-Strawberry Salad

2 (10 ounce) packages baby spinach	2 (280 g)
1 pint fresh strawberries, halved	.5 kg
1 (8 ounce) bottle poppy seed salad dressing	227 g
½ cup slivered almonds, toasted	120 ml

• In salad bowl, combine spinach and strawberries and toss. When ready to serve, toss with salad dressing and sprinkle almonds on top. Serves 6 to 8.

Broccoli-Ham-Topped Potatoes

5 - 6 large potatoes	
2 cups cooked deli ham, diced	480 ml
1 (10 ounce) can cream of broccoli soup	280 g
1 (8 ounce) package shredded cheddar cheese	227 g

- Cook potatoes in microwave until done. With knife, cut potatoes down center and fluff insides with fork. In saucepan over low heat, combine remaining ingredients, heat and stir until they blend well. Spoon generous amounts of ham-soup mixture into potatoes and reheat in microwave for 2 to 3 minutes, if necessary. Serves 4 to 6.

Spinach-Orange Salad

1 (10 ounce) package fresh baby spinach	280 g
2 (11 ounce) cans mandarin oranges, drained	2 (312 g)
½ small jicama, peeled, julienned	
⅓ cup slivered almonds, toasted	80 ml
1 bunch fresh green onions, sliced	
Vinaigrette salad dressing	

- In salad bowl, combine all salad ingredients and toss with vinaigrette dressing. Serves 4.

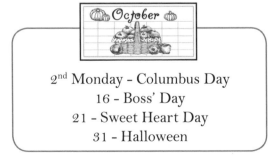

October

2nd Monday – Columbus Day
16 – Boss' Day
21 – Sweet Heart Day
31 – Halloween

1
2
3
4
5
6
7
8
9
10
11
12
13
14
15
16
17
18
19
20
21
22
23
24
25
26
27
28
29
30
31

1
2
3
4
5
6
7
8
9
10
11
12
13
14
15
16
17
18
19
20
21
22
23
24
25
26
27
28
29
30
31

Beef and Broccoli

1 pound beef sirloin steak	.5 kg
1 onion, chopped	
1 (10 ounce) can cream of broccoli soup	280 g
1 (10 ounce) package frozen chopped broccoli, thawed	280 g
1 (12 ounce) package medium noodles, cooked	340 g

• Slice beef across grain into very thin strips. In large skillet brown steak strips and onion in a little oil and stir several times. Reduce heat and simmer 10 minutes. Stir in soup and broccoli and heat. When ready to serve, spoon beef mixture over hot, cooked noodles. Serves 4 to 6.

Fantastic Fried Corn

2 (16 ounce) packages frozen whole kernel corn	2 (.5 kg)
½ cup (1 stick) butter	120 ml
1 cup whipping cream	240 ml
1 tablespoon sugar	15 ml

• Place corn in large skillet, turn on medium heat and add butter, whipping cream, sugar and 1 teaspoon (5 ml) salt.

• Stirring constantly and heat until most of whipping cream and butter absorbs into corn. Serves 4 to 6.

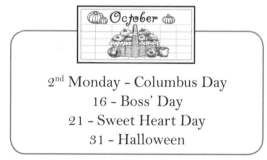

October

2nd Monday – Columbus Day
16 – Boss' Day
21 – Sweet Heart Day
31 – Halloween

Savory Chicken and Mushrooms

1 (16 ounce) package frozen chopped onions and peppers	.5 kg
1 (8 ounce) package fresh mushrooms, sliced	227 g
1 (10 ounce) can cream of mushroom soup	280 g
1 cup milk	240 ml
1 rotisserie chicken, skinned, boned, chopped	
3 cups instant brown rice	710 ml

- In large skillet with a little oil, cook onions, peppers and mushrooms about 5 minutes or until onions are translucent and stir frequently. Stir in mushroom soup and milk, mix well and add chicken pieces with a little salt and pepper. Boil, reduce heat and cook for about 10 minutes. Serve over hot, cooked rice. Serves 4 to 6.

Broccoli-Pepper Salad

5 cups cut broccoli florets, stemmed	1.3 L
1 sweet red bell pepper, julienned	
1 cup diagonally sliced celery	240 ml
1 (8 ounce) package cubed Monterey Jack cheese	227 g
½ cup honey-mustard salad dressing	120 ml

- In bowl with lid, combine all salad ingredients and mix well. Toss with honey-mustard salad dressing. Serves 4 to 6.

1
2
3
4
5
6
7
8
9
10
11
12
13
14
15
16
17
18
19
20
21
22
23
24
25
26
27
28
29
30
31

Meatball Subs

1 (18 ounce) package frozen meatballs, thawed	**510 g**
1 (28 ounce) jar chunky spaghetti sauce	**794 g**
6 submarine or hoagie buns	
1 (12 ounce) package shredded mozzarella cheese	**340 g**

- Preheat oven to 450° (230° C). In saucepan, combine meatballs and spaghetti sauce and heat until hot. Shave thin layer off top of each roll. With fork, remove some of soft interior of bun to make a "trough". Place rolls on large baking pan and spoon about 3 heaping tablespoons (45 ml) cheese in bottom of roll. Bake about 5 minutes or until buns are light brown and cheese melts. Spoon about ¼ cup (60 ml) spaghetti sauce and 2 to 3 meatballs in each bun. Top subs with little more sauce and generous topping of cheese. Serve hot. Serves 4 to 6.

Corny Salad

3 (11 ounce) cans Mexicorn®, drained, chilled	**3 (312 g)**
1 (15 ounce) can green peas, drained, chilled	**425 g**
2 yellow bell peppers, chopped	
1 (8 ounce) bottle Italian dressing, chilled	**227 g**

- In serving bowl with lid, combine corn, peas and peppers and pour dressing over vegetables. Refrigerate. When serving, use slotted spoon. Serves 4 to 6.

Caesar-Salad Pizza

1 (12 inch) Italian pizza crust	32 cm
1 (8 ounce) package shredded mozzarella cheese	227 g
1 (6 ounce) package, cooked chicken breast strips	168 g
2 cups shredded lettuce	480 ml
3 fresh green onions, sliced	
¾ cup shredded cheddar and colby cheese	180 ml
½ (8 ounce) bottle Caesar dressing	½ (227 g)

- Preheat oven to 400° (204° C). Top pizza crust with mozzarella cheese and bake 8 minutes or until cheese melts. In bowl, combine chicken strips, lettuce, onions and cheese. Pour about half of Caesar dressing over salad and toss. Top hot pizza with salad and cut into wedges. Serve immediately. Serves 4.

Fluffy Fruit Salad

2 (20 ounce) cans pineapple tidbits, drained	2 (567 g)
1 (16 ounce) can whole cranberry sauce	.5 kg
2 (11 ounce) cans mandarin oranges, drained	2 (312 g)
½ cup chopped pecans	120 ml
1 (8 ounce) carton whipped topping	227 g

- In bowl, combine pineapple, cranberries, oranges and pecans and fold in whipped topping. Serves 4.

1
2
3
4
5
6
7
8
9
10
11
12
13
14
15
16
17
18
19
20
21
22
23
24
25
26
27
28
29
30
31

1
2
3
4
5
6
7
8
9
10
11
12
13
14
15
16
17
18
19
20
21
22
23
24
25
26
27
28
29
30
31

Speedy Taco Soup

2 (14 ounce) cans chicken broth	2 (396 g)
1 (12 ounce) can chunk chicken breast with broth	340 g
1 (16 ounce) jar mild thick-and-chunky salsa	.5 kg
2 (15 ounce) cans pinto beans with liquid	2 (425 g)
1 (15 ounce) can whole kernel corn, drained	425 g

- In large saucepan, combine broth, chicken with broth, salsa, beans and corn. Heat to boiling, reduce heat and simmer 15 minutes. Serves 4 to 6.

Pound Cake Deluxe

1 bakery pound cake	
1 (15 ounce) can crushed pineapple with juice	.5 kg
1 (3.4 ounce) package coconut instant pudding mix	100 g
1 (8 ounce) carton whipped topping	227 g
½ cup flaked coconut	120 ml

- Slice cake horizontally to make 3 layers. Mix pineapple, pudding and whipped topping and blend well. Spread on each layer and sprinkle top of cake with coconut and chill. Serves 6 to 8.

Simple Bread Idea: Hot Flour Tortillas

- Heat flour tortillas and serve with butter.

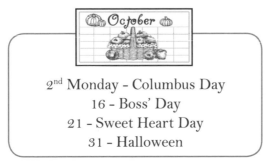

October

2nd Monday - Columbus Day
16 - Boss' Day
21 - Sweet Heart Day
31 - Halloween

Loaded Potatoes

6 large baking potatoes, washed
1 (1 pound) package bulk pork sausage .5 kg
1 (8 ounce) package cubed Velveeta® cheese 227 g
1 (10 ounce) can diced tomatoes and green chilies,
   drained 280 g

• Cook potatoes in microwave until tender. In skillet
  over medium heat, brown sausage and drain fat. Add
  cheese and diced tomatoes and green chilies and
  stir well. With knife, cut potatoes down center and
  fluff insides with fork. Spoon generous amounts of
  sausage-cheese mixture on each potato and reheat in
  microwave 2 to 3 minutes, if necessary. Serves 4 to 6.

Italian Green Salad

1 (10 ounce) package Italian-blend salad greens 280 g
1 seedless cucumber, sliced
1 small zucchini with peel, sliced
Creamy Italian dressing
⅓ cup sunflower seeds 80 ml

• In salad bowl, combine salad greens, cucumber and
  zucchini. When ready to serve, toss with creamy
  Italian dressing and sprinkle sunflower seeds on top.
  Add croutons, if desired. Serves 4.

Skillet Chicken and More

4 - 5 boneless, skinless chicken breast halves
2 (10 ounce) cans cream of chicken soup   **2 (280 g)**
2 cups instant white rice   **480 ml**
1 (16 ounce) package broccoli florets   **.5 kg**
Paprika

- In very large skillet with a little oil, brown chicken breasts on both sides and simmer 10 minutes. Remove chicken and keep warm. Add soup and 2 cups (480 ml) water to skillet. Heat to boiling.
- Stir in instant rice and broccoli. Top with chicken sprinkled with a little pepper and paprika. Cover and cook on low 15 minutes or until liquid evaporates. Serves 4 to 6.

Asparagus Salad

2 (15 ounce) cans asparagus spears, drained   **2 (425 g)**
1 cup shredded Swiss cheese   **240 ml**
3 fresh green onions, chopped

- Place asparagus on serving plate and sprinkle cheese and onions on top. Serve room temperature. Serves 4 to 6.

Pork and Veggie Stir-Fry

1 (16 ounce) whole pork tenderloin, thinly sliced	.5 kg
2 tablespoons peeled, grated fresh ginger	30 ml
1 (10 ounce) package frozen snow peas	280 g
2 small zucchini, halved lengthwise, sliced	
1 bunch green onions, cut in (3-inch) pieces	8 cm
1 (14 ounce) can chicken broth	396 g
2 tablespoons teriyaki sauce	30 ml
1 tablespoon cornstarch	15 ml

- In large skillet with a little oil over medium-high heat, stir-fry pork slices and ginger just until pork loses its pink color. Transfer to serving bowl and keep warm. In same skillet with a little more oil, cook snow peas, zucchini and onions until tender-crisp. In small bowl, combine broth, teriyaki sauce and cornstarch and mix well. Pour into skillet with vegetables and heat to boiling. Boil, stirring constantly, until sauce thickens. Return pork to skillet, stir to coat with sauce and heat thoroughly. Serves 4 to 6.

Cottage Fruit Salad

1 (16 ounce) carton small curd cottage cheese	.5 kg
1 (6 ounce) package orange gelatin	168 g
2 (11 ounce) cans mandarin oranges, drained	2 (312 g)
1 (20 ounce) can chunk pineapple, drained	567 g
1 (8 ounce) carton whipped topping	227 g

- Sprinkle gelatin over cottage cheese and mix well. Add oranges and pineapple and mix well. Fold in whipped topping and chill. Serves 6 to 8.

1
2
3
4
5
6
7
8
9
10
11
12
13
14
15
16
17
18
19
20
21
22
23
24
25
26
27
28
29
30
31

Cheesy Chicken Soup

1 (10 ounce) can fiesta nacho cheese soup	280 g
1 (10 ounce) can cream of chicken soup	280 g
2 (14 ounce) cans chicken broth	2 (396 g)
1 cup half-and-half cream	240 ml
2 (12 ounce) cans white chicken breast with broth	2 (340 g)

• In saucepan over medium heat, combine all ingredients and stir until soup is hot. Serves 4 to 6.

Broccoli-Stuffed Tomatoes

4 medium tomatoes	
1 (10 ounce) package frozen chopped broccoli	280 g
1 (6 ounce) roll garlic cheese, softened	168 g
½ teaspoon garlic salt	2 ml

• Preheat oven to 350° (176° C). Cut tomato tops off and scoop out pulp. Cook frozen broccoli in microwave according to package directions and drain well. Combine broccoli, cheese and garlic salt. Heat just until cheese melts, stuff broccoli mixture into tomatoes and place on sprayed baking sheet. Bake about 10 minutes. Serves 4 to 6.

October

2nd Monday – Columbus Day
16 – Boss' Day
21 – Sweet Heart Day
31 – Halloween

Chili-Pepper Chicken

¼ cup (½ stick) butter	60 ml
6 boneless, skinless chicken breast halves	
1 (6 ounce) box spicy chicken coating mix	168 g
1 (16 ounce) jar mild salsa	.5 kg

• Preheat oven to 400° (204° C). In 9 x 13-inch (23 x 33 cm) glass baking dish, melt butter in oven and remove. In shallow bowl, place coating mix and coat each chicken breast on both sides. Place chicken in baking dish and arrange so pieces are not touching. Bake 20 minutes or until chicken browns lightly. Serve with heaping spoon of salsa. Serves 4 to 6.

Ranch-Style Mashed Potatoes

1 (1 ounce) packet ranch dressing mix	28 g
¼ cup (½ stick) butter, melted	60 ml
¾ cup sour cream	180 ml
5 - 6 cups prepared instant mashed potatoes with no salt or butter	1.3 L

• In large, heavy saucepan over low heat, combine all ingredients. Stir until potatoes heat through. Serves 4 to 6.

Simple Side Dish: **Easy Bean Salad**

• Drain 2 (15 ounce/425 g) cans 3-bean salad and serve chilled.

Baked Orange Roughy

1 egg, beaten
¼ cup milk   60 ml
1½ cups cracker crumbs   360 ml
⅓ cup grated parmesan cheese   80 ml
4 large orange roughy fillets

•   Preheat oven to 425° (220° C). In shallow bowl,
beat egg and milk. In another shallow bowl, combine
cracker crumbs and parmesan cheese. Dip fillets in
egg mixture, then dredge both sides of fillets in crumb
mixture and press to use all crumb mixture. Place in
sprayed 9 x 13-inch (23 x 33 cm) baking pan. Bake
uncovered for 15 to 20 minutes or until fish flakes
easily with fork. Serves 4 to 6.

Green Rice and Spinach

1 cup instant rice   240 ml
1 (10 ounce) package frozen chopped spinach   280 g
1 onion, finely chopped
3 tablespoons butter   45 ml
¾ cup shredded cheddar cheese   180 ml

•   Preheat oven to 350° (176° C). Cook rice in large
saucepan. Punch holes in box of spinach and cook in
microwave about 3 minutes. Reserve 3 tablespoons
(45 ml) cheese for topping and add spinach, onion,
butter, cheese and ¼ teaspoon (1 ml) salt to rice.
(If rice mixture seems a little dry, add several
tablespoons water.) Pour into sprayed 2-quart (2 L)
baking dish and bake for 25 minutes. Serves 4.

Sassy Red Pepper Chicken

4 boneless, skinless chicken breast halves	
1½ cups seasoned breadcrumbs	**360 ml**
1 teaspoon garlic powder	**5 ml**
1 large egg, beaten	
½ cup oil, divided	**120 ml**

Red Pepper Sauce:

¾ cup drained, diced roasted red peppers	**180 ml**
½ cup vinegar	**120 ml**
½ cup ketchup	**120 ml**
⅔ cup sugar	**160 ml**
1 teaspoon paprika	**5 ml**

- Place chicken breasts between 2 sheets plastic wrap and use meat mallet to flatten chicken to ¼-inch (.6 cm). Set aside. In shallow bowl, combine breadcrumbs and garlic and place beaten egg with 2 tablespoons (30 ml) water in second shallow bowl. Dip chicken in egg mixture then dredge in breadcrumbs. Pour half oil in skillet and cook 2 chicken breasts for 5 minutes one each side. Remove from skillet. Repeat procedure. Place all pepper sauce ingredients in saucepan, bring to a boil and reduce heat. Cook 25 minutes and stir often. Serve with chicken. Serves 4 to 6.

Vanilla Pudding

2 (16 ounce) cartons refrigerated vanilla pudding	**2 (.5 kg)**
1 (12 ounce) jar chocolate ice cream topping	**340 g**

- Place pudding in sherbet dishes and drizzle chocolate topping over pudding. Serves 4 to 6.

1
2
3
4
5
6
7
8
9
10
11
12
13
14
15
16
17
18
19
20
21
22
23
24
25
26
27
28
29
30
31

Easy Meaty Minestrone

2 (20 ounce) cans minestrone soup	2 (567 g)
1 (15 ounce) can pinto beans with liquid	425 g
1 (18 ounce) package frozen Italian meatballs, thawed	510 g
1 (5 ounce) package grated parmesan cheese	143 g

- In large saucepan, combine soup, beans, meatballs and ½ cup (120 ml) water. Bring a to boil, reduce heat to low and simmer about 15 minutes. To serve, sprinkle each serving with parmesan cheese. Serves 4 to 6.

Pear-Cheese Salad

Shredded lettuce	
2 (15 ounce) cans pear halves	2 (425 g)
1 (8 ounce) package shredded cheddar cheese	227 g

- On individual salad plates, place shredded lettuce and top with 2 pear halves. Sprinkle with cheese. Serves 4.

Simple Bread Idea: **Easy Cornbread Twists**

- Bake 1 (11.5 ounce/320 g) package refrigerated cornbread twist according to package directions.

Crunchy Pork Chops

1 cup crushed saltine crackers	240 ml
¼ cup biscuit mix	60 ml
1 egg, beaten	
5 - 6 (½ inch/1.2 cm) thick boneless pork chops	

• In shallow bowl, combine crushed crackers, biscuit mix and ¾ teaspoon (4 ml) salt. In second shallow bowl, combine beaten egg and 2 tablespoons (30 ml) water. Dip pork chops into egg mixture and dredge in cracker mixture. Heat a little oil in heavy skillet, cook pork chops about 15 minutes and turn once. Serves 4 to 6.

Broccoli-Wild Rice

2 (10 ounce) packages frozen chopped broccoli	2 (280 g)
1 (6 ounce) box long grain-wild rice	168 g
1 (6 ounce) jar processed cheese spread	168 g
1 (10 ounce) can cream of chicken soup	280 g

• Preheat oven to 350° (176° C). Cook broccoli and rice according to package directions. Combine all ingredients and pour into sprayed 2-quart (2 L) baking dish. Cover and bake for 25 to 30 minutes or until bubbly. Serves 4 to 6.

Chile Bread

1 loaf unsliced Italian bread	
½ cup (1 stick) butter, melted	120 ml
1 (4 ounce) can diced green chilies, drained	114 g
¾ cup shredded Monterey Jack cheese	180 ml

• Preheat oven to 350° (176° C). Slice bread almost through. Combine melted butter, chilies and cheese. Spread between bread slices. Cover loaf with foil. Bake for 15 minutes. Serves 4 to 6.

1
2
3
4
5
6
7
8
9
10
11
12
13
14
15
16
17
18
19
20
21
22
23
24
25
26
27
28
29
30
31

Chicken Taco Pie

1 pound boneless, skinless chicken breast halves	**.5 kg**
1 (1 ounce) packet taco seasoning mix	**45 g**
1 green and 1 red bell pepper, finely chopped	
1½ cups shredded Mexican 3-cheese blend	**360 ml**
1 (8 ounce) package corn muffin mix	**227 g**
1 egg	
⅓ cup milk	**80 ml**

- Preheat oven to 400° (204° C). Cut chicken into 1-inch (2.5 cm) chunks and cook on medium-high heat in large skillet with a little oil. Cook about 10 minutes. Drain and stir in taco seasoning, bell peppers and ¾ cup (180 ml) water. Reduce heat, simmer and cook for additional 10 minutes. Stir several times. Spoon into sprayed 9-inch (23 cm) deep-dish pie pan and sprinkle with cheese. Prepare corn muffin mix with egg and milk and mix well. Spoon over top of pie and bake for 20 minutes or until top is golden brown. Let stand about 5 minutes before serving. Serves 4 to 6.

Peachy Cottage Cheese

Shredded lettuce	
1 - 2 (15 ounce) cans peach halves	**1 - 2 (425 g)**
1 (16 ounce) carton small curd cottage cheese	**.5 kg**
¼ cup dried sweetened cranberries	**60 ml**

- Place about half shredded lettuce on individual salad plates with 1 or 2 peach halves. Spoon 1 heaping tablespoon (15 ml) cottage cheese over peaches and sprinkle cranberries over top. Serves 4 to 6.

Shrimp Florentine

2 (10 ounce) boxes frozen creamed spinach, thawed	2 (280 g)
1 (12 ounce) package penne pasta	340 g
2 tablespoons oil	30 ml
1 pound large shrimp, peeled, veined	.5 kg
¼ cup grated parmesan cheese	60 ml

- Cook spinach and past according to package directions. Place oil, shrimp and a little pepper in large skillet over medium-high heat. Cook 3 minutes or until shrimp turns pink. Add cooked spinach, pasta and parmesan cheese and toss gently. If pasta is too dry, gradually add 1 to 2 tablespoons (15 ml/30 ml) hot water. Spoon into serving bowl and serve hot. Serves 4 to 6.

City-Slicker Salad

2 (10 ounce) packages fresh spinach	2 (280 g)
1 quart fresh strawberries, halved	1 L
½ cup slivered almonds, toasted	120 ml
Poppy seed dressing	

- Tear spinach into smaller pieces and add strawberries and almonds. Refrigerate until ready to serve. Toss with poppy seed dressing. Serves 4 to 6.

Ranch French Bread

1 loaf French bread	
½ cup (1 stick) butter, softened	120 ml
1 tablespoon ranch dressing mix	15 ml

- Preheat oven to 350° (176° C). Cut loaf in half horizontally. Blend butter and dressing mix. Spread butter mixture on bread. Wrap bread in foil. Bake for 15 minutes. Serves 4 to 6.

1
2
3
4
5
6
7
8
9
10
11
12
13
14
15
16
17
18
19
20
21
22
23
24
25
26
27
28
29
30
31

Zesty Orange Chicken

½ cup white wine	120 ml
½ cup orange juice concentrate	120 ml
½ cup orange marmalade	120 ml
½ teaspoon ground ginger	2 ml
½ teaspoon cinnamon	2 ml
1 large fryer chicken, quartered	
2 (11 ounce) cans mandarin oranges, drained	2 (312 g)
½ cup halved green grapes	120 ml
1½ cups instant brown rice, cooked	360 ml

- Preheat oven to 325° (162° C). Combine wine, orange juice concentrate, marmalade, ginger and cinnamon in sprayed 9 x 13-inch (23 x 33 cm) baking dish. Add chicken quarters and turn to coat chicken. Bake uncovered and baste occasionally, for 40 minutes. Add oranges and grapes to dish during last 5 minutes of cooking. Serve over hot, cooked, buttered rice. Serves 4 to 6.

Hawaiian Coleslaw

1 (16 ounce) package shredded coleslaw mix	.5 kg
1 (8 ounce) can crushed pineapple, drained	227 g
1 (8 ounce) bottle coleslaw dressing, chilled	227 g
¼ cup flaked coconut, optional	60 ml

- In salad bowl, toss slaw mix, pineapple, dressing and a little coconut and chill. Serves 4 to 6.

Simple Bread Idea: Hawaiian Bread

- Slice 1 round loaf Hawaiian bread into pie wedges, heat and serve with butter.

Chicken-Wild Rice Special

1 (6 ounce) package long grain-wild rice mix	168 g
4 - 5 boneless, skinless chicken breast halves	
2 (10 ounce) cans French onion soup	2 (280 g)
1 red and 1 green bell pepper, seeded, julienned	

• In saucepan, cook rice according to package directions and keep warm. Brown chicken breasts on both sides in large skillet with a little oil over medium-high heat. Add soup, ¾ cup (180 ml) water and bell peppers. Reduce heat to medium-low, cover and cook 15 minutes. To serve, place rice on serving platter with chicken breasts on top. Serve sauce in gravy boat to spoon over chicken and rice. Serves 4 to 6.

Popovers

2 cups flour	480 ml
6 eggs, beaten	
2 cups milk	480 ml
Butter	

• Preheat oven to 425° (220° C). Combine flour and 1 teaspoon (5 ml) salt in bowl. Add eggs and milk and mix. (The batter will be like thick cream.) Coat popover pans with butter and heat in oven. Fill each cup half full. Bake for 20 minutes. Reduce heat to 375° (190° C) and bake for additional 25 minutes. Serve immediately. Serves 4.

1
2
3
4
5
6
7
8
9
10
11
12
13
14
15
16
17
18
19
20
21
22
23
24
25
26
27
28
29
30
31

1
2
3
4
5
6
7
8
9
10
11
12
13
14
15
16
17
18
19
20
21
22
23
24
25
26
27
28
29
30
31

Tortellini Soup

3 (14 ounce) cans chicken broth	3 (396 g)
2 (9 ounce) packages refrigerated cheese tortellini	2 (255 g)
1 (15 ounce) can cannellini beans, rinsed, drained	425 g
1 (4 ounce) jar chopped pimento	114 g
1 teaspoon dried basil	5 ml
1 tablespoon balsamic vinegar	15 ml

• In large saucepan, bring chicken broth to boiling. Add tortellini and cook about 6 minutes or until tender. Stir in beans, pimento, basil, vinegar and a little salt and pepper. Simmer for 8 to 10 minutes. Serves 4 to 6.

Spicy Cornbread Twists

½ cup (1 stick) butter, melted	120 ml
¾ cup yellow cornmeal	180 ml
½ teaspoon cayenne pepper	2 ml
1 (11 ounce) can refrigerated breadsticks	312 g

• Preheat oven to 375° (190° C). Melt butter in pie pan in oven. Remove pan from oven. In small mixing bowl, combine cornmeal and cayenne pepper and spread on wax paper. Roll breadsticks in melted butter, then in cornmeal mixture. Twist breadsticks according to package directions, place on sprayed baking sheet and bake 16 to 18 minutes or until breadsticks are light brown. Serves 4 to 6.

Baked Halibut Fillets

4 fresh halibut fillets	
2 tablespoons lime juice	30 ml
1 (10 ounce) can diced tomatoes and green chilies	280 g
1 cup salsa	120 ml
6 green olives, thinly sliced	
3 tablespoons butter, melted	45 ml
1 (6 ounce) box couscous with toasted pine nuts	168 g

• Preheat oven to 350° (176° C). Place fillets on shallow plate and spoon lime juice over fillets. Let stand 5 minutes. Place tomatoes and green chilies in sprayed 9 x 13-inch (23 x 33 cm) baking dish. Stir in salsa and olives and season with a little salt and pepper. Place fillets on top of sauce and drizzle with melted butter. Bake for 15 to 18 minutes or until fish flakes easily with fork. Serve over hot cooked couscous and spoon sauce over each fillet. Serves 4.

Tossed Salad Surprise

1 (10 ounce) package spring-mix salad greens	280 g
½ small jicama, peeled, julienned	
1 small red onion, sliced	
10 cherry tomatoes, halved	
2 small zucchini, sliced	
Honey-mustard dressing	

• In salad bowl, toss greens, jicama, red onion and zucchini. Spoon about 2 tablespoons (30 ml) honey-mustard dressing on each serving. Serves 4.

1
2
3
4
5
6
7
8
9
10
11
12
13
14
15
16
17
18
19
20
21
22
23
24
25
26
27
28
29
30
31

Fried Chicken Breasts

4 - 6 boneless, skinless chicken breast halves
2 eggs, beaten
30 saltine crackers, finely crushed

- Pound chicken breasts to ¼-inch (.6 cm) thickness. (If chicken breasts are very large, cut in half.) In shallow bowl, combine beaten eggs, a little salt and pepper and 3 tablespoons (45 ml) water. Dip chicken in egg mixture and crushed crackers to coat well. Deep fry until golden brown. Drain on paper towels. Serves 4 to 6.

Divine Strawberries
This is wonderful served over pound cake
or just served in sherbet glasses.

1 quart fresh strawberries	**1 L**
1 (20 ounce) can pineapple chunks, well drained	**567 g**
2 bananas, sliced	
1 (18 ounce) carton strawberry glaze	**510 g**

- Cut strawberries in half or in quarters, if strawberries are very large. Add pineapple chunks and bananas. Fold in strawberry glaze and chill. Serves 4.

Simple Side Dish:
Fast Mashed Potatoes and Gravy

- Prepare 1 (24 ounce/680 g) package frozen mashed potatoes and 1 (1 ounce/28 g) packet cream gravy mix according to package directions.

Tuna-Biscuit Melts

1 (10 ounce) can refrigerated buttermilk biscuits	280 g
1 (12 ounce) can chunk light tuna packed in water,	
drained	340 g
¾ cup chopped celery	180 ml
½ cup sweet pickle relish	120 ml
⅓ cup refrigerated honey-mustard dressing	80 ml
4 slices Swiss cheese	

- Preheat oven to 350° (176° C). Bake biscuits according to can directions and cool slightly. Split biscuits and arrange cut-side up on same baking pan.
- In large bowl, combine tuna, celery, pickle relish and dressing. Divide tuna mixture among split biscuits and place half slice cheese over top of tuna.
- Bake 6 to 7 minutes or until filling is hot and cheese melts. Serves 4 to 6.

Brandied Apples

1 loaf pound cake	
1 (20 ounce) can apple pie filling	567 g
½ teaspoon allspice	2 ml
2 tablespoons brandy	30 ml
Vanilla ice cream	

- Slice pound cake and place on individual dessert plates. In saucepan, combine pie filling, allspice and brandy. Heat and stir just until hot. Place several spoonfuls over cake and top with scoop of vanilla ice cream. Serves 6 to 8.

1
2
3
4
5
6
7
8
9
10
11
12
13
14
15
16
17
18
19
20
21
22
23
24
25
26
27
28
29
30
31

1
2
3
4
5
6
7
8
9
10
11
12
13
14
15
16
17
18
19
20
21
22
23
24
25
26
27
28
29
30

Chilly Night's Turkey Bake

1 (6 ounce) package chicken stuffing mix	168 g
1½ pounds deli turkey, cut into (1 inch/2.5 cm)) strips	.7 kg
1 (10 ounce) can cream of chicken soup	280 g
½ cup sour cream	120 ml
1 (16 ounce) bag frozen mixed vegetables, thawed, drained	.5 kg

- Preheat oven to 375° (190° C). Sprinkle ½ cup (120 ml) dry stuffing mix evenly in sprayed 9 x 13-inch (23 x 33 cm) baking dish and set aside. In bowl, combine remaining stuffing and 1 cup (240 ml) water and stir just until moist. Set aside. Place turkey strips over dry stuffing mix in baking dish. In bowl, mix soup, sour cream and vegetables, spoon over turkey strips and top with prepared stuffing. Bake uncovered for 25 minutes. Serves 6 to 8.

Cranberry Mousse

1 (15 ounce) can jellied cranberry sauce	425 g
1 (8 ounce) can crushed pineapple, drained	227 g
1 (8 ounce) carton sour cream	227 g
1 tablespoon mayonnaise	15 ml

- In saucepan, place cranberry sauce and crushed pineapple. Cook until cranberry sauce liquefies. Fold in sour cream and mayonnaise. Pour into molds or muffin cups and freeze. Serves 4 to 6.

Chicken Couscous

1¼ cups chicken broth	300 ml
1 (6 ounce) package pine nut couscous mix	168 g
1 rotisserie chicken, boned, cut up	
1 (4 ounce) can chopped pimento	114 g
½ cup crumbled feta cheese	120 ml
1 (10 ounce) package frozen green peas, thawed	280 g
1 tablespoon dried basil	15 ml
1 tablespoon lemon juice	15 ml

- Heat broth and seasoning packet from couscous in microwave on HIGH for 4 minutes or until broth begins to boil. Place couscous in large bowl and stir in broth. Cover and let stand 5 minutes. Fluff couscous with fork and add chicken, pimento, cheese, peas, basil and lemon juice. Toss to blend well. Serve warm. Serves 4 to 6.

Raspberry-Spinach Salad

2 (10 ounce) packages baby spinach	2 (280 g)
1 cup fresh raspberries	240 ml
½ red onion, sliced in rings	
¼ cup real bacon bits	60 ml
1 (8 ounce) bottle raspberry salad dressing	227 g

- Mix all salad ingredients and toss with dressing. Serves 4 to 6.

November

1st Sunday - End of Daylight Savings
11 - Veterans' Day
4th Thursday - Thanksgiving

1
2
3
4
5
6
7
8
9
10
11
12
13
14
15
16
17
18
19
20
21
22
23
24
25
26
27
28
29
30

Crunchy Baked Fish

1 cup mayonnaise	240 ml
2 tablespoons fresh lime juice	30 ml
1 - 1½ pounds haddock fillets	.5 kg
2 cups finely crushed corn chips	480 ml

- Preheat oven to 425° (220° C). In small bowl, mix mayonnaise and lime juice. Spread on both sides of fish fillets. Place crushed corn chips on wax paper and dredge both sides of fish in chips. Place fillets on foil-covered baking sheet and bake 15 minutes or until fish flakes easily. Serves 4 to 6.

Crunchy Broccoli

2 (10 ounce) packages frozen broccoli florets	2 (280 g)
1 (8 ounce) can sliced water chestnuts, drained, chopped	227 g
½ cup (1 stick) butter, melted	120 ml
1 (1 ounce) packet dry onion soup mix	28 g

- Place broccoli in microwave-safe dish, cover and microwave on HIGH for 5 minutes. Turn dish and cook another 4 minutes. Add water chestnuts. Combine melted butter and soup mix and blend well. Toss with cooked broccoli. Serves 4 to 6.

Simple Side Dish:
Fast Macaroni and Cheese

- Prepare 1 (24 ounce/680 g) package frozen macaroni and cheese according to package directions.

Shrimp Marinara

1½ pounds shelled, veined medium shrimp, tails removed	.7 kg
1 (16 ounce) jar refrigerated marinara sauce	.5 kg
1 tablespoon lime juice	15 ml
1 teaspoon minced garlic	5 ml

- In large skillet with a little oil, cook shrimp over medium heat 2 to 3 minutes or until shrimp turn pink. Stir in marinara sauce, lime juice and minced garlic. Simmer 5 minutes or until sauce heats through. Serve over angel hair pasta. (See below.) Serves 4 to 6.

Angel Hair Pasta

1 (8 ounce) package angel hair pasta	227 g
2 tablespoons butter	30 ml
2 tablespoons cream	30 ml

- Cook pasta according to package directions. Drain well and stir in butter, cream and a little salt. Pour onto serving platter and spoon marinara shrimp on top of pasta. Serves 4 to 6.

Green Salad

1 (10 ounce) package spring-mix salad greens	280 g
1 bunch red radishes, sliced	
1 small zucchini with peel, sliced	
1 cup fresh broccoli florets, stemmed	240 ml
Honey-mustard vinaigrette dressing	

- In salad bowl, combine salad greens, radishes, zucchini and broccoli florets. Toss with honey-mustard vinaigrette dressing. Serves 4 to 6.

1
2
3
4
5
6
7
8
9
10
11
12
13
14
15
16
17
18
19
20
21
22
23
24
25
26
27
28
29
30

A Different Chili

2 onions, coarsely chopped	
3 (15 ounce) cans great northern beans, drained	3 (425 g)
2 (14 ounce) cans chicken broth	2 (396 g)
2 tablespoons minced garlic	30 ml
1 (7 ounce) can chopped green chilies	198 g
1 tablespoon ground cumin	15 ml
3 cups cooked, diced chicken breasts	710 ml
1 (8 ounce) package shredded Monterey Jack cheese	227 g

• In large, heavy pot with a little oil, cook onions, about 5 minutes, but do not brown. Place 1 can beans in shallow bowl and mash with fork. Add mashed beans, 2 remaining cans beans, chicken broth, garlic, green chilies and cumin. Bring to boil and reduce heat. Cover and simmer 30 minutes. Add chopped chicken, stir to blend well and heat until chili is thoroughly hot. When serving, top each bowl with 3 tablespoons (45 ml) Jack cheese. Serves 4 to 6.

Simple Bread Idea:
Hot, Buttered Flour Tortillas

• Heat flour tortillas and serve with butter and salsa.

November

1st Sunday - End of Daylight Savings
11 - Veterans' Day
4th Thursday - Thanksgiving

Chicken-Waldorf Salad

1 pound boneless, skinless chicken breasts	.5 kg
1 red and 1 green apple with peels, sliced	
1 cup sliced celery	240 ml
½ cup chopped walnuts	120 ml
2 (6 ounce) cartons orange yogurt	2 (168 g)
½ cup mayonnaise	120 ml
1 (6 ounce) package shredded lettuce	168 g

• Place chicken in large saucepan and cover with water. On high heat, cook about 15 minutes. Drain and cool. Cut into 1-inch (2.5 cm) chunks and season with a little salt and pepper. Place in large salad bowl. Add sliced apples, celery and walnuts. Stir in yogurt and mayonnaise. Toss to mix well. Serve over shredded lettuce. (May be served room temperature or chilled several hours). Serves 4 to 6.

Poppy Seed Bread

3¾ cups biscuit mix	890 ml
1½ cups shredded cheddar cheese	360 ml
1 tablespoon poppy seeds	15 ml
1 egg, beaten	
1½ cups milk	360 ml

• Preheat oven to 350° (176° C). Combine all ingredients and beat vigorously for 1 minute. Pour into sprayed, floured loaf pan. Bake for 50 to 60 minutes or when toothpick inserted in center comes out clean. Remove from pan and cool before slicing. Serves 4 to 6.

1
2
3
4
5
6
7
8
9
10
11
12
13
14
15
16
17
18
19
20
21
22
23
24
25
26
27
28
29
30

Taco Pie

1 pound lean ground beef	**.5 kg**
1 (11 ounce) can Mexicorn®, drained	**312 g**
1 (8 ounce) can tomato sauce	**227 g**
1 (1 ounce) packet taco seasoning	**28 g**
1 (9 inch) frozen piecrust	**23 cm**
1 cup shredded cheddar cheese	**240 ml**

• Preheat oven to 350° (176° C). In large skillet, brown and cook ground beef until no longer pink. Stir in corn, tomato sauce and taco seasoning. Keep warm. Place piecrust in pie pan and bake 5 minutes. Remove from oven and spoon ground beef mixture onto piecrust, spread evenly. Sprinkle cheese over top and bake another 20 minutes or until filling is bubbly. Let stand 5 minutes before slicing to serve. Serves 4 to 6.

Baked Beans

2 (15 ounce) cans pork and beans, slightly drained	**2 (425 g)**
½ onion, finely chopped	
⅔ cup packed brown sugar	**160 ml**
¼ cup chili sauce	**60 ml**
1 tablespoon Worcestershire sauce	**15 ml**
2 strips bacon	

• Preheat oven to 325° (162° C). In bowl, combine beans, onion, brown sugar, chili sauce and Worcestershire. Pour into sprayed 2-quart (2 L) baking dish and place bacon strips over bean mixture. Bake uncovered for 50 minutes. Serves 4 to 6.

Sweet-And-Sour Pork Cutlets

¾ cup flour	180 ml
4 (3 ounce) pork cutlets	4 (84 g)
2 tablespoons butter, divided	30 ml
¾ cup orange juice	180 ml
⅓ cup dried sweetened cranberries	80 ml
1 tablespoon dijon-style mustard	15 ml
1 tablespoon brown sugar	15 ml

- Place flour in shallow bowl and dredge cutlets in flour. Brown pork cutlets and turn once in heavy skillet with 1 tablespoon (15 ml) butter. Add orange juice, cranberries, mustard, brown sugar and remaining butter. Cook on high until mixture bubbles. Reduce heat and simmer about 5 minutes. Serves 4.

Cherry-Cranberry Salad

1 (6 ounce) package cherry gelatin	168 g
1 (20 ounce) can cherry pie filling	567 g
1 (16 ounce) can whole cranberry sauce	.5 kg

- In mixing bowl, combine cherry gelatin and 1½ cups (360 ml) boiling water and mix until gelatin dissolves. Mix pie filling and cranberry sauce into gelatin. Pour into 9 x 13-inch (23 x 33 cm) dish. Place salad in freezer to congeal for 45 minutes. Serves 4 to 6.

Simple Side Dish: **Fast Veggies-Rice**

- Prepare 1 (4.3 ounce/128 g) box garden vegetable rice and pasta according to package directions.

1
2
3
4
5
6
7
8
9
10
11
12
13
14
15
16
17
18
19
20
21
22
23
24
25
26
27
28
29
30

A Different Sandwich

1 (9 inch) round loaf focaccia bread	23 cm
3 ounces deli ham slices	84 g
6 slices Swiss cheese	
⅓ cup bottled roasted red bell peppers, drained	80 ml
1 (6 ounce) package baby spinach	168 g
3 tablespoons Italian or romano-basil vinaigrette	45 ml

- Preheat oven to 350° (176° C). Place bread on cutting board and slice horizontally. Place 1 layer ham and cheese on bread and top with red bell peppers and heavy layer of spinach. Top with remaining bread. Drizzle with vinaigrette and wrap in foil. Bake for 16 minutes. To serve, cut focaccia into six wedges and serve immediately. Serves 2 to 4.

Stuffed-Cucumber Slices

2 cucumbers, peeled	
1 (8 ounce) package cream cheese, softened	227 g
½ cup stuffed green olives, finely chopped, drained	120 ml

- Half cucumbers lengthwise and scoop out seeds. (Use grapefruit spoon to scrape down middle of cucumbers to leave hollow in each half.) In mixing bowl with mixer, beat cream cheese until creamy. Fold in olives and ½ teaspoon (2 ml) salt and mix well. Fill cucumber hollows to top with cream cheese mixture. Press halves together, wrap tightly in plastic wrap and chill. Cut crosswise in ⅓-inch (.8 cm) slices to serve. Serves 2 to 4.

Super Supper Frittata

2 cups cooked white rice	480 ml
1 (10 ounce) box frozen green peas, thawed	280 g
1 cup cooked, cubed ham	240 ml
8 large eggs, beaten	
1 cup shredded pepper-Jack cheese, divided	240 ml
1 teaspoon dried thyme	5 ml
1 teaspoon sage	5 ml

• In large cast-iron skillet with a little oil, heat rice, peas and ham 3 to 4 minutes or until mixture is thoroughly hot. In separate bowl, whisk eggs, three-fourths cheese, thyme, sage and 1 teaspoon (5 ml) salt. Add to mixture in skillet and shake pan gently to distribute evenly. On medium heat, cover and cook, without stirring, until set on bottom and sides.

• Eggs will still be runny in center. Sprinkle remaining cheese over top. Place in oven and broil about 5 minutes or until frittata is firm in center. Serves 4 to 6.

Serendipity Salad

1 (6 ounce) package raspberry gelatin	168 g
1 (15 ounce) can fruit cocktail with juice	425 g
1 (8 ounce) can crushed pineapple with juice	227 g
2 bananas, cut into small chunks	
1 cup miniature marshmallows	240 ml

• Dissolve gelatin in 1½ cups (360 ml) boiling water and mix well. Add fruit cocktail and pineapple and chill until gelatin begins to thicken. Add bananas and marshmallows and pour into sherbet dishes. Cover with plastic wrap and refrigerate. (You could also pour salad into 7 x 11-inch/18 x 28 cm glass dish and cut into squares to serve.) Serves 4 to 6.

1
2
3
4
5
6
7
8
9
10
11
12
13
14
15
16
17
18
19
20
21
22
23
24
25
26
27
28
29
30

Alfredo-Chicken Spaghetti

1 (8 ounce) package thin spaghetti, broken in thirds	227 g
2 teaspoons minced garlic	10 ml
1 (16 ounce) jar alfredo sauce	.5 kg
¼ cup milk	60 ml
1 (10 ounce) box broccoli florets, thawed	280 g
2 cups cooked, diced chicken	480 ml

• Cook spaghetti according to package directions and drain. Place back in saucepan and stir in garlic, alfredo sauce and milk and mix well. Add drained broccoli florets and cook on medium heat (about 5 minutes), stir several times or until broccoli is tender. Add more milk if mixture gets too dry. Stir in diced chicken and spoon into serving bowl. Serves 4 to 6.

Green and White Salad

1 (16 ounce) package frozen green peas, thawed	.5 kg
1 head cauliflower, cut into bite-size pieces	
1 (8 ounce) carton sour cream	227 g
1 (1 ounce) packet dry ranch salad dressing	28 g

• In large bowl, combine peas and cauliflower. Combine sour cream and salad dressing. Toss with vegetables. Refrigerate. Serves 4 to 6.

November

1st Sunday – End of Daylight Savings
11 – Veterans' Day
4th Thursday – Thanksgiving

Home-Made Tomato Soup

3 (15 ounce) cans whole tomatoes with liquid	3 (425 g)
1 (14 ounce) can chicken broth	396 g
1 tablespoon sugar	15 ml
1 tablespoon minced garlic	15 ml
1 tablespoon balsamic vinegar	15 ml
¾ cup whipping cream	180 ml

• With blender, puree tomatoes (in batches) and pour into large saucepan. Add chicken broth, sugar, garlic, balsamic vinegar and a little salt and bring to boiling. Reduce heat and stir in whipping cream. Cook, stirring constantly, for 2 to 3 minutes or until soup is hot. You might want to garnish each serving with 1 tablespoon (15 ml) ready-cooked, crumbled bacon. Serves 4 to 6.

Pizza Sandwich

1 (14 ounce) package English muffins	396 g
1 pound bulk sausage, cooked, drained	.5 kg
1½ cups pizza sauce	360 ml
1 (4 ounce) can mushrooms, drained	114 g
1 (8 ounce) package shredded mozzarella cheese	227 g

• Split muffins and layer ingredients on each muffin half ending with cheese. Broil until cheese melts. Serves 4 to 6.

1
2
3
4
5
6
7

Spicy Glazed Pork Tenderloin

½ cup orange juice	120 ml
¼ cup lime juice	60 ml
½ cup packed brown sugar	120 ml
1 teaspoon ground cumin	15 ml
1 teaspoon cayenne pepper	15 ml
2 (1 pound) pork tenderloins	2 (.5 kg)

8
9
10
11
12
13
14
15
16

• In small bowl, combine orange juice, lime juice, brown sugar, cumin and cayenne pepper. Pat tenderloins dry and season with a little salt and pepper. Heat oil in skillet and cook tenderloins, turning on all sides, about 9 to 10 minutes. Reduce heat to medium, add orange juice mixture and cook, rolling tenderloins to coat, until mixture is thick and syrupy, about 10 minutes. Transfer to cutting board and cover tenderloins with foil. Let stand 10 minutes before slicing crosswise into ½-inch (1.2 cm) slices. Arrange on serving plate and pour glaze over slices. Serves 6 to 8.

17
18
19
20
21

Parmesan Peas

2 (10 ounce) packages frozen green peas	2 (280 g)
3 tablespoons butter, melted	45 ml
1 tablespoon lemon juice	15 ml
⅓ cup grated parmesan cheese	80 ml

22
23
24
25
26

• Microwave peas, butter and lemon juice in 2 tablespoons (30 ml) water for 6 minutes and rotate once. Leave in oven several minutes. Sprinkle with parmesan cheese. Serve hot. Serves 6 to 8.

27
28
29
30

Tequila-Lime Chicken

6 boneless, chicken breast halves with skins

Marinade:

½ cup lime juice	**120 ml**
¼ cup tequila	**60 ml**
1½ teaspoons chili powder	**7 ml**
1½ teaspoons minced garlic	**7 ml**
1 teaspoon seeded, diced jalapeno pepper	**5 ml**

• In large sealable plastic bag, combine all marinade ingredients. Add chicken breasts, seal bag and turn to coat. Refrigerate 10 hours or overnight. Remove breasts from marinade and sprinkle chicken with a little salt and pepper. Discard marinade. Grill skin side down 5 to 7 minutes. Turn and cook 10 minutes or until it cooks thoroughly. Remove to platter, cover and let stand 5 minutes before serving. Serves 4 to 6.

Favorite Pasta

1 (8 ounce) package spinach linguine	**227 g**
1 cup whipping cream	**240 ml**
1 cup chicken broth	**240 ml**
½ cup grated parmesan cheese	**120 ml**
½ cup frozen English peas	**120 ml**

• Cook linguine according to package directions, drain and keep warm. Combine whipping cream and chicken broth in saucepan and bring to boil. Reduce heat and simmer mixture 25 minutes or until it thickens and reduces to 1 cup (240 ml). Remove from heat. Add cheese and peas and stir until cheese melts. Toss with linguine and serve immediately. Serves 4 to 6.

1
2
3
4
5
6
7
8
9
10
11
12
13
14
15
16
17
18
19
20
21
22
23
24
25
26
27
28
29
30

Grilled T-Bone Steaks

4 (1 inch) thick T-bone steaks	**4 (2.5 cm)**

Marinade:

⅓ cup Worcestershire sauce	**80 ml**
2 teaspoons minced garlic	**10 ml**
1 tablespoon vinegar	**15 ml**
1 teaspoon sugar	**5 ml**

- Place steaks in large resealable plastic bag. Combine all marinade ingredients and pour in plastic bag. Turn to coat well. Refrigerate 1 hour and turn occasionally. Heat charcoal to medium hot. Remove steaks from marinade and grill, turning once, about 3 minutes per side. Let steaks stand 5 minutes before serving. Serves 4 to 6.

Spinach-Apple Salad

⅓ cup frozen orange juice concentrate, thawed	**80 ml**
¾ cup mayonnaise	**180 ml**
2 (10 ounce) packages fresh spinach	**2 (280 g)**
1 red apple with peel, diced	
5 slices bacon, fried, crumbled	

- Mix orange juice concentrate and mayonnaise and toss with spinach and apple. Top with bacon. Serves 4 to 6.

Shrimp and Rice Casserole

2 cups instant rice	480 ml
1½ pounds frozen cooked shrimp	.7 kg
1 (10 ounce) carton alfredo sauce	280 g
1 (4 ounce) can chopped pimento, drained	114 g
4 fresh green onions with tops, chopped	
1 (8 ounce) package shredded cheddar cheese, divided	227 g

- In saucepan, cook rice according to package directions and place in sprayed 9 x 13-inch (23 x 33 cm) baking dish. Thaw shrimp in colander under cold running water, drain well, remove tails and set aside. In saucepan on medium heat, combine alfredo sauce, pimento and green onions. Stir in shrimp and spoon mixture over rice. Cover with half cheese and bake about 15 minutes. Remove from oven, sprinkle remaining cheese and return to oven for 5 minutes. Serves 4 to 6.

TIP: Thawing shrimp under running water is better than thawing in refrigerator. It can get a fishy smell if thawed in refrigerator.

Romaine-Artichoke Salad

1 (10 ounce) package romaine lettuce	280 g
1 (6 ounce) jar artichoke hearts, drained, chopped, chilled	168 g
1 sweet red bell pepper, julienned, chilled	
Garlic-vinaigrette dressing	
⅓ cup sunflower seeds, toasted	80 ml

- In salad bowl, combine romaine, artichoke hearts and bell pepper. Add about ½ (8 ounce/227 g) bottle garlic-vinaigrette dressing (more if needed) and toss. Sprinkle sunflower seeds over top of salad. Serves 6 to 8.

1
2
3
4
5
6
7
8
9
10
11
12
13
14
15
16
17
18
19
20
21
22
23
24
25
26
27
28
29
30

Chicken-Vegetable Chili

1 (16 ounce) package frozen, chopped onions and bell pepper	.5 kg
2 tablespoons minced garlic	30 ml
2 tablespoons chili powder	30 ml
3 teaspoons ground cumin	15 ml
2 pounds boneless, skinless chicken breast halves, cubed	1 kg
2 (14 ounce) cans chicken broth	2 (396 g)
3 (15 ounce) cans pinto beans with jalapenos, divided	3 (425 g)

• Cook onions and bell peppers about 5 minutes, stirring occasionally, in skillet with a little oil. Add garlic, chili powder, cumin and cubed chicken and cook another 5 minutes. Stir in broth and a little salt. Bring to a boil and reduce heat. Cover and simmer for 15 minutes. Place 1 can beans in shallow bowl and mash with fork. Add mashed beans and remaining 2 cans beans to pot. Bring to boil, reduce heat and simmer for 10 minutes. Serves 4 to 6.

Pineapple-Lemon Pie

1 (14 ounce) can sweetened condensed milk	306 g
1 (20 ounce) can lemon pie filling	567 g
1 (20 ounce) can crushed pineapple, well drained	567 g
1 (8 ounce) carton whipped topping	227 g
2 (9 inch) cookie-flavored piecrusts	2 (23 cm)

• With mixer, combine condensed milk and lemon pie filling and beat until smooth. Add pineapple and whipped topping and gently fold into pie filling mixture. Pour into 2 piecrusts. Refrigerate. Serves 6 to 8.

Crab-Corn Chowder

1 (1 ounce) packet leek soup mix	28 g
2 cups milk	480 ml
1 (8 ounce) can whole kernel corn	227 g
½ (8 ounce) package cubed Velveeta® cheese	½ (227 g)
1 (7 ounce) can crabmeat, drained, flaked	198 g

- In large saucepan, combine soup mix and milk and cook over medium heat, stirring constantly, until soup thickens. While still on medium heat, stir in corn and cheese until cheese melts. Just before serving, add crab and stir until hot. Serves 4 to 6.

Cheddar Cornbread

2 (8 ounce) packages cornbread muffin mix	2 (227 g)
2 eggs, beaten	
½ cup milk	120 ml
½ cup plain yogurt	120 ml
1 (15 ounce) can cream-style corn	425 g
½ cup shredded cheddar cheese	120 ml

- Preheat oven to 400° (204° C). In bowl, combine cornbread mix, eggs, milk and yogurt until they blend. Stir in corn and cheese. Pour into sprayed 9 x 13-inch (23 x 33 cm) baking dish. Bake for 18 to 20 minutes or until light brown. Serves 6 to 8.

November

1st Sunday - End of Daylight Savings
11 - Veterans' Day
4th Thursday - Thanksgiving

1
2
3
4
5
6
7
8
9
10
11
12
13
14
15
16
17
18
19
20
21
22
23
24
25
26
27
28
29
30

1
2
3
4
5
6
7
8
9
10
11
12
13
14
15
16
17
18
19
20
21
22
23
24
25
26
27
28
29
30

Creamy Chicken And Veggies

6 small boneless, skinless chicken breast halves
1 (16 ounce) bottle creamy Italian dressing .5 kg
1 (16 ounce) package frozen broccoli, cauliflower
   and carrots, thawed .5 kg

- Sprinkle chicken with a little salt and pepper. Place a little oil in large, heavy non-stick skillet over medium-high heat. Add chicken breasts and cook 2 minutes on each side. Pour about three-fourths dressing over chicken. Cover and simmer for about 8 minutes. Add vegetables, cover and cook another 10 minutes or until vegetables are tender. Serves 4 to 6.

Baked Tomatoes

2 (16 ounce) cans diced tomatoes, drained 2 (.5 kg)
1½ cups breadcrumbs, toasted, divided 360 ml
¼ cup sugar 60 ml
½ onion, chopped
¼ cup (½ stick) butter, melted 60 ml

- Preheat oven to 325° (162° C). Combine tomatoes, 1 cup (240 ml) breadcrumbs, sugar, onion and butter. Pour into sprayed baking dish and cover with remaining breadcrumbs. Bake for 25 to 30 minutes or until crumbs are light brown. Serves 4 to 6.

Cheesy Potatoes

1 (5 ounce) box three-cheese potatoes 143 g
½ cup milk 120 ml
1 tablespoon butter 15 ml

- Prepare and bake according to package directions. Serves 4 to 6.

Skillet Nachos

½ (16 ounce) package tortilla chips	½ (.5 kg)
1 (8 ounce) can whole kernel corn, drained	227 g
½ (15 ounce) can chili beans	½ (425 g)
½ cup thick and chunky salsa	120 ml
1 (8 ounce) package shredded 4-cheese blend	227 g
1 (4 ounce) can sliced ripe olives	114 g

• Arrange tortilla chips in single layer in large 12-inch (32 cm) skillet. In saucepan, combine corn, beans and salsa and heat just until hot and bubbly. Spoon salsa mixture over tortilla chips and sprinkle on about three-fourths cheese. Cover skillet and cook on medium-high for about 5 minutes or until cheese melts. To serve, sprinkle ripe olives and remaining cheese over top. (You may want to serve with more salsa.) Serves 4 to 6.

Guacamole Salad

1 (16 ounce) carton refrigerated guacamole	.5 kg
Shredded lettuce	
Remaining chips from package above	

• Place lettuce on individual salad plates with 2 heaping tablespoons (30 ml) guacamole. Serves 4 to 6.

Haystacks

1 (12 ounce) package butterscotch chips	340 g
1 cup salted peanuts	240 ml
1½ cups chow mein noodles	360 ml

• Melt butterscotch chips in top of double boiler. Remove from heat and stir in peanuts and noodles. Drop by teaspoonfuls on wax paper. Cool and store in airtight container. Serves 4 to 6.

1
2
3
4
5
6
7
8
9
10
11
12
13
14
15
16
17
18
19
20
21
22
23
24
25
26
27
28
29
30

1
2
3
4
5
6
7
8
9
10
11
12
13
14
15
16
17
18
19
20
21
22
23
24
25
26
27
28
29
30

Quick Skillet

1½ pounds lean ground beef	**.7 kg**
2 (3 ounce) packages Oriental-flavored ramen	
noodles	**2 (84 g)**
⅔ cup stir-fry sauce	**160 ml**
1 (16 ounce) package frozen Oriental stir-fry	
vegetables	**.5 kg**

• In large skillet, brown and crumble ground beef. Add
   2½ cups (600 ml) water, seasoning packets, stir-fry
   sauce to taste and vegetables. Cook and stir on
   medium-low heat about 5 minutes. Break noodles,
   add to beef-vegetable mixture and cook another 6
   minutes. Stir and separate noodles as they soften.
   Serves 4 to 6.

Cherry Crush

1 (6 ounce) box cherry gelatin	**168 g**
1 (8 ounce) package cream cheese, softened	**227 g**
1 (20 ounce) can cherry pie filling	**567 g**
1 (15 ounce) can crushed pineapple with juice	**425 g**

• Dissolve gelatin with 1½ cups (360 ml) boiling water.
   With electric mixer beat in cream cheese very slowly
   at first. Fold in pie filling and crushed pineapple.
   Pour into 9 x 13-inch (23 x 33 cm) baking dish.
   Refrigerate. Serves 6 to 8.

Simple Bread Idea:
Whole Wheat, French Bread

• Butter each slice of 1 loaf whole wheat French bread.
   Restack loaf and roll in foil. Heat at 350° (176° C) for
   15 minutes.

Hearty Bean And Ham Soup

¼ cup (½ stick) butter	60 ml
1 (15 ounce) can sliced carrots, drained	425 g
1 cup chopped celery	240 ml
1 cup chopped green bell pepper	240 ml
2 - 3 cups cooked, diced ham	480 ml
2 (15 ounce) cans navy beans with liquid	2 (425 g)
2 (15 ounce) cans jalapeno pinto beans with liquid	2 (425 g)
2 (14 ounce) cans chicken broth	2 (396 g)
2 teaspoons chili powder	10 ml

- In soup pot with butter, cook carrots, celery and bell pepper about 8 minutes until tender-crisp. Add diced ham, navy beans, pinto beans, chicken broth, chili powder and a little salt and pepper. Bring to a boil, stirring constantly, for 3 minutes. Reduce heat and simmer for 15 minutes. Serves 6 to 8.

Fantastic Fruit Salad

2 (11 ounce) cans mandarin oranges	2 (312 g)
2 (15 ounce) cans pineapple chunks	2 (425 g)
1 (16 ounce) carton frozen strawberries, thawed	.5 kg
1 (20 ounce) can peach pie filling	567 g
1 (20 ounce) can apricot pie filling	567 g

- Drain oranges, pineapple and strawberries. Combine all ingredients and fold together gently. Spoon into glass serving bowl. Refrigerate. Serves 6 to 8.

1
2
3
4
5
6
7
8
9
10
11
12
13
14
15
16
17
18
19
20
21
22
23
24
25
26
27
28
29
30

Honey-Mustard Grilled Chicken

¾ cup mayonnaise	180 ml
2 tablespoons dijon-style mustard	30 ml
¼ cup honey	60 ml
4 - 5 boneless, skinless chicken breast halves	

- In bowl, combine mayonnaise, mustard and honey and mix well. Brush about half mayonnaise mixture over each piece of chicken and grill over hot coals until done. Serve with remaining mayonnaise-mustard mixture. Serves 4.

Cauliflower Medley

1 head cauliflower, cut into florets	
1 (15 ounce) can Italian stewed tomatoes	425 g
1 bell pepper, chopped	
1 onion, chopped	
¼ cup (½ stick) butter	60 ml
1 cup shredded cheddar cheese	240 ml

- Preheat oven to 350° (176° C). In large saucepan, place cauliflower, stewed tomatoes, bell pepper, onion and butter with about 2 tablespoons (30 ml) water and some salt and pepper. Cook in saucepan with lid until cauliflower is done, about 10  minutes. (Do not let cauliflower get mushy.) Place in sprayed 2-quart (2 L) baking dish and sprinkle cheese on top. Bake just until cheese melts. Serves 4.

Colorful Sausage Supper

4 tablespoons olive oil, divided	60 ml
1 pound cooked Polish sausage, cut into	
(¼ inch/.6 cm) slices	.5 kg
1 sweet red bell pepper, julienned	
3 small zucchini, sliced	
3 small yellow squash, sliced	
1 (16 ounce) package penne pasta	.5 kg
1 (26 ounce) jar spaghetti sauce, heated	737 g

• In large skillet with 2 tablespoons (30 ml) oil, saute sausage, bell pepper, zucchini and squash until vegetables are tender-crisp. Keep warm. Cook pasta according to package directions, drain and stir in remaining oil. Add a little salt and pepper. Spoon into large serving bowl and spread heated spaghetti sauce over pasta. Use slotted spoon to top with sausage-vegetable mixture. Serve immediately. Serves 4 to 6.

Peachy Fruit Salad

2 (20 ounce) cans peach pie filling	2 (567 g)
1 (20 ounce) can pineapple chunks, drained	567 g
1 (11 ounce) can mandarin oranges, drained	312 g
1 (8 ounce) jar maraschino cherries, drained	227 g
1 cup miniature marshmallows	240 ml

• Combine all ingredients in large bowl, fold together gently and refrigerate. (Bananas may be added, if you like.) Serves 4 to 6.

1
2
3
4
5
6
7
8
9
10
11
12
13
14
15
16
17
18
19
20
21
22
23
24
25
26
27
28
29
30

Florentine Shrimp-Pasta

2 (9 ounce) frozen boil-in-bags creamed spinach	**2 (255 g)**
1 (12 ounce) package penne pasta	**340 g**
¼ cup whipping cream	**60 ml**
1 teaspoon Cajun seasoning	**5 ml**
2 tablespoons olive oil	**30 ml**
1 pound peeled, medium shrimp, cooked	**.5 kg**

• Bring large pot of water to a boil, add spinach pouches and cook according to package directions. In another large saucepan, cook pasta according to package directions. Drain, add cream and Cajun seasoning and mix until they blend well. In skillet with olive oil, cook shrimp about 3 minutes or until pink. Cut spinach pouches and add to pasta. Stir in shrimp and transfer to serving dish. Serves 4 to 6.

Sesame-Romaine Salad

1 large head romaine lettuce	
2 tablespoons sesame seeds, toasted	**30 ml**
6 strips bacon, fried, crumbled	
½ cup grated Swiss cheese	**120 ml**
Creamy Italian salad dressing	

• Wash and dry lettuce. Tear into bite-size pieces. When ready to serve, sprinkle sesame seeds, bacon and cheese over lettuce and toss with creamy Italian salad dressing. Serves 4 to 6.

Southwest Pizza

1 (12 inch) pre-baked pizza crust	32 cm
¾ cup prepared guacamole	180 ml
1 (10 ounce) package cooked southwest-style chicken breasts	280 g
½ cup roasted red peppers, drained, sliced	120 ml
1 (4 ounce) can sliced ripe olives, drained	114 g
1 (8 ounce) package shredded Mexican 4-cheese blend	227 g

• Preheat oven to 350° (176° C). Place pizza crust on sprayed cookie sheet and spread guacamole over crust. Top with chicken, red peppers and olives and spread evenly. Top with cheese. Bake 15 minutes or just until cheese bubbles and is light brown. Cut pizza into wedges to serve. Serves 4.

Marinated Corn Salad

3 (15 ounce) cans whole kernel corn, drained	3 (425 g)
1 red bell pepper, chopped	
1 cup chopped walnuts	240 ml
¾ cup chopped celery	180 ml
1 (8 ounce) bottle Italian salad dressing	227 g

• In bowl with lid, combine corn, bell pepper, walnuts and celery. (For a special little zip, add several dashes hot sauce.) Pour salad dressing over vegetables. Refrigerate several hours before serving. Serves 4 to 6.

Chicken-Noodle Soup Supper

1 (3 ounce) package chicken-flavored ramen noodles, broken	84 g
1 (10 ounce) package frozen green peas, thawed	280 g
2 teaspoons butter	10 ml
1 (4 ounce) jar sliced mushrooms, drained	114 g
3 cups cooked, cubed chicken	710 ml

- In large saucepan, heat 2¼ cups (540 ml) water to boiling. Add ramen noodles, contents of seasoning packet and peas. Heat to boiling, reduce heat to medium and cook about 5 minutes. Stir in mushrooms and chicken and continue cooking over low heat until all ingredients are hot. To serve, spoon into serving bowl. Serves 6 to 8.

Souper-Sausage Cornbread

1 (10 ounce) can golden corn soup	280 g
2 eggs	
¼ cup milk	60 ml
2 (6 ounce) package corn muffin mix	2 (168 g)
¼ pound pork sausage, cooked, drained, crumbled	114 g

- Preheat oven to 400° (204° C). In bowl, combine soup, eggs and milk. Stir in muffin mix just until they blend. Fold in sausage. Spoon mixture into sprayed 9 x 13-inch (23 x 33 cm) baking pan. Bake for about 20 minutes or until light brown. Serves 6 to 8.

Creamy Chicken-Pasta

1 (10 ounce) package penne pasta	280 g
1 tablespoon olive oil	15 ml
2 (12 ounce) cans white chicken meat, drained	2 (340 g)
2 tablespoons prepared pesto	30 ml
¾ cup whipping cream	180 ml

• In large saucepan, cook penne pasta according to package directions. Drain and place back in saucepan. Gently stir in oil, chicken, pesto (for a stronger basil or garlic taste, you might want to use little more than 2 tablespoons/30 ml pesto), whipping cream and a little salt and pepper. Place saucepan over low-medium heat and simmer, but do not let mixture boil until cream absorbs into pasta. Spoon into serving bowl and serve immediately. Serves 6 to 8.

Creamed-Spinach Bake

2 (10 ounce) packages frozen chopped spinach	2 (280 g)
2 (3 ounce) packages cream cheese, softened	2 (84 g)
3 tablespoons butter	45 ml
1 cup seasoned breadcrumbs	240 ml

• Preheat oven to 350° (176° C). Cook spinach according to package directions and drain well. Combine cream cheese and butter with spinach and heat until they melt and mix well with spinach. Pour into sprayed baking dish and sprinkle a little salt over spinach. Cover with breadcrumbs and bake for 15 to 20 minutes. Serves 6 to 8.

1
2
3
4
5
6
7
8
9
10
11
12
13
14
15
16
17
18
19
20
21
22
23
24
25
26
27
28
29
30

Sweet-And-Sour
Chicken and Veggies

1 (3 ounce) package chicken-flavored ramen noodles	84 g
1 (16 ounce) package frozen broccoli,	
cauliflower and carrots	.5 kg
⅔ cup sweet-and-sour sauce	160 ml
1 tablespoon soy sauce	15 ml
3 boneless, skinless, chicken breast halves, cooked,	
cut in strips	

• In large saucepan, cook noodles and vegetables in 2 cups (480 ml) water (reserve seasoning packet) for 3 minutes or until liquid absorbs. Add seasoning packet, chicken, sweet-and-sour sauce, soy sauce and a little salt and pepper. Heat on low-medium heat and stir until hot. Serves 4 to 6.

Black Bean Salad

2 (15 ounce) cans black beans, rinsed,	
drained, chilled	2 (425 g)
2 (11 ounce) cans Mexicorn®, drained, chilled	2 (312 g)
1 green pepper, chopped	
1 small red onion, chopped, chilled	
1 (8 ounce) bottle garlic-vinaigrette salad dressing	227 g

• In bowl with lid, combine all salad ingredients and cover with dressing. Serves 6 to 8.

November

1ˢᵗ Sunday - End of Daylight Savings
11 - Veterans' Day
4ᵗʰ Thursday - Thanksgiving

Hurry-Up Enchiladas

2 cups cooked, cubed chicken breasts	480 ml
1 (10 ounce) can cream of chicken soup	280 g
1 (16 ounce) jar chunky salsa, divided	.5 kg
8 (6 inch) flour tortillas	8 (15 cm)
1 (10 ounce) can fiesta nacho cheese soup	280 g

• In saucepan, heat and stir chicken, chicken soup and ¾ cup (180 ml) salsa. Spoon about ½ cup (120 ml) chicken mixture down center of each tortilla. Use all of chicken mixture. Roll tortillas around filling and place seam-side down in sprayed 9 x 13-inch (23 x 33 cm) glass baking dish. In saucepan, combine fiesta nacho soup, remaining salsa and ½ cup (120 ml) water and pour over enchiladas. Cover with wax paper and microwave, turning twice, on HIGH 5 minutes or until filling bubbles. Serves 6 to 8.

Spanish Rice

2 (15 ounce) cans Spanish rice	2 (425 g)
1 cup shredded cheddar cheese	240 ml

• Preheat oven to 325° (162° C). Place rice in sprayed 7 x 11-inch (18 x 28 cm) baking dish and heat for 20 minutes. Sprinkle cheese over top and return to oven for 5 minutes. Serves 6 to 8.

Guacamole Salad

Shredded lettuce	
1 (16 ounce) carton frozen guacamole, thawed	.5 kg
1 bunch fresh green onions, chopped	

• For each serving, place shredded lettuce on individual salad plates with about ⅓ cup (80 ml) guacamole and top with green onions. Serve with chips.

1
2
3
4
5
6
7
8
9
10
11
12
13
14
15
16
17
18
19
20
21
22
23
24
25
26
27
28
29
30
31

After-Thanksgiving Day Salad

1 (10 ounce) package romaine lettuce, torn	280 g
1 (15 ounce) can black beans, rinsed, drained	425 g
1 (8 ounce) package cheddar cheese, cubed	227 g
2 - 3 cups cooked, diced turkey	480 ml
⅓ cup pre-cooked, crumbled bacon	80 ml

Dressing:
½ cup mayonnaise	120 ml
¾ cup salsa	180 ml

- In salad bowl, combine lettuce, black beans, cheese and turkey and mix well. Combine mayonnaise, salsa and ¾ teaspoon (4 ml) pepper. Spoon over salad and toss. Serves 4 to 6.

Chive-Potato Souffle

3 eggs, separated	
2 cups cooked, hot instant mashed potatoes	480 ml
½ cup sour cream	120 ml
2 heaping tablespoons chopped chives	30 ml

- Preheat oven to 350° (176° C). Beat egg whites until stiff and set aside. Beat yolks until smooth and add to potatoes. Fold beaten egg whites, sour cream, chives and 1 teaspoon (5 ml) salt into potato-egg yolk mixture and pour into sprayed 2-quart baking dish. Bake for 45 minutes. Serves 4 to 6.

Stove-Top Ham Supper

1 (12 ounce) package spiral pasta	340 g
3 tablespoons butter, sliced	45 ml
2 - 3 cups cooked, cubed ham	480 ml
1 teaspoon minced garlic	5 ml
1 (16 ounce) package frozen broccoli, cauliflower and carrots	.5 kg
½ cup sour cream	120 ml
1 (8 ounce) package shredded cheddar cheese, divided	227 g

- Preheat oven to 375° (190° C). Cook pasta in large saucepan, according to package directions, drain and stir in butter while still hot. Add ham, garlic and 1 teaspoon (5 ml) salt. Cook vegetables in microwave according to package directions and stir, with liquid, into pasta-ham mixture. Stir in sour cream and half cheese. Mix until they blend well. Spoon into sprayed 3-quart (3 L) baking dish. Bake 15 minutes or just until bubbly around edges. Sprinkle remaining cheese on top and let stand just until cheese melts. Serves 6 to 8.

Bean-Onion-Pepper Salad

2 (15 ounce) cans cut green beans, drained	2 (425 g)
1 (15 ounce) can yellow wax beans, drained	425 g
1 small red onion, chopped, chilled	
1 orange bell pepper, julienned, chilled	
Italian dressing	

- In container with lid, combine green beans, wax beans, onion and bell pepper. Pour Italian dressing over vegetables just to cover. Chill several hours. Serves 6 to 8.

1
2
3
4
5
6
7
8
9
10
11
12
13
14
15
16
17
18
19
20
21
22
23
24
25
26
27
28
29
30
31

Chicken Salsa

Chicken:
6 boneless, skinless chicken breast halves
1 tablespoon cornstarch   **15 ml**

Marinade:
1 (16 ounce) jar salsa	**.5 kg**
¾ cup honey	**180 ml**
½ cup light soy sauce	**120 ml**
2 tablespoons oil	**30 ml**
½ teaspoon dried ginger	**2 ml**

- Preheat oven to 350° (176° C). Dry each chicken piece with paper towels. In bowl, combine all marinade ingredients and mix well. Pour 1½ cups (360 ml) marinade into sealable plastic bag, add chicken and refrigerate 2 to 3 hours. Cover and refrigerate remaining marinade.

- Place drained chicken (discard chicken marinade) in sprayed 9 x 13-inch (23 x 33 cm) baking dish. Top with remaining refrigerated marinade and bake uncovered for 25 to 30 minutes or until juices run clear. Remove chicken and keep warm. In small saucepan, combine cornstarch with 2 tablespoons (30 ml) water and stir in pan juices. Bring to a boil and cook about 2 minutes, stirring constantly, until it thickens. To serve, pour sauce over chicken. Serves 4 to 6.

Chile-Rice Bake

1 cup instant rice	**240 ml**
1 (1 pint) carton sour cream	**.5 kg**
1 (7 ounce) can chopped green chilies	**198 g**
1 (8 ounce) package shredded Monterey Jack cheese	**227 g**

(Continued on page 349.)

(Continued from page 348.)

- Preheat oven to 325° (162° C). Cook rice according to package directions. Add remaining ingredients plus ½ teaspoon (2 ml) salt. Place mixture in sprayed 7 x 11-inch (18 x 28 cm) baking dish. Bake covered for 15 to 20 minutes or until hot. Serves 4 to 6.

Mandarin Chicken

1 (11 ounce) can mandarin oranges, drained	312 g
1 (6 ounce) can frozen orange juice concentrate	168 g
1 tablespoon lemon juice	15 ml
1 tablespoon cornstarch	15 ml
4 boneless, skinless chicken breast halves	
2 tablespoons garlic-and-herb seasoning	30 ml
2 tablespoons butter	30 ml

- In saucepan, combine oranges, orange juice concentrate, lemon juice, ⅔ cup (160 ml) water and cornstarch. Cook on medium heat, stirring constantly, until mixture thickens. Set aside. Sprinkle chicken breasts with seasoning and place in skillet with butter. Cook about 7 minutes on each side until brown. Lower heat and spoon orange juice mixture over chicken, cover, simmer about 20 minutes and add a little water if sauce gets too thick. Serves 4 to 6.

Mushroom Rice

1 (6 ounce) package chicken rice and pasta	168 g
1 (4 ounce) can sliced mushrooms, drained	114 g
⅓ cup slivered almonds	80 ml
1 (8 ounce) carton sour cream	227 g

- Preheat oven to 350° (176° C). Prepare rice according to package directions. Fold in mushrooms, almonds and sour cream. Place in sprayed 3-quart (3 L) baking dish. Bake covered for 25 to 30 minutes. Serves 4 to 6.

1
2
3
4
5
6
7
8
9
10
11
12
13
14
15
16
17
18
19
20
21
22
23
24
25
26
27
28
29
30
31

1
2
3
4
5
6
7
8
9
10
11
12
13
14
15
16
17
18
19
20
21
22
23
24
25
26
27
28
29
30
31

Hearty 15-Minute Turkey Soup

1 (14 ounce) can chicken broth	396 g
3 (15 ounce) cans navy beans, rinsed, drained	3 (425 g)
1 (28 ounce) can diced tomatoes with liquid	794 g
2 - 3 cups cooked, cubed white turkey meat	480 ml
2 teaspoons minced garlic	10 ml
¼ teaspoon cayenne pepper	1 ml
Freshly grated parmesan cheese	

• Mix all ingredients except cheese and heat. Garnish with parmesan cheese. Serves 6 to 8.

Cornbread Muffins

2 (8 ounce) boxes corn muffin mix	2 (227 g)
⅔ cup milk	160 ml
2 eggs	

• Preheat oven to 400° (204° C). In mixing bowl, combine all ingredients and pour into sprayed 12 to 14-cup (3 L) muffin pan. Bake 20 minutes or until light brown. Serves 6 to 8.

Cherry Cobbler

2 (20 ounce) cans cherry pie filling	2 (567 g)
1 (18 ounce) box white cake mix	510 g
¾ cup (1½ sticks) butter, melted	180 ml
1 (4 ounce) package almonds, slivered	114 g

• Preheat oven to 350° (176° C). Spread pie filling in sprayed 9 x 13-inch (23 x 33 cm) baking pan. Sprinkle cake mix over cherries. Drizzle melted butter over top. Sprinkle almonds over top. Bake for 45 minutes. Top with whipped topping, if you like. Serves 6 to 8.

Turkey Burgers

2 pounds ground turkey	1 kg
1 (16 ounce) jar hot chipotle salsa, divided	.5 kg
8 slices Monterey Jack cheese	
Sesame seed hamburger buns	

• In large mixing bowl, combine ground turkey with 1 cup (240 ml) salsa. Mix well and shape into 8 patties. Place patties on broiler pan and broil 12 to 15 minutes. Turn once during cooking. Top each patty with cheese slice and grill just long enough to melt cheese. Place burgers on buns, spoon heaping tablespoon (15 ml) salsa over cheese and top with half of bun. Serves 6 to 8.

Quickie Pasta Salad

1 (24 ounce) carton deli-pasta salad	680 g
1 bunch fresh green onions, sliced	
1 (4 ounce) jar chopped pimento, drained	114 g
3 vine-ripened tomatoes	

• In large bowl, combine salad, green onions and pimento. Quarter each tomato and place around edge of salad. Serves 6 to 8.

Blueberry Cobbler

2 (20 ounce) cans blueberry pie filling	2 (567 g)
1 (18 ounce) box white cake mix	510 g
1 egg	
½ cup (1 stick) butter, softened	120 ml

• Preheat oven to 350° (176° C). Spread pie filling in sprayed 9 x 13-inch (23 x 33 cm) baking dish. With mixer, combine cake mix, egg and butter and blend well. Mixture will be stiff. Spoon over filling. Bake for 45 minutes or until brown. Serves 6 to 8.

1
2
3
4
5
6
7
8
9
10
11
12
13
14
15
16
17
18
19
20
21
22
23
24
25
26
27
28
29
30
31

Chicken-Parmesan Spaghetti

1 (14 ounce) package frozen, cooked, breaded chicken cutlets, thawed	396 g
1 (28 ounce) jar spaghetti sauce	794 g
2 (5 ounce) packages grated parmesan cheese, divided	2 (143 g)
1 (8 ounce) package thin spaghetti, cooked	227 g

- Preheat oven to 400° (204° C). In sprayed 9 x 13-inch (23 x 33 cm) baking dish, place cutlets and top each with about ¼ cup (60 ml) spaghetti sauce and heaping tablespoon (15 ml) parmesan. Bake 15 minutes. Place cooked spaghetti on serving platter and top with cutlets. Sprinkle remaining cheese over cutlets. Heat remaining spaghetti sauce and serve with chicken and spaghetti. Serves 6 to 8.

Fluffy Fruit Salad

2 (20 ounce) cans pineapple tidbits, drained	2 (567 g)
1 (16 ounce) can whole cranberry sauce	.5 kg
2 (11 ounce) cans mandarin oranges, drained	2 (312 g)
½ cup chopped pecans	120 ml
1 (8 ounce) carton whipped topping	227 g

- In bowl, combine pineapple, cranberries, oranges and pecans and fold in whipped topping. Serve in pretty crystal bowl. Serves 6 to 8.

Simple Bread Idea: **Garlic Toast**

- Heat 1 (11 ounce/8 slices/312 g) frozen French garlic toast according to package directions.

Pepper Steak

1¼ pounds sirloin steak, cut into strips	567 g
1 (14 ounce) can beef broth	396 g
1 (16 ounce) package frozen chopped bell peppers and onions, thawed	.5 kg
2 tablespoons cornstarch	30 ml
Beef-flavored rice	

- Sprinkle pepper over steak. In large skillet with a little oil, brown steak strips. Pour beef broth over steak and add bell pepper-onion mixture, ¾ cup water (180 ml) and 1 teaspoon (5 ml) salt. Bring to a boil, reduce heat and simmer 15 minutes. In small bowl, combine cornstarch and ½ cup water (120 ml) into skillet. Stir and cook over medium heat until mixture thickens. Serves 4.

Potato Souffle

2⅔ cups dry instant mashed potatoes	640 ml
2 eggs, beaten	
1 cup shredded cheddar cheese	240 ml
1 (3 ounce) can french-fried onion rings	84 g

- Preheat oven to 350° (176° C). Prepare mashed potatoes according to directions. Fold in beaten eggs and cheese and stir well. Spoon into sprayed 2-quart (2 L) baking dish. Sprinkle with onion rings. Bake uncovered for 20 to 25 minutes. Serves 4.

1
2
3
4
5
6
7
8
9
10
11
12
13
14
15
16
17
18
19
20
21
22
23
24
25
26
27
28
29
30
31

Spaghetti Soup

1 (7 ounce) package pre-cut spaghetti	198 g
1 (18 ounce) package frozen, cooked meatballs, thawed	510 g
1 (28 ounce) jar spaghetti sauce	794 g
1 (15 ounce) can Mexican stewed tomatoes	425 g

• In soup pot with 3 quarts (3 L) boiling water and a little salt, cook spaghetti about 6 minutes (no need to drain). When spaghetti is done, add meatballs, spaghetti sauce and stewed tomatoes and cook until mixture is hot. Serves 4 to 6.

Ambrosia Dessert

2 (11 ounce) cans mandarin oranges, drained, chilled	2 (312 g)
1 (20 ounce) can pineapple tidbits, drained, chilled	567 g
1 (7 ounce) can flaked coconut, chilled	198 g
1 cup miniature marshmallows	240 ml

• In bowl with lid, combine oranges, pineapple and coconut. Fold in marshmallows. (Make sure marshmallows are separated so they do not stick together.) Refrigerate. Serves 4 to 6.

Simple Bread Idea: **Soup Crackers**

• Serve 1 (10 ounce/280 g) package oysters crackers with soup.

December

7 - Pearl Harbor Day
24 - Christmas Eve
25 - Christmas Day
31 - New Year's Eve

Spiced Chicken

Spice Mix:

1 tablespoon paprika	15 ml
1 teaspoon ground cumin	5 ml
½ teaspoon cayenne pepper	2 ml
½ teaspoon coriander	2 ml
½ teaspoon oregano	2 ml

Chicken:

4 - 5 boneless, skinless chicken breasts, halved lengthwise
Extra-virgin olive oil

- In small bowl combine paprika, cumin, cayenne pepper, coriander, oregano and 1 teaspoon (5 ml) salt. In large shallow baking dish, place chicken pieces and drizzle with olive oil to coat. Rub each piece with spice mix and let stand about 10 minutes. Heat large skillet over medium-high heat and brown chicken pieces. Reduce heat, cover and simmer about 10 minutes on each side. Transfer to serving platter. Serves 4 to 6.

Pistachio Salad

1 (4 ounce) package instant pistachio pudding	114 g
1 (15 ounce) can crushed pineapple with juice	425 g
1 (8 ounce) carton whipped topping	227 g

- Stir instant pudding and pineapple together and fold in whipped topping. Refrigerate until ready to serve. Serves 4 to 6.

1
2
3
4
5
6
7
8
9
10
11
12
13
14
15
16
17
18
19
20
21
22
23
24
25
26
27
28
29
30
31

1
2
3
4
5
6
7
8
9
10
11
12
13
14
15
16
17
18
19
20
21
22
23
24
25
26
27
28
29
30
31

Italian Sausages And Ravioli

1 (16 ounce) package sweet Italian pork sausage,	
casing removed	.5 kg
1 (28 ounce) jar chunky mushroom and green pepper	
spaghetti sauce	794 g
1 (24 ounce) package frozen cheese-filled ravioli,	
cooked, drained	680 g
Grated parmesan cheese	

• In large skillet over medium heat, cook sausage according to package directions. Brown and stir until meat is no longer pink. Stir in spaghetti sauce and heat to boiling. Add ravioli and stir gently until it is hot. Pour into serving dish and sprinkle with parmesan cheese. Serves 6 to 8.

Grape Fluff

1 cup grape juice	240 ml
2 cups miniature marshmallows	480 ml
2 tablespoons lemon juice	30 ml
1 (8 ounce) carton whipping cream, whipped	227 g

• In saucepan, heat grape juice to boiling. Add marshmallows and stir constantly until they melt. Add lemon juice and cool. Fold in whipped cream and spoon into individual serving dishes. Refrigerate. Serves 6.

Ham and Yams

1 (1 pound) fully cooked center-cut ham steak	**.5 kg**
3 tablespoons frozen orange juice concentrate	**45 ml**
3 tablespoons honey	**45 ml**
¼ teaspoon ginger	**1 ml**

• Place ham steak in large skillet. In small bowl, combine orange juice concentrate, honey and ginger. Spread mixture over ham steak and cook on low-medium heat for 4 minutes. Turn steak and brush again with juice mixture. Cook another 4 to 5 minutes over low heat to slightly brown ham. Serve with Sweet Sugared Potatoes. (See recipe below.) Serves 4.

Sweet Sugared Potatoes

1 (28 ounce) can sweet potatoes with liquid	**794 g**
¼ cup (½ stick) butter, melted	**60 ml**
1 cup packed brown sugar	**240 ml**
2 eggs, beaten	
1 teaspoon cinnamon	**5 ml**
Chopped pecans	

• In mixing bowl, beat yams, butter, brown sugar, eggs and cinnamon until fluffy. Cover with paper towel and microwave on HIGH for 5 minutes. Turn once during cooking. To serve, place ham on serving platter and spoon yams around ham steak. Garnish with ½ cup (120 ml) chopped pecans. Serves 4 to 6.

1
2
3
4
5
6
7
8
9
10
11
12
13
14
15
16
17
18
19
20
21
22
23
24
25
26
27
28
29
30
31

Crispy Oven Fish

¾ cup biscuit mix	180 ml
⅓ cup yellow cornmeal	80 ml
1½ teaspoons chili powder	7 ml
1 egg, beaten	
1½ pounds orange roughy fillets	.7 kg

- Preheat oven at 425° (220° C). Pour several tablespoons (30 ml) oil into 9 x 13-inch (23 x 33 cm) baking pan and place in oven to heat oil. In shallow bowl, combine biscuit mix, cornmeal and chili powder. Add 1 tablespoon (15 ml) water to egg and mix well. Dip each piece of fish in egg and in biscuit-cornmeal mixture to coat well. Place in heated pan. Bake 20 to 25 minutes or until fish flakes easily with fork. Serves 4.

Simple Side Dish: **Fast Mashed Potatoes**

- Prepare 1 (7 ounce/198 g) box sour cream and chives mashed potatoes according to package directions.

Simple Bread Idea: **Hush Puppies**

- Heat 1 (16 ounce/.5 kg) package frozen hush puppies according to package directions.

December

7 - Pearl Harbor Day
24 - Christmas Eve
25 - Christmas Day
31 - New Year's Eve

Tuna Noodles

1 (8 ounce) package wide noodles, cooked, drained	227 g
2 (6 ounce) cans white tuna, drained	2 (168 g)
1 (10 ounce) can cream of chicken soup	280 g
¾ cup milk	180 ml

- Preheat oven to 300° (148° C). Place half noodles in sprayed 2-quart (2 L) baking dish. In saucepan, combine tuna, soup and milk and heat just enough to mix well. Pour half soup mixture over noodles and repeat layers. Cover and bake for 20 minutes. Serves 4.

Cucumber-Jicama Salad

1 (1 pound) jicama	.5 kg
1 small cucumber, sliced	
½ cup red onion, slivered	120 ml
Lemon-vinaigrette dressing	
Shredded lettuce	

- Peel jicama, cut lengthwise into wedges and cut crosswise into thin sticks.   In bowl, combine jicama, cucumber and red onion. Toss with lemon-vinaigrette dressing and spoon into salad bowl lined with shredded lettuce. Serves 4.

Simple Bread Idea: **Sour Dough Bread**

- Slice 1 round loaf sour dough bread in wedges and butter each wedge. Place on baking sheet and heat at 325° (162° C) for 15 minutes.

1
2
3
4
5
6
7
8
9
10
11
12
13
14
15
16
17
18
19
20
21
22
23
24
25
26
27
28
29
30
31

Beefy Vegetable Soup

1 pound lean ground beef	.5 kg
1 (46 ounce) can cocktail vegetable juice	1.25 kg
1 (1 ounce) packet onion soup mix	28 g
1 (3 ounce) package beef-flavored ramen noodles	84 g
1 (16 ounce) package frozen mixed vegetables	.5 kg

- In large soup pot over medium heat, cook beef until no longer pink. Drain. Stir in cocktail juice, soup mix, contents of noodle seasoning packet and mixed vegetables. Heat mixture to boiling, reduce heat and simmer uncovered 6 minutes or until vegetables are tender-crisp. Return to boiling, stir in noodles and cook 3 minutes. Serves 4 to 6.

Cheese Muffins

3¾ cups buttermilk biscuit mix	890 ml
1¼ cups shredded cheddar cheese	300 ml
1 egg, beaten	
1¼ cups milk	300 ml
Dash chili powder	

- Preheat oven to 325° (162° C). In large bowl, combine all ingredients and beat vigorously by hand. Pour into sprayed muffin cups. Bake for 35 minutes. Serves 4 to 6.

Lemon Tarts

1 (3.5 ounce) box instant lemon pudding mix	100 g
1 (8 ounce) package graham cracker tart shells	227 g
1 (8 ounce) carton whipped topping	227 g

- Whip pudding mix according to package directions and spoon into tart shells. Top with whipped topping. Serves 4 to 6.

Classy Chicken

4 boneless, skinless chicken breast halves	
¼ cup lime juice	**60 ml**
1 (1 ounce) packet dry Italian salad dressing mix	**28 g**
¼ cup (½ stick) butter, melted	**60 ml**

- Preheat oven to 325° (162° C). Season chicken with a little salt and pepper and place in shallow baking dish.
- Combine lime juice, salad dressing mix and butter and pour over chicken.
- Cover and bake for 1 hour. Remove cover for last 15 minutes of cooking. Serves 4 to 6.

Mexican-Fiesta Rice

1 (6 ounce) package Mexican fiesta rice	**168 g**
2 tablespoons butter	**30 ml**
1 cup chopped celery	**240 ml**
1 (8 ounce) package shredded Mexican Velveeta®	
cheese	**227 g**

- In saucepan, heat 2 cups (480 ml) water to boiling and add rice and butter. Return to boiling, reduce heat and simmer 5 minutes. Stir occasionally. Add celery, stir to mix and place in serving dish. Cover with cheese. Serves 4 to 6.

1
2
3
4
5
6
7
8
9
10
11
12
13
14
15
16
17
18
19
20
21
22
23
24
25
26
27
28
29
30
31

Warm-Your-Soul Soup

3 (14 ounce) cans chicken broth	3 (396 g)
2 (15 ounce) cans Italian stewed tomatoes	2 (425 g)
1 onion, chopped	
1 rib celery, chopped	
1 (8 ounce) package fettuccine	227 g

- In large soup pot, combine chicken broth, tomatoes, onion, celery and 2 cups (480 ml) water. Bring to a boil, reduce heat and simmer until onion and celery are tender-crisp. Add fettuccine and cook according to package directions. Season with a little salt and pepper. Serves 4 to 6.

Deviled Eggs

6 eggs, hard-boiled	
2 tablespoons sweet pickle relish	30 ml
3 tablespoons mayonnaise	45 ml
½ teaspoon mustard	2 ml
Paprika	

- Peel eggs and cut in half lengthwise. Take yolks out and mash with fork. Add relish, mayonnaise and mustard to yolks and mix well. Place yolk mixture back into egg white halves. Sprinkle with paprika. Serves 4 to 6.

Mayo Muffins

1¼ cups self-rising flour	300 ml
3 tablespoons mayonnaise	45 ml
1 cup whole milk	240 ml

- Preheat oven to 375° (190° C). Mix all ingredients and spoon into sprayed muffin cups. Bake for 20 minutes or until light brown. Serves 4 to 6.

Apricot-Glazed Tenderloin

2 (1 pound) pork tenderloins	**2 (.5 kg)**
1½ cups apricot preserves	**360 ml**
⅓ cup chili sauce	**80 ml**
2 small onions, sliced	

• Cut each pork tenderloin crosswise in ¼-inch (.6 cm) slices. In skillet, heat about 2 tablespoons (30 ml) oil over medium-high heat and add pork slices. Cook and stir about 10 minutes or until pork is no longer pink. Remove from skillet and keep warm. Add apricots, chili sauce and onion slices to skillet. Cook about 5 minutes. Return pork slices to skillet and add about ¼ cup (60 ml) water. Cover and cook over medium-low heat 10 to 15 minutes. Stir occasionally during cooking. Serve over couscous. Serves 4 to 6.

Creamed Spinach Bake

2 (10 ounce) packages frozen chopped spinach	**2 (280 g)**
2 (3 ounce) packages cream cheese, softened	**2 (84 g)**
3 tablespoons butter	**45 ml**
1 cup seasoned breadcrumbs	**240 ml**

• Preheat oven to 350° (176° C). Cook spinach according to package directions and drain. Combine cream cheese and butter with spinach. Heat until cream cheese and butter melt and mix well with spinach. Pour into sprayed baking dish and sprinkle a little salt over spinach. Cover with breadcrumbs and bake for 15 to 20 minutes. Serves 4 to 6.

1
2
3
4
5
6
7
8
9
10
11
12
13
14
15
16
17
18
19
20
21
22
23
24
25
26
27
28
29
30
31

Buttered Flounder

2 pounds flounder fillets	**1 kg**
⅔ cup butter	**160 ml**
3 tablespoons fresh cilantro leaves	**45 ml**
1 tablespoon lime juice	**15 ml**

- Preheat broiler. Place fillets in large, sprayed broiler pan. Broil about 3 to 4 minutes and carefully turn fillets over with tongs and not with fork. Broil 3 minutes more or until fish flakes easily when tested with fork. In saucepan, heat and stir butter, cilantro leaves and lime juice. Just before serving, spoon mixture over flounder. Serves 4 to 6.

Red and Green Salad

1 (12 ounce) package mixed salad greens	**340 g**
3 fresh green onions with tops, chopped	
2 medium red apples with peels, diced	
½ cup poppy seed salad dressing	**120 ml**

- In mixing bowl, toss salad greens, onions and apples. Drizzle with dressing and toss. Serves 4.

Simple Side Dish:
Toasted Pine-Nut Couscous

- Prepare 1 (6 ounce/168 g) package toasted pine nut couscous according to package directions.

Grilled-Lemon Chicken

6 boneless, skinless chicken breast halves	
2 teaspoons garlic salt	**10 ml**
1 tablespoon freshly grated lemon peel	**15 ml**
2 teaspoons dried thyme leaves	**10 ml**

• In small bowl, combine garlic salt, lemon peel, thyme leaves and a little pepper. Spray grill with cooking spray and heat coals. Sprinkle seasoning mixture over chicken breasts. Grill chicken 20 to 25 minutes or until chicken is no longer pink and juices run clear. Turn once during cooking. Serves 6 to 8.

Vegetable Salad

1 (16 ounce) package frozen green peas, thawed, drained	**.5 kg**
1 small head cauliflower, cut into bite-size pieces	
1 (8 ounce) carton sour cream	**227 g**
⅓ cup mayonnaise	**80 ml**
1 (1 ounce) packet dry ranch salad dressing mix	**28 g**

• In large bowl with lid, combine peas and cauliflower. In separate bowl, combine sour cream, mayonnaise and dressing mix and toss with vegetables. Serves 4 to 6.

December

7 - Pearl Harbor Day
24 - Christmas Eve
25 - Christmas Day
31 - New Year's Eve

1
2
3
4
5
6
7
8
9
10
11
12
13
14
15
16
17
18
19
20
21
22
23
24
25
26
27
28
29
30
31

Orange-Dijon Chops

1 cup orange marmalade	240 ml
3 tablespoons dijon-style mustard	45 ml
3 tablespoons soy sauce	45 ml
8 (¾ inch) thick pork loin chops	8 (1.8 cm)

- In small saucepan over low heat, stir marmalade, dijon-style mustard and soy sauce until preserves melt. When ready to grill, sprinkle both sides of pork chops with salt and pepper. Place chops on grill about 5 inches (13 cm) from heat. Cook about 15 minutes or until pork is no longer pink in center. Turn once during cooking and brush with preserve mixture last 2 minutes of cooking time. When ready to serve, heat preserves mixture to boiling and serve hot with pork chops. Serves 8.

Spinach Bake

2 (8 ounce) packages cream cheese, softened	2 (227 g)
1 (10 ounce) can cream of chicken soup	280 g
2 (16 ounce) packages frozen chopped spinach, thawed, well drained	2 (.5 kg)
1 cup crushed round, buttery crackers	240 ml

- Preheat oven to 325° (162° C). In mixing bowl, beat cream cheese until smooth. Add soup and mix well. Stir in spinach. Spoon into sprayed 3-quart (3 L) baking dish. Sprinkle cracker crumbs over top of casserole. Bake uncovered for 35 minutes. Serves 6 to 8.

Skillet Chicken and Peas

4 - 5 boneless, skinless chicken breast halves	
2 (10 ounce) cans cream of chicken soup	2 (280 g)
½ teaspoon paprika	2 ml
2 cups instant rice	480 ml
1 (10 ounce) package frozen green peas	280 g

- Heat a little oil in very large skillet. Add chicken and cook until brown. Transfer chicken to plate and keep warm. To skillet, add soup, 1¾ cups (420 ml) water, paprika and ½ teaspoon (2 ml) pepper. Heat to boiling, stir in rice and peas and reduce heat. Top with chicken and cook on low heat for 15 minutes. Serves 4 to 6.

Super Corn Casserole

1 (15 ounce) can whole kernel corn, drained	425 g
1 (15 ounce) can cream-style corn	425 g
½ cup (1 stick) butter, melted	120 ml
1 (8 ounce) carton sour cream	227 g
1 (6 ounce) package jalapeno cornbread mix	168 g

- Preheat oven to 350° (176° C). Mix all ingredients and pour into sprayed 9 x 13-inch (23 x 33 cm) baking dish. Bake uncovered for 35 minutes. Serves 6 to 8.

Deluxe Dinner Nachos

Nachos:

1 (14 ounce) package tortilla chips, divided	396 g
1 (8 ounce) package shredded Velveeta® cheese, divided	227 g
1 (8 ounce) can chopped jalapenos, divided	227 g

- Place about three-quarters tortilla chips in sprayed baking dish. Sprinkle half cheese and lots of jalapenos on top. Heat at 400° (204° C) just until cheese melts.

Deluxe Dinner Topping:

1 (11 ounce) can Mexicorn® with liquid	312 g
1 (15 ounce) can jalapeno pinto beans, drained	425 g
2 cups skinned, chopped rotisserie chicken	480 ml
1 bunch fresh green onions, chopped	

- Combine corn, beans and rotisserie chicken in saucepan. Heat over medium heat, stirring constantly, until mixture is hot. Spoon mixture over nachos, place dish in oven and heat for about 10 minutes. Sprinkle remaining cheese and green onions over top and serve immediately. Garnish with remaining jalapenos, remaining tortillas and salsa. Serves 4 to 6.

Country Baked Beans

4 (15 ounce) cans baked beans, drained	4 (425 g)
1 (12 ounce) bottle chili sauce	340 g
1 large onion, chopped	
½ pound bacon, cooked, crumbled	227 g
2 cups packed brown sugar	480 ml

- Preheat oven to 325° (162° C). In unsprayed 3-quart (3 L) baking dish, combine all ingredients and stir until they blend. Bake uncovered for 55 minutes or until hot throughout. Serves 6 to 8.

Steakhouse Stew

1 pound boneless beef sirloin steak, cubed	.5 kg
1 (15 ounce) can stewed tomatoes	425 g
1 (10 ounce) can French onion soup	280 g
1 (10 ounce) can tomato soup	280 g
1 (16 ounce) package frozen stew vegetables, thawed	.5 kg

• In skillet with a little oil, cook steak cubes until juices evaporate. Transfer to soup pot or roaster. Add 1 cup (240 ml) water, tomatoes, soups and vegetables and heat to boiling. Reduce heat to low and cook on medium for about 15 minutes or until vegetables are tender. Serves 4.

Cream-Style Corn Sticks

2 cups biscuit mix	480 ml
3 fresh green onions, finely chopped	
1 (8 ounce) can cream-style corn	227 g
½ cup (1 stick) butter, melted	120 ml

• Preheat oven to 400° (204° C). In medium bowl, combine biscuit mix, green onions and cream-style corn and stir well. On floured surface, roll out dough and cut into 3 x 1-inch (8 x 2.5 cm) strips. Roll dough in melted butter, place on sprayed baking sheet and bake 15 to 17 minutes. Serves 4 to 6.

Stuffed Celery

1 stalk celery, trimmed	
1 (16 ounce) carton pimento cheese	.5 kg

• Break off celery ribs and cut in 3-inch (8 cm) pieces. Fill generously with cheese.

1
2
3
4
5
6
7
8
9
10
11
12
13
14
15
16
17
18
19
20
21
22
23
24
25
26
27
28
29
30
31

1
2
3
4
5
6
7
8
9
10
11
12
13
14
15
16
17
18
19
20
21
22
23
24
25
26
27
28
29
30
31

Chiffon-Cheese Breakfast Souffle

12 slices white bread with crusts trimmed
2 (5 ounce) jars Old English cheese spread,
   softened   2 (143 g)
6 eggs, beaten
3 cups milk   710 ml
¾ cup (1½ sticks) butter, melted   180 ml

- Cut each slice of bread into 4 triangles. Place dab of cheese on each triangle and place triangles evenly in layers in sprayed 9 x 13-inch (23 x 33 cm) baking dish. (You could certainly prepare this in a souffle dish if you have one.) Combine eggs, milk, butter and a little salt and pepper. Pour over layers, cover and chill 8 hours. Remove from refrigerator 10 to 15 minutes before baking. Bake at 350° (176° C) uncovered for 1 hour. Serves 6.

Bacon Nibblers

1 (1 pound) package sliced bacon   .5 kg
1½ cups packed brown sugar   360 ml
1½ teaspoons dry mustard   7 ml

- Preheat oven to 325° (162° C). Cut each slice of bacon in half. Combine remaining ingredients and ¼ teaspoon (1 ml) pepper in shallow bowl. Dip each half slice of bacon in brown sugar mixture and press down so sugar coats well on bacon. Place each slice on sprayed baking sheet with sides.
- Bake for 25 minutes, turning once, until bacon browns. Immediately remove with tongs to several layers of paper towels. Bacon will harden and can be broken in pieces. Serves 4 to 6.

Breakfast or Brunch

Turkey Casserole

1 (6 ounce) package herb-seasoned stuffing mix	168 g
1 cup canned whole cranberry sauce	240 ml
6 (¼ inch) thick slices turkey	6 (.6 cm)
1 (15 ounce) jar turkey gravy	425 g

- Preheat oven to 375° (190° C). Prepare stuffing according to package directions. In medium bowl, combine stuffing and cranberry sauce and set aside. Place turkey slices in sprayed 9 x 13-inch (23 x 33 cm) baking dish and pour gravy on top. Spoon stuffing mixture over casserole. Bake about 15 minutes or until hot and bubbly. Serves 4 to 6.

Asparagus Bake

3 (15 ounce) cans asparagus	3 (425 g)
3 eggs, hard-boiled, sliced	
⅓ cup milk	80 ml
1½ cups shredded cheddar cheese	360 ml
1¼ cups cheese cracker crumbs	300 ml

- Preheat oven to 350° (176° C). Place asparagus in sprayed 7 x 11-inch (18 x 28 cm) baking dish, layer hard-boiled eggs on top and pour milk over casserole. Sprinkle cheese on top and add cracker crumbs. Bake uncovered for 30 minutes. Serves 4 to 6.

Peanut Butter Brownies

1 (20 ounce) package brownie mix	567 g
1 cup peanut butter chips	240 ml

- Preheat oven to 350° (176° C). Prepare brownie mix according to package directions and stir in peanut butter chips. Spoon mixture into sprayed 9 x 13-inch (23 x 33 cm) baking pan. Bake for 35 minutes. Cool and cut into squares.

1
2
3
4
5
6
7
8
9
10
11
12
13
14
15
16
17
18
19
20
21
22
23
24
25
26
27
28
29
30
31

Skillet Beef And Pasta

1 (8 ounce) package spiral, rotini pasta	227 g
1 (14 ounce) can beef broth	396 g
1 pound lean ground beef	.5 kg
2 (11 ounce) cans Mexicorn®, drained	2 (312 g)
1 (16 ounce) package cubed Mexican Velveeta® cheese	.5 kg

• Cook pasta according to directions, but use 4½ cups (1.2 L) water and 1¾ cups (420 ml) beef broth instead of 6 cups (1.5 L) water. While pasta cooks, brown beef in large skillet and drain. Stir in corn and cheese and cook on low heat until cheese melts. Gently stir cooked pasta into beef mixture until pasta coats well. Spoon mixture into serving bowl and garnish with sprigs of parsley, if desired. Serves 4 to 6.

Chile-Cheese Squash

1 pound yellow squash, cubed	.5 kg
⅔ cup mayonnaise	160 ml
1 (4 ounce) can diced green chilies, drained	114 g
⅔ cup shredded longhorn cheese	160 ml
⅔ cup breadcrumbs	120 ml

• Cook squash in salted water just until tender-crisp and drain. Return to saucepan, stir in mayonnaise, chilies, cheese and breadcrumbs. Serve hot. Serves 4 to 6.

December

7 - Pearl Harbor Day
24 - Christmas Eve
25 - Christmas Day
31 - New Year's Eve

Easy Smothered Steak

Flour	
2 pounds round steak, cubed	1 kg
2 (12 ounce) jars home-style beef gravy	2 (340 g)
2 tablespoons oil	30 ml

- Lightly flour cubed steak on all sides and brown in large skillet with oil. Drain fat, pour gravy over steak, cover and simmer for 15 minutes. Serves 6 to 8.

Herbed New Potatoes

1½ pounds new potatoes	.7 kg
6 tablespoons (¾ stick) butter, sliced	90 ml
¼ teaspoon thyme	1 ml
½ cup chopped fresh parsley	120 ml
½ teaspoon rosemary	2 ml

- Scrub potatoes and cut in halves, but do not peel. In medium saucepan, boil potatoes in lightly salted water for about 20 minutes or until tender and drain. Add butter, thyme, parsley and rosemary and toss gently until butter melts. Serve hot. Serves 4 to 6.

Caesar Salad

2 (8 ounce) packages romaine lettuce	2 (227 g)
1 (8 ounce) package shredded mozzarella cheese	227 g
1 (8 ounce) bottle Caesar salad dressing	227 g
1 (6 ounce) box seasoned croutons	168 g

- Combine lettuce and cheese and toss with dressing. Sprinkle croutons over salad and serve. Serves 4 to 6.

1
2
3
4
5
6
7
8
9
10
11
12
13
14
15
16
17
18
19
20
21
22
23
24
25
26
27
28
29
30
31

Sweet 'N Spicy Chicken Over Rice

1 pound boneless, skinless chicken breasts, cubed	.5 kg
1 (1 ounce) packet taco seasoning	38 g
1 (16 ounce) jar chunky salsa	.5 kg
1 (8 ounce) jar peach preserves	227 g

• Place cubed chicken in resealable plastic bag, add taco seasoning and toss to coat. In large skillet with a little oil, brown chicken and cook on medium-low for 5 minutes. In saucepan, combine salsa, preserves and ¼ cup (60 ml) water. Heat and stir until salsa and preserves mix well. Stir into skillet with chicken. Bring mixture to boil. Reduce heat, cover and simmer 15 minutes. Serve on Hot, Cooked Rice. (See recipe below.) Serves 4 to 6.

Hot, Cooked Rice

2 cups instant white rice	480 ml
Butter	
1½ cups chopped walnuts	360 ml
1 bunch fresh green onions, chopped	

• Cook rice according to package directions. Stir in walnuts and onions and serve chicken over rice. Serves 4 to 6.

Cauliflower And Green Peas

1 (16 ounce) package frozen cauliflower, thawed	.5 kg
1 cup chopped celery	240 ml
¼ cup (½ stick) butter	60 ml
1 (15 ounce) can green peas	425 g

• Cook cauliflower according to package directions and drain. Saute celery in butter and stir in peas and cauliflower. Heat thoroughly. Serves 4 to 6.

Cheesy Chicken And Potatoes

1 (20 ounce) package frozen hash browns with peppers and onions, thawed	567 g
1 tablespoon minced garlic	15 ml
2 - 2½ cups bite-size chunks rotisserie chicken	480 ml
1 bunch green onions, sliced	
1 cup shredded cheddar cheese	240 ml

• Add a little oil to large skillet over medium-high heat, cook potatoes for 7 minutes and turn frequently. Add garlic, chicken, green onions and ⅓ cup (80 ml) water and cook 5 to 6 minutes. Remove from heat and stir in cheese. Serve immediately right from skillet. Serves 4 to 6.

Tossed Italian Green Salad

1 (10 ounce) package Italian-blend mixed greens	280 g
1 seedless cucumber, sliced	
1 rib celery, sliced	
2 small zucchini, sliced	

• In salad bowl, combine mixed greens, cucumber, celery and zucchini and toss. Dress with creamy Italian or favorite dressing. Serves 4 to 6.

7 - Pearl Harbor Day
24 - Christmas Eve
25 - Christmas Day
31 - New Year's Eve

1
2
3
4
5
6
7
8
9
10
11
12
13
14
15
16
17
18
19
20
21
22
23
24
25
26
27
28
29
30
31

1
2
3
4
5
6
7
8
9
10
11
12
13
14
15
16
17
18
19
20
21
22
23
24
25
26
27
28
29
30
31

Turkey For Supper

4 (¼ inch) thick smoked deli turkey breast slices	4 (.6 cm)
1 (8 ounce) package cream cheese, softened	227 g
¼ cup mayonnaise	60 ml
1½ cups hot, chunky salsa	360 ml

• Place turkey slices on serving platter. In mixing bowl with mixer, combine cream cheese and mayonnaise. Fold in salsa. Place one-fourth cream cheese mixture on each slice turkey. Serve cold. Serves 4.

Dinner Rice

2 cups cooked white rice	480 ml
1 onion, chopped	
¼ cup (½ stick) butter, melted	60 ml
1 (8 ounce) package shredded Mexican Velveeta® cheese	227 g

• Preheat oven to 325° (162° C). Combine all ingredients and mix well. Spoon mixture into sprayed 2-quart (2 L) baking dish. Bake covered for 30 minutes. Serves 4.

Swiss-Spinach Salad

1 (10 ounce) bag baby spinach	280 g
½ red onion, chopped	
1 (8 ounce) package shredded Swiss cheese	227 g
Wild berry vinaigrette dressing	
½ cup sunflower seeds, toasted	120 ml

• In salad bowl, combine spinach, onion and Swiss cheese. Toss with wild berry vinaigrette dressing. Sprinkle sunflower seeds over top of salad. Serves 4.

Index

Bread

Index

Index

Index

Index

Index

Index

Main Dishes

Index

Index

Index

Index

Index

Index

Index

Index

Sandwiches

Index

Index

Index

Soups

Index

Index

Index

Cookbook Resources, LLC
Bringing Families and Friends To The Table

The Best of Cooking with
3 Ingredients

The Ultimate Cooking with
4 Ingredients

Easy Cooking with 5 Ingredients

Diabetic Cooking with
4 Ingredients

Healthy Cooking with
4 Ingredients

Gourmet Cooking with
5 Ingredients

4-Ingredient Recipes for
30-Minute Meals

Essential 3-4-5 Ingredient
Recipes

The Best 1001 Short,
Easy Recipes

The Best 1001 Fast Easy Recipes

Easy Slow Cooker Cookbook

Easy One-Dish Meals

Easy Potluck Recipes

Easy Casseroles

Easy Desserts

Sunday Night Suppers

365 Easy Meals

365 Easy Chicken Recipes

365 Easy Soups and Stews

Quick Fixes with Cake Mixes

Kitchen Keepsakes/More Kitchen
Keepsakes

Gifts for the Cookie Jar

All New Gifts for the Cookie Jar

Muffins In A Jar

Brownies In A Jar

Gifts in a Pickle Jar

The Big Bake Sale Cookbook

Classic Tex-Mex and Texas Cooking

Classic Southwest Cooking

Southern Family Favorites

Miss Sadie's Southern Cooking

The Great Canadian Cookbook

Texas Longhorn Cookbook

Cookbook 25 Years

The Best of Lone Star Legacy
Cookbook

A Little Taste of Texas

A Little Taste of Texas II

Trophy Hunters' Wild Game
Cookbook

Italian Family Cookbook

Old-Fashioned Cookies

Grandmother's Cookies

Quilters' Cooking Companion

Mother's Recipes

Recipe Keeper

Cookie Dough Secrets

Casseroles to the Rescue

Holiday Recipes

Mealtimes and Memories

Southwest Sizzler

Southwest Olé

Class Treats

Leaving Home

cookbook *resources*® LLC
Bringing Families To The Table

To Order: *365 Easy Meals*

Please send_____ hardcover copies @ $19.95 (U.S.) each $ _____
        Texas residents add sales tax @ $1.60 each $ _____

Please send _____ paperback copies @ $16.95 (U.S.) each $ _____
        Texas residents add sales tax @ $1.34 each $ _____

Plus postage/handling @ $6.00 (1ˢᵗ copy) $ _____
        $1.00 (each additional copy) $ _____

     Check or Credit Card (Canada-credit card only)   **Total** $ _____

Charge to:
_____ MasterCard _____Visa
Account # _____
Expiration Date _____
Signature_____

Mail or Call:
Cookbook Resources
541 Doubletree Drive
Highland Village, TX 75077
Toll Free (866) 229-2665
Fax   (972) 317-6404

Name _____
Address_____
City_____State_____Zip_____
Telephone (Day)_____(Evening)_____

To Order: *365 Easy Meals*

Please send_____ hardcover copies @ $19.95 (U.S.) each $ _____
        Texas residents add sales tax @ $1.60 each $ _____

Please send _____ paperback copies @ $16.95 (U.S.) each $ _____
        Texas residents add sales tax @ $1.34 each $ _____

Plus postage/handling @ $6.00 (1ˢᵗ copy) $ _____
        $1.00 (each additional copy) $ _____

     Check or Credit Card (Canada-credit card only)   **Total** $ _____

Charge to:
_____ MasterCard _____Visa
Account # _____
Expiration Date _____
Signature_____

Mail or Call:
Cookbook Resources
541 Doubletree Drive
Highland Village, TX 75077
Toll Free (866) 229-2665
Fax   (972) 317-6404

Name _____
Address_____
City_____State_____Zip_____
Telephone (Day)_____(Evening)_____

Order online at www.cookbookresources.com